CW00801389

# FOREWORD

I have been privileged to know Tracey since she was a youngster growing up on her family's farm at Widecombe-in-the-Moor. This beautiful spot is located in the south west region of the United Kingdom amongst barren moorland called Dartmoor. In addition to a deep affection and respect for horses, her infectious energy and zest for life has always been evident.

Whilst many would have been content to take such powerful gifts for granted, Tracey wanted to share them with anyone and everyone. Through years of diligence and perseverance she developed a photographic skill that is the envy of others and has built a successful business selling her work in the United Kingdom and abroad. Underlying this artistic talent has been her faith in God, coupled with the strong sense that 'You can achieve anything you want, if you set your mind to it.' The source of her motivation, therefore, is realising dreams and giving inspiration to others.

Tracey became involved in what I call 'long haul' riding, and introduced the Riding By Faith series after her first expedition through New Zealand. Long distance riding is challenging at the best of times; to ride solo for months on end with only the wilderness and your horses for company would seriously test most of us.

Riding Across America is her most demanding ride yet from the Rio Grande in Mexico to Montana's border with Alberta, Canada. Her experiences during the time in the saddle with her two quarter horses, Smoky and Pistol, will have appeal in the United States, but also to horse lovers throughout the world. In six months the trio covered several thousands of miles across desert, prairies and mountains. But they also navigated their way across the territories of snakes, drug smugglers, wild animals and battled through all manner of weather.

Apart from some equipment, Tracey has not sought sponsorship for her rides. She relies, instead, on an increasingly wide network of honest to goodness horse loving people with a deep understanding of their environment; and she has her strong faith in God to help overcome challenges confronting her.

The pages of this book feature breathtaking photographs of the Wild West, its animals and many friends, who helped her as she made her way north. Not only is it a delightful read, but she cleverly relates to the environment and aspects of American history associated with the States she rides through. I am left with a strong sense that this lady has the courage and perseverance that would be the envy of many soldiers … and that coming from a former commander in Her Majesty's Forces must be saying something.

Brigadier Simon Young CBE

# THANKS TO: –

MY FAITHFUL GOD FOR THIS ADVENTURE!

My parents, Elizabeth and Rod for providing a wonderful way of life
on a farm, surrounded by animals, especially Dartmoor ponies –
And a spacious place for dreaming!

The friendship and commitment of the following;
Jonathan Constant for your valuable advice and editing.
Marian Constant for your ideas and dedicated proofing.
Robert and Joan Knight and Simon Young.
Greg Scott for your extensive assistance on the US front.
Faith Russell for your steadfast prayer support.
Shan Palmes for your great encouragement.

Designed and published by Tracey Elliot-Reep 2009
Photographs © by Tracey Elliot-Reep and friends
Text and sketches © Tracey Elliot-Reep
Shilstone Rocks
Widecombe-in-the-Moor
Dartmoor
Devon TQ13 7TF
England

www.traceyelliotreep.com

ISBN  798-0-9538231-7-8

Printed through 1010 Printing International in China

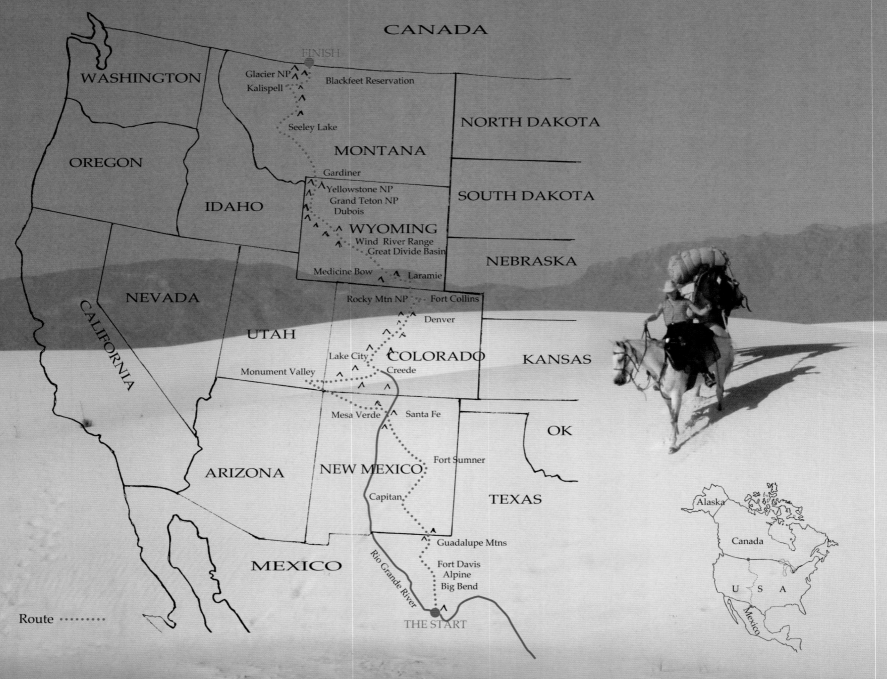

# THE ROUTE

CANADA

WASHINGTON

FINISH

Glacier NP
Kalispell
Blackfeet Reservation

NORTH DAKOTA

OREGON

Seeley Lake

MONTANA

IDAHO

Gardiner
Yellowstone NP
Grand Teton NP
Dubois

SOUTH DAKOTA

WYOMING

Wind River Range
Great Divide Basin

NEBRASKA

Medicine Bow    Laramie

NEVADA

Rocky Mtn NP    Fort Collins

Denver

CALIFORNIA

UTAH

Lake City    COLORADO    KANSAS

Monument Valley    Creede

Mesa Verde    Santa Fe

ARIZONA    NEW MEXICO    Fort Sumner

Capitan    TEXAS

Guadalupe Mtns

MEXICO    Fort Davis
Alpine
Big Bend

Rio Grande River

THE START

OK

Route ·········

Alaska

Canada

U S A

Mexico

6

It is not enough for an artist to
see, he must make others see
- Degas

In this book I want to take you on a journey, riding by faith across the United States of America. To show you some of the spectacular and diverse scenery of the America West, its hospitable people and their way of life.

P.S As an English girl I have kept to English spelling – I hope my American friends will forgive me! As George Bernard Shaw stated:

England and America are two countries separated by a common language

# THE DREAM

*For it is God who works in you both to will and do for His good pleasure. Phil 2v13NKJ*

I had this growing certainty that I was going to be riding in North America. "But where?" was my question. Previously, I had ridden the length of New Zealand, from the top to the bottom of Britain and all around Southern Ireland. But where in the United States? It is such a huge expanse of land!

Then Sandy a friend, lent me a video based on a true story, which described the moment when machines were replacing horsepower in the US Cavalry, and several hundred surplus horses were ordered to be taken south to Mexico to be destroyed. The officer and soldiers couldn't bear to see their horses killed so they kidnapped them and herded them north into the Rockies. It was when the soldiers asked the officer, "where are we going?", and he replied "Canada", that my heart leapt. Suddenly, I knew I was riding to Canada! And I would leave from the Mexico/Texas border.

I knew no one in Texas connected with horses until I visited the Bible Christian Chapel in Haselbury Plucknett in Somerset, England, where I met Tanya Fallin. She invited me to stay at her home in Palo Pinto County Texas, while looking for horses.

Then, just two weeks before I was leaving England a friend, introduced me to another Texan, Philip Dautrich – this time in Dartmoor National Park, South West England, where I grew up. Philip was a minister in the famous Princetown Prison, set in the middle of Dartmoor, and built in the early nineteenth century to house thousands of French prisoners of war, who were later joined by many Americans. He suggested that I get in touch with his uncle, who bred quarter horses in East Texas.

As a child, growing up on my mother's Shilstone Rocks Dartmoor Pony stud farm, I had often dreamt of being a cowboy or a native American Indian. I have especially strong memories of my seventh birthday, because although I had already been riding ponies, this was when I was given one of my very own, called Little Goose. He came into the kitchen wrapped up in brown parcel paper! I would charge around on Little Goose, riding bareback – one day as an Indian, with my bow and arrow, the next as a cowboy, with my toy gun in a smart white holster on my belt!

*God matches the dream to the dreamer - Robert H Schuller*

You saw me before I was born.
Every day of my life was recorded in your book.
Every moment was laid out before a single day had passed.
How precious are your thoughts about me, O God!
They are innumerable! Psalm 139v16 NLT

Every man dies, not every man really lives. - William Wallace in the film Braveheart

Twenty three years later, after my reoccuring thoughts of cowboys and Indians, I was living in a small caravan (7ft by 10ft) with my Jack Russell dog. The magazine that I worked for had gone bust, owing me thousands of pounds, and around the same time my fiancé gave me the ultimatum: "God or me". Although I loved this man I also loved God and I knew my choice of God, would echo throughout eternity. With my dreams seemingly dashed, instead of allowing myself to be swallowed up in depression I decided to trust God, fight for my life and live life to the fullest. I began my own business based solely on faith, hard work, six postcards and no money!

Let your hopes, not your hurts, shape your future - Robert H.Schuller

# TEXAS START

Some men see things as they are and say 'Why?' I dream things that never were and say 'Why not?' - George Bernard Shaw

"Isn't that rather a long way?" One acquaintance remarked when I mentioned I was going for a ride across America.

"All power to your elbow!" exclaimed Margie Goodfellow, the friend who introduced me to Philip Dautrich.

I started my adventure at Dallas airport where I was met by Tanya. She passed me onto Larry Joiner, Philip's uncle, who drove me to his home near Huntington in south east Texas.

"Most little boys dream of growing up and becoming a cowboy," Larry remarked in his Texan drawl, which I began to get attuned to during the journey of several hours. "It has lots to do with independence. They don't like the office chair confines. They like the open, their horse and the elements. I do too and this is one of the reasons I chose ag (agriculture)." As we travelled eastwards the land began to become greener, more rolling and wooded with large conifer trees.

"Here's Huntington. We've got one light (traffic light) and two hamburger places!" Larry told me, as we neared his place, home to his KL quarter horse stud. Over the next couple of days he and his wife Karon took me to look at horses in the area. I tried a grey they called Smoky, who was a bit over qualified as a roping horse for trekking up the country and would cost more than I had budgeted to pay. However, he stood at 15 hands high, and was what I was looking for in size and type.

Then they showed me a neighbour's red roan horse. "He's called Pistol - he's very fast!" Larry remarked, and he would know, because Eli, their son had broken him in. Pistol wasn't friendly and was taller than Smoky, maybe 16 hands high. I didn't want a high horse or a race horse, but I agreed to try them both.

The saddles were very uncomfortable and the stirrups couldn't be shortened to suit my height of five foot five inches, so I had to stand on tiptoes in Eli's six foot three length stirrups. I would lose them frequently, and then gave up altogether, finding it easier without them. However, Smoky and Pistol who were trained to chop and change direction abruptly meant that it was not a smooth ride, as both western horses and English rider experienced communication problems as we circled one way then the other under two huge fans.

"God please," I whispered, experiencing the hard saddle, "I really need a comfortable saddle to ride to Canada!"

"And this is the girl who's riding to Canada!" Larry called out.

"On your own?" asked Mike Coleman, the owner of the indoor arena.

"Not exactly," I replied, "I've got God, His angels, two horses and maybe a dog too!"

"Why are you going to Canada?"

"Why not?" I replied and Larry chuckled.

"Mike could be right. I think you might be crazy!"

After visiting Larry and Karon Joiner in Texas, I then needed to do some business in New Zealand where I have completed several long rides. I arrived in Auckland for the first ride 17 years earlier, accompanied by a Scottish friend, Ali, just £60 (US $100) and a dream to ride the 2,000 mile length of both the North and South Island. Since that first amazing adventure, I have published several photographic 'journey books' and started a greeting card business in England and New Zealand.

Three months later, in early March, I was back in Texas, but without my luggage! Tanya found me at the Dallas airport lost luggage counter, where I was describing the contents of my suitcases: "There's a beige dress and high heeled shoes in one and camping equipment in the other, including walking boots."

"Hiking boots she means!" added Tanya. I continued to discover that although Americans spoke English, there were so many different meanings and spellings. As one man told me after a misunderstanding: "We speak another language."

So there I was, with nothing but the clothes I stood up in and my hand luggage, and within a month I would be starting my ride.(Several days later my bags turned up!) Organisation had never been my strong point! Nor was administration or filling in forms. Never, on any of my previous rides, had I been faced with so much paperwork – in this case, it involved National Park permits and fees. To make matters worse, I had decided to arrange for a two-man film crew to meet me in five locations, and this seemed to double the paperwork.

Fortunately, Tanya had a good brain for all this, whereas it just gave me a headache. All I wanted to do was to get on a horse and ride like I usually did… although this was a much tougher country to ride across with many more dangers, and large areas with no water or grazing for horses.

The Brazos River flooding
at Lone Camp after a tornado.

# CREEPY CRAWLIES

Courage is resistance to fear, mastery of fear - not absence of fear - Mark Twain

"They may start rattlin' when you stop right by them and then you've got to learn to fly." Steve, Tanya's husband, replied to my question about snakes rattling during my time at Lone Camp in Palo Pinto County.

"Yes Ma-am," he said, in his Texas drawl, "You know what a tree locust sounds like? Like that, but louder. But we do have snakes that don't rattle, they just get you. There are also water moccasins and copper head snakes. They come out of the water at night. They can be everywhere. You have to get used to it. Look a little and then go."

"Just don't be looking out there," he added, motioning at the horizon. "You need to be paying attention. You've got to look at your trail, not far off. It's beside the little cattle trails that the snakes wait for a rabbit to run by, then they strike it, put the venom in it and they know it'll die further down the trail."

"If you get a snake bite, you'd better have a lot of money!" Steve added, handing me a magazine with an article written by a woman.

"The charges for tempting fate in my flip flops to feed my chickens amounted to a whopping $40,470. The price of the anti-venom treatment alone was $36,102," I read out loud.

"Oooh, my gosh!" Tanya exclaimed, and I didn't dare mention that I wasn't insured.

I had never been insured on any of my previous rides. I hadn't even thought of it when I rode through New Zealand and Ireland, but for the first time in my life I was riding through the United States, famous for its legal system and astronomically high medical expenses. I did make several enquiries about insurance, but they declined when they heard details of my US expedition.

"We can insure you only off the horse, but not on the horse," one of them said, after I told them I was riding across America. So that settled it. As usual I would be trusting God, the biggest insurer around with my horses and my life! The only insurance I had to have for the filming in the National Parks was for liability for my horses, and I did manage to obtain that... at a price!

"Do you know what crawdads are?" Steve asked.

"Never heard of them!" I replied.

"Crawdads pick the tart out of you (bite you).They swim in the rivers, like a crab swimming backwards."

"I want you to be frightened," one woman told me. "south west Texas is the most desolate area. At night the earth moves and things come out of the ground – crawling things. Be careful where you put your hands at night," warned another. "The killer bees are really bad where you're going. There are big swarms, you'll hear them and they will bite you. They had to revive one man three times."

"You've got a lot of creepy crawlies down here haven't you!" I said, trying to keep my British stiff upper lip, which was quivering slightly in the face of all these dangers. I almost expected to trip over a snake with every step! "But rattle snakes are mostly in west Texas." Steve added having had experience as a government trapper.

"Well great, that was where I was starting," I said sarcastically. As thunder and lightning caused Tanya and Steve's wooden house to rattle, and a tornado ripped through Lone Camp, I asked myself: "why didn't I choose somewhere a little more hospitable to begin my trek, without all these intimidating dangers?" I wasn't used to all these perils, severe weather, creepy crawlies, fire ants, poisonous snakes and drug smugglers coming up from Mexico. All my other rides seemed suddenly rather tame in comparison to what I was now attempting.

I will not allow your facts to interfere with my vision!
- Don Quixote in the film Man of La Mancha

# THE LONGHORN

These majestic cattle carry a massive set of horns that can stretch over eight feet from tip to tip. The longhorn have a reputation for being more dangerous than grizzly bears, and no predator would take on a healthy animal. Built for speed, with coats of many colours, they can travel long distances to water, but they can also be spooked and stampeded more easily than any other breed of cattle.

Originally Spanish, the longhorn were first brought to New Spain (now Mexico) in the early 1500s, possibly with Columbus, although Cortez brought more in the 1520s. The first cattle and horses walked into Texas and North America in 1541 with conquistador Francisco Vasquez de Coronado and his company in search for gold. The story has it, they were caught in a wild thunderstorm which caused the cattle to stampede. Many escaped and were never rounded up, and several hundred years later, they had multiplied into millions.

The Spanish missions, agents of the Crown and church, also brought cattle and horses to Texas, but were driven out by the Native Americans, leaving the cattle behind, which multiplied over the open grasslands. When Moses Austin arrived with American colonials to settle this part of Mexico, which is now in Texas, before the Mexican Revolution, they found thousands of free roaming, wild cattle.

Before I had decided to leave from the Big Bend area in southern Texas, one of my thoughts had been to follow the Goodnight and Loving Cattle Trail from Oliver Loving's home ranch in Palo Pinto County, as Tanya and Steve lived close by, near Fort Worth. I would then trek across the desert to the Pecos river and follow it north to Fort Sumner on the trail of the longhorn cattle drives.

The long drives took the longhorn cattle from their breeding grounds in Texas as far as California and Oregon. After the war, the cattle business boomed as the railroad and settlers moved west and, between 1866 and 1890, ten million cattle were driven over the trails of Texas along the main routes, called the Chisholm, Shawnee and Western Trails. It was a very risky business with many dangers of river crossings, bandits and hostile Native Americans and the trail operators could gain or lose a lot, due to the uncertainty of rain, grass and the price fluctuations at their destination.

The trail I had thought to follow was named after the famous partnership of Oliver Loving, one of the first cowboys, and Charles Goodnight, a former Texas ranger, who left the frontier of Texas in June 1866 with 2,000 head of mixed cattle and 18 armed men to cross the Llano Estacado – a waterless desert of 80 miles – in order to reach the Pecos River. Usually a herd could only move 10 to 15 miles a day, but theirs was so thirsty and restless that they feared a stampede, so kept them going for three days and nights. On the approach to the Pecos, the thirst-craved cattle smelt the water and stampeded, galloping right over the cliffs, into the river, and piling in on top of one another, so that many of them drowned. Others became stuck in the quicksand and banks where they landed and had to be left behind.

They had intended to move the herd north into Colorado and sell them in Denver, but as they travelled up the Pecos River, they passed a reservation at Fort Sumner, New Mexico Territory, where 8,500 Navajo Indians were being held by the Army and were starving after a failed farming plan. The army bought the steers to save the Navajos for the vast sum of $12,000 in gold. Others, having heard of their success, planned to follow their trail to Fort Sumner. Hearing of the competition, Loving and Goodnight quickly assembled a herd back in Texas, buying cattle with gold.

Indian attacks stampeded the herd and delayed their progress. Loving, doubting whether they would be the first to reach the Army to win the beef contract, went on ahead with One-Armed Bill Wilson, travelling at night. Not seeing any Indians after several days, they rode on in daylight but were spotted by the Comanches, and chased to the banks of the Pecos, where Loving was shot in the wrist and side.

Wilson escaped down the river, and made it back to the herd, seeking help. Goodnight and his men saddled up and rode hard all night, but when they arrived, there was no sign of Loving. They came to the conclusion that he must have killed himself to avoid capture.

Loving made it up river, where some Mexicans had taken him to a doctor in Fort Sumner. The wound in Loving's side healed, but gangrene had set into his wrist by the time Goodnight arrived. While he was dying, he made two requests of his friend and partner: that Goodnight would continue their partnership for at least two more years to keep Loving's family free of debt, and also to ensure that his body was taken back to Texas.

Goodnight had the casket put in a box made of hammered tin, constructed from oil cans, and loaded on a wagon. He returned it to Loving's family at Wetherford hundreds of miles, along their Goodnight-Loving Trail, which made the most touching funeral cortege in the history of the cattle drives.

# GETTING SET

Man looks at the outward appearance, but the Lord looks at the heart. 1 Samuel 16v7 NIV

"She's fixin' to ride from the Big Bend to Canada," Tanya commented to a large man in a cowboy hat, looking down on me.
"What, her?!" his look implied. I had picked up the American expression and felt like indignantly replying: "Hey man, do you realise who's backing me?"

Tanya was a gifted administrator and an efficient shopper, who could find just about anything, so I just stuck with her, especially in the huge American shopping malls, so I wouldn't get lost! As Tanya whisked me around I got confused as to whether I was in Fort Worth, or Dallas, or Mineral Wells! She knew where the good value Goodwill shops were located. It must have been one of their fastest ever sales when Tanya took me into one, asked where the shirts were and within five minutes I was out of the door with an emerald silk shirt for $3.95!

"Phone, English riding clothes, including long-sleeved shirts, hat, two comfortable saddles, bridle, halters, woollen saddle blankets, saddle bags for my camera…" I read from my long shopping list. "…Oh, and breeching."

"The deal that goes round the horse's butt?" Tanya asked, and Steve answered, "correct!"

"Everyone says I should get a GPS," I grimaced, not just because they were expensive, but also because I doubted that I could use one, being rather non-technically minded. I didn't want to be irresponsible, but even the thought of all the technical gear that I had been advised to take was already weighing me down – satellite phone, beacons, GPS… "The pioneers never had all this stuff," I grumbled, thinking there would just be more for me to lose.

Back in England, Stephen, a friend and an adventure expedition leader, had given me a compass-reading lesson. After explaining, he looked at my blank face and asked: "Do you have trouble spelling?" I admitted: "Yes."

"Ok, you're kinesthetic. You need to learn by doing it. Come on let's go out on Dartmoor and practise!"

# AUSSIE SADDLE

*The Lord is my shepherd. I shall not want. Psalm 23v1 NKJ*

Tanya took me to Teskeys, a large saddlery outlet in Parker County, the quarter horse capital of the world. I was gobsmacked by almost three hundred saddles, some techni-coloured with seats of pink, blue, green ostrich leather. One was tooled with an intricate pattern of pink and green flowers and leaves.

"I've never seen anything like it!" I exclaimed, and Tanya laughed. Under the eye of an enthusiastic sales person I tried sitting in some of the plainer saddles, but I didn't find them comfortable. One summer, when I was 19, I had worked on trail rides in Michigan, and even then I never found Western saddles comfortable. The conclusion I came to was that as I had grown up riding bareback and English style, my bones and muscles had grown that way.

"Take a look at that." An assistant showed me an Australian stock saddle, hidden behind other rows of equipment, called a Bronco Poley.

"God, this is what I want," I said, as I moulded myself into it and examined all the many and useful attachments. I didn't have the finance to buy such a luxurious saddle, so summoning courage, I asked the store owner if he would like to sponsor me. He declined, so I plucked up courage again and called the saddle maker himself, Colin Dangaard of the Australian Stock Saddle Company, based in California.

"When do you want it by?" he asked in his Australian accent, which was so noticeable after all the Texas drawls.

"Next week," I replied.

"What kind of horses are you taking and what size are you?"

"Quarter horses. One's 15 hands and the other almost 16 hands high. I'm five foot five and about nine stone." Then I remembered that in America they didn't weigh themselves in stones, as we do in England, so I added: "A stone is 14 pounds… so times nine."

"I will see what I can find," came his reply. I waited in anticipation, as this was the saddle I really wanted.

# SHOPPING IN DALLAS

*My God will supply all your needs. Philippians 4v19 NIV*

Tanya passed me on to Lois, her son Larry and daughter-in-law, Ketty Doolen, in Fort Worth, who chauffeured me around Dallas to find some more equipment. Lois is a dear friend in her eighties, who I had lodged and attended Andrew Wommack's Charis Bible College with, in Colorado Springs, ten years previously.

"They don't have English here. This is the West! Cowboys wear jeans," were the replies when I asked around for jodhpurs.

"Jodpants?" Ketty asked.

"No, they're called jodhpurs," I replied, laughing. "Pants are underwear in England!"

"Well, we're expecting some hot days!" joked Larry who was driving, and passed two girls riding horses on the central reservation.

"Hey, there are some girls wearing English pants!" he exclaimed enthusiastically, did a U-turn and pulled up alongside them.

"I got these from a magazine," said one of the girls. I knew I wouldn't have time to order them.

"There's a new shop just opened up the road!" the other girl exclaimed, pointing. "It's called 'All About The Horse' and they sell English clothing!"

"We were in the plan!" Ketty confirmed as we followed their directions. I bought two pairs of jodhpurs in my size, a pair of half chaps (leggings covering the lower leg) and some gloves.

"Now I just need some saddles!" I said with satisfaction, as I patted my bag, leaving the shop. Larry drove us in search of a local market, but it wasn't open that day. We eventually found a second hand saddlery shop, but could only peer in through the windows at the piles of saddles, as it was closed.

"We know God wants you to have our saddle," said Larry and Ketty, later that night. "There's no doubt about it." I was so touched by their generous gesture that I felt like crying and laughing at the same time, for I could use their Western saddle to carry Steve's panniers.

"Just one more to get!" I sighed, trusting that Colin would have one of those Aussie ones, "otherwise I may be jumping into the Rio Grande from the Mexican border bareback!"

Smoky wearing a hay rack!

# BLACK JACK SMOKE
## – barn name Smoky

*...if you are simply content to be yourself
your life will count for plenty.*
Matt 23v12TM

"We're getting the horses legged up pretty good," Larry said over the phone (by which he meant getting them fit!) as Lois and I drove to east Texas. However, I was gutted to find that Smoky had saddle sores and girth galls, after being borrowed by a rough rider the previous weekend. It looked as if I needed to find a replacement, for one has to avoid saddle sores at all costs during a long distance ride, especially not start with them. And sadly, his beautiful tail had also been chewed off at the end of his dock.

"Once we came back and found him wearing his hayrack!" remarked Larry adding, "You can see he has a scar on the bridge of his nose. He ran into a pipe fence and busted his face. The bone was cracked, which required a metal plate and many stitches. I also stitched him up after he was playing and reared up and came down on a fence post, which sliced his neck open, but was not too serious. He really has some cuttin' ability, but we just rope off of him. He's probably the most charismatic horse we have had. He's sure to keep you entertained and on your toes! He's always getting into something, he was worse than a pet raccoon!"

*Always be a first-rate version of yourself,
instead of a second-rate version
of somebody else - Judy Garland*

19

# SMOOTH EASY PISTOL ~ barn name Pistol

"That's the horse you're riding to Canada!" Larry said with a chuckle, as Pistol rather over reacted to having hobbles put on for the first time.

"Well, his name Pistol seems to suit him!" I remarked at his explosive behaviour, daunted by the challenge ahead of riding him several thousand miles to Canada and surviving. Rather lost for words I added, "Smoky and Pistol are good Wild West names!"

"Smoky is pretty laid back. You don't want them both laid back. Pistol's drive will keep Smoky going – their personalities complement each other," Larry confirmed, adding: "It's a pretty hard ride. It's not like you are going to be party pushing, but it's not the pony express ride either."

Larry, Karon and Eli helped me to gather equipment and organise the farrier and the vet, as the horses had to have a list of vaccinations including west nile, rabies, tetanus, as well as the coggins test and health papers.

Security is a myth – it doesn't exist.
oiding danger is no safer in the long run than outright exposure.
Life is either a daring adventure or nothing at all.
Helen Keller

Be free all worthy spirits, and stretch yourselves,
for greatness and for height – George Chapman

# NEEDING A PARACHUTE!

*Don't use your energy to worry use your energy to believe.*
*– Joel Osteen*

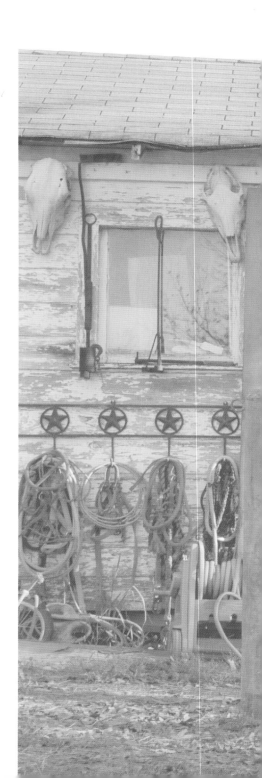

"This one will be alright. You don't need a parachute to ride him!" commented Delbert Reynolds, the farrier and patted Smoky on the hindquarters. Meanwhile Pistol, tied to the trailer, was striking out with his forefeet. My heart sank. How could I take a horse that was so bad at being shod?

"Do you want me to leave him?" Delbert Reynolds asked. "I saw the look on your face."

"I don't have time to find another horse. I'm leaving in a few days," I replied in quiet desperation.

"Tell them 'he's a light taper', as he hasn't been shod before. Maybe you'll be able to swap him for a good mule," Delbert suggested, passing me a handful of nails and an extra set of horseshoes, on which he had welded boriem (hard metal) to make them last a lot longer.

"Always keep the diamond of the nail nearest the frog," he indicated. Although I had shod quiet horses on previous rides, I doubted whether I would be able to get one on Pistol. It didn't help when Delbert showed me where a nail had gone through his thumb, after a horse had pulled back its hoof.

"God, please keep their shoes on as long as possible," I pleaded.

"A capful of gas will take any soreness out of the hoof," advised Delbert, showing me where it should go.

Later, I was sitting on a fence, as that was the only place there was a signal for my phone in the falling snow (this was unusual as it had been a humid 84 degrees Fahrenheit the prevous day) and confided in a friend:

"Pistol is wild and Smoky is accident prone. He has saddle sores and his tail has been chewed off at the end of his dock while Pistol has a great gap of missing mane – and they're meant to be film stars! And how am I going to get shoes on him anyway?

"Are you going to get other horses?" My friend replied.

"I don't have time! I have to leave in four days to meet the film people in Big Bend, in south west Texas. I've had to pay them a huge amount of money up front – the proceeds from more than a year of my business – whether I turn up or not. So I have to make every minute count!" I added, feeling worried and stretched in several different directions with the task I was undertaking, "I thought the horses were expensive, but they're small compared with the film costs!"

"It's by faith," she reminded me. "It's all happening – it's really exciting!"

"But I'm worn out," I replied, "and I haven't even started the ride!" I was thinking I still had to wade through and understand a wad of American legal jargon about liability insurance for my horses, just to enter the National Parks as I couldn't get permits to film without it.

I began to wonder why I was making a documentary anyway? Why not just stick to a book, the easier option which didn't involve extra people, complications and a huge amount of money? But I felt sure that a documentary, along with a book would reach and inspire a wider audience to live their dreams despite the obstacles.

*For a dream comes with much business and painful effort. Ecclesiastes 5v3Amp*

*Diary 5th April: God, I'm feeling overwhelmed! Are these really the horses I am meant to take?*

Eli, Karon and Larry Joiner.

23

In his 1939 Christmas broadcast , King George VI read these words to the British people,

"I said to the man who stood at the gate of the year, "Give me a light that I may tread safely into the unknown," and he replied,

"Go out into the darkness and put your hand into the hand of God. That shall be to you better than light. And safer than a known way."

# THE VISION

While we do not look at things that are seen but at the things which are
not seen....For we walk by faith not by sight.
2 Corinthians 4v18, 5v7 NKJ

   I was aware of the prophesy I was given, when Bruce and Barbara Thompson
were praying for me before I left New Zealand to return to Texas, and this was
how I knew that Smoky, with his saddle sores, and Pistol, who was wild at being
shod, were the horses I should ride from Mexico to Canada.
   "I see a white horse and a red horse. The red horse is to do with the battles. I
see the red horse going ahead of you fighting off the enemy. A warhorse taking the
darts that the enemy throw at you, deflecting and protecting."

"The white horse is alongside you, to minister to you, to strengthen you, to draw
you into deeper intimacy, faith, all along the way. Intimacy and relationship,
holiness and purity, strengthening you. And being horses they know how to
minister to your horses."

Trust in the Lord with all your heart;
do not depend on your own understanding.
Seek his will in all you do, and he will direct your paths.
Proverbs 3v5&6 NLT

...And I looked, and behold a white horse.
He who sat on it had a bow; and a crown was given to him,
and he went out conquering and to conquer
When he opened the second seal,
I heard the second living creature saying,
"Come and see."
Another horse, fiery red, went out....

Revelations 6v2-4 NKJ

# EVE OF DEPARTURE ~ NEW BEGINNINGS

To everything there is a season, and a time for every matter or purpose
under heaven: A time to be born .....
He has made everything beautiful in its time.
He also has planted eternity in men's hearts and mind,
(a divinely implanted sense of a purpose working through the ages
which nothing under the sun but God alone can satisfy).
Ecclesiastes 3v1,2,11 Amp

# TO WEST TEXAS

*"She may be riding by faith, but I'll be riding with Smith and Wesson!"*

"Are you taking a gun?" Howard, Pistol's owner asked, as I handed him a cheque in payment for his horse.

"No, I'm riding by faith with God."

"She may be riding by faith, but I'll be riding with Smith and Wesson!" Larry chuckled, as Howard showed him, on the map, the best way to Big Bend and remarked about the rough terrain and drug smugglers.

"What are Smith and Wesson?" I inquired.

"A 45 automatic pistol and a 44 magnum saddle rifle – a little easier to handle. It's got good knock down. If you hit something it's gonna get knocked down," Larry explained.

"Get up in there," Larry told Smoky, throwing the lead rope over his neck and patting him on the hindquarters as he stepped into the trailer, at 3am in the morning, followed by Pistol.

"If you can ride to Canada, I can at least drive you out there to West Texas to get you started," said Larry, as we started our 12-hour, 800-mile journey across Texas. "Alaska is bigger than Texas, but we still think it's the largest state regardless. If all the ice melted Texas would be bigger!". The United States purchased Alaska from Russia in 1867 for $7.2 million in gold, which amounted to approximately 1.9 cents per acre of land.

"I'm just amazed how fast you got organised!" he added.

"So am I!" I laughed. "God's helping me!"

"Evidently," Larry said giving me his quizzical look. "Someone's got to be in charge! Maybe the good Lord had told us this is how you live by faith!"

"Is there a napkin, or handkerchief in there?" asked Larry, motioning for me to open the glove box.

"Oh, there's a gun!" I said, a little surprised, for we don't carry guns in our glove boxes in England!

At 5am we got a puncture, right by a filling station, but as hard as we tried, we just couldn't remove the spare tyre.

"I figured everyone in a small town would get up early!" Larry remarked, as we both looked out for one-ton Ford trucks (four wheel drive).

"Evidently no one gets punctures around here, as no one carries a spare, observed Larry… but just then a work truck pulled up alongside us and offered to cut the spare off. At last, Larry could change the tyre.

"We're off like a herd of turkeys," said Larry, in a relieved tone. "So much for adventure! I'm riding by your faith now!"

I came that they may have and enjoy life, and have it in abundance (to the full, till it overflows).

John 10v10 Amp

"Americans are geared to work. What you are doing is beyond our comprehension," said Larry.

"I was the same for many years," I replied, remembering a day, after years of driving myself too hard, when I sat at the kitchen table, my mind totally blank. I didn't recover for days and it was a warning to me – one which I heeded by going for a long ride to get life into perspective.

"Now I work hard and take time out to go a little slower, enjoy life and have some space. Having a horseback adventure is good for the soul!" I replied with a smile.

It was a pretty drive through the rolling hills of mid Texas, full of small trees, Indian paintbrush flowers and blue bonnets. But once we dropped down on the western side the scenery changed abruptly to a baked brown colour as far as the eye could see.

"A long stretch of nothin' isn't it?" commented Larry. He told me about Texas history, and how rivers provide the natural state boundaries. They included the Rio Grande River, towards which we were heading, which borders Texas and Mexico.

Prior to the arrival of European explorers, there were already several established American civilisations: the Pueblo from the upper Rio Grande region, the Mound Builders of the Mississippi Valley, the Mexican and central American cultures and 17 different tribes of Native Americans. The name Texas comes from a word from the Hasinai tribe of Native Americans meaning 'friends' or 'allies'. At that time, no one culture dominated the present day area of Texas. Some tribes were hospitable while others were hostile to the European explorers.

The Texas Declaration of Independence was decreed in 1836, creating the Republic of Texas. A few days later, the Battle of the Alamo ended when Mexican General Antonio Lopez de Santa Anna's forces defeated 200 Texans defending the small mission, which became the city of San Antonio. Later that year, near the present day city of Houston, the Battle of San Jacinto was fought and General Santa Anna's entire force of 1,600 men were beaten by General Sam Houston's army of 800 Texans, which resulted in Texas' independence from Mexico. In 1845 the US government authorised the annexation of the Republic of Texas. One of the prime motivations was that the Texas government had huge debts, which the US Federal Government agreed to take on in exchange for a large portion of Texas-claimed territory – now parts of Colorado, Kansas, Oklahoma, New Mexico and Wyoming.

Face your deficiencies and acknowledge them,
but do not let them master you. - Helen Keller

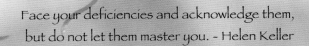

29

# BIG BEND – TEXAS

"With your accent they might not let you in. You don't sound Texan!" joked Larry as we approached the border patrol.

"Who actually has the accent? I retorted with a laugh, adding: "You Texans sure do shorten up and chop words a bit!" To which Larry added, with a chuckle: "Texans shorten things and chop them a lot!"

We were waved through and approached Big Bend National Park. I had never heard of Big Bend until six months previously, in England, when a conversation turned to the migration of birds, flying up through Mexico and the Big Bend area of Southern Texas.

"But you won't want to start there as it's too far south," I was told, but this aroused my curiosity, so I looked up Big Bend on the internet, and learnt that it is located in the northern part of the Chihuahuan Desert of Mexico. An area of interesting and dramatic scenery, including sheer canyon walls bordering the Rio Grande River and the Chisos Mountains, shooting upwards out of the plains – making a great backdrop for photos!

I was so glad to be there in early April as the cacti were flowering in intense vivid colours – an extreme contrast to the stark mountainous desert all around. Although it felt hot in the middle of the day to me, it wasn't near to the one hundred degree temperatures, which can last for five months of the year. I was intrigued to know how anything could survive in the heat. The cactus' spines, which are modified leaves, protect the plant from the hot drying sun and they preserve water in their succulent pads, small leaves and stems, which are cleverly angled to minimise loss of moisture. For their part, jack rabbits handle the desert heat with their long ears, and their long legs keep them high off the ground.

The first people to settle here were hunters and gatherers. After 1700, the Apache, Kiowa and Comanche came to the Big Bend. The Kiowa and Comanche crossed to Mexico using routes known as the 'Great Comanche War Trail', capturing livestock and slaves. The Spaniards attempted to establish protective forts and later US cavalry established camps along the Rio Grande to protect the settlers.

In 1944, Big Bend became a National Park to preserve the great canyons, mountains and desert. Unlike Dartmoor National Park, where I grew up and many people live, few people live in the National Parks in the United States and most of the residents in the Big Bend, due to the difficult economics of ranching in this dry area, sold their land to the government.

Santa Elena Canyon

# THE RIO GRANDE

If God can inspire me to believe it, He can help me to achieve it.
- Robert H.Schuller

I thought of starting my ride with a big splash by jumping Smoky and Pistol into the Rio Grande, and so into North America, from the Mexican bank. But the threat of a $5,000 fine or a year in prison made me think again!

The Rio Grande is 1,885 miles long, making it the second longest river in North America, flowing from Colorado to the Gulf of Mexico, and I expected it to be as massive as its name implies. However, where I crossed, my horses hardly got their knees wet in the brown shallow water, until I selected a deeper section to swim across for our momentous start!

The river can get low after dry spells as it is used extensively both upstream and downstream by agriculture and industry. Thunderstorms bring most of the rainfall and after a wet summer the river can run 25 to 30 feet higher. So it was quite pleasant to paddle across in early April! I thought: "No wonder so many drug smugglers and people from Central America illegally enter the United States (nicknamed wetbacks) – all they have to do is to walk across the Rio Grande border!" On the other hand, they do then have to negotiate a vast area of desert with no water and dodge the United States' extensive border patrol.

*Diary: 11th April. Wow, the start of my journey. It's both scary and thrilling! The film crew, Bob Garner and Trip Uhalt, didn't make it for filming yesterday evening as planned, but the light was good early this morning when we met at 6.30am at the Rio Grande River. Swimming Smoky was like riding a sea horse, as he was so upright and I really had to grip his mane to stay on! I don't think Pistol has ever swum before! My head feels like it got too much sun as I couldn't wear my hat for the filming because of the shadow. Good thing I'm here in spring, not in early summer when it's way over 100 degrees – this English girl would melt!*

You are today where your thoughts have brought you.
You will be tomorrow where your thoughts take you.
- James Allen

*If people knew how hard I work to gain my mastery, it would not seem so wonderful at all.*
*- Michelangelo*

"Can I give you some photo tips? I suggested.
"You mean criticism!" said Larry, giving me his quizzical look.

"Constructive criticism!" I assured him with a chuckle, as I looked at the back of my digital camera. It had taken me years of deliberation to change from a film camera and I missed the colour saturation of transparency film. However, one of the biggest advantages with digital, apart from cost, was that you could see the image instantly and it enabled other people to take shots for me. I could direct them how I would like the composition and then immediately view the picture and ask them to try again, with slight exposure or composition adjustment.

"That's why photographers' friends or acquaintances have to be patient!" I said with a laugh, and handed my camera to Trip the film cameraman.

"Can you take some too Trip?" I asked, as I wanted to take advantage of the dramatic scenery, softly lit by the sinking sun. "Maybe from a higher angle?" I suggested inspecting the photos showing on the back of the camera, adding "I want you to get those layers of the buttes looking towards Mexico."

"You see Larry, she doesn't like my photos either!"

"Well, you should know what photographers are like!" I replied.

# THE BRONCO POLEY

*Only be strong and very courageous; do not be afraid nor be dismayed,*
*for the Lord your God is with you wherever you go.*
Joshua 1v7&9 NKJ

"A buzzard and a lizard could starve to death out here!" Larry exclaimed, as we discussed what to do.

I had borrowed Larry's saddle while waiting on the Aussie one. "I could post your saddle back," I suggested.

"Post?!" said Larry, looking at me with his puzzled expression. "When we post something we put it on a stick! Oh… you mean mail it! No, let's go and get your Australian one."

"Shee, by the look of your face, you'd think it was Christmas!" remarked Judy, one of the assistants at the Big Bend Saddlery in Alpine, as I unpacked a Bronco Poley saddle sent by Colin Dangaard from the Australian Saddle Company.

"Oh, this is the saddle I really wanted!" I exclaimed as I lifted out the lightweight, shining, conker-coloured saddle, smelling of rich leather. "It's so comfortable, and look at all these extra useful attachments!" I noticed a water bottle and a torch (flashlight), and then I pulled out some sturdy saddlebags and found an unexpected extra bridle and breastplate enclosed.

"I'll guarantee if you don't have water out here, you're not going to live very long," confirmed Garry Dunshee, proprietor of the Big Bend saddlery, and offered his corrals for my horses, 12 miles south of Alpine at Ash Creek.

"This is a notorious area for drug smugglers and thieves kill people to rob them. I suggest you take a gun and just lay it across the front of your saddle," he advised, and continued to tell of some horrific incidents involving unscrupulous drug smugglers. Coming from a quiet little village in the south west of England I was shocked. I didn't have a TV and never watched thrillers, but I felt I might be riding into a thriller situation.

"Now you've got your saddle, you're all set to go. You won't be needing me any more," remarked Larry. He helped me unload and handed me some paste for Smoky's back sores, adding: "Good for frost and sunburn too!"

"What you're doing, you have to have enormous faith. I don't think I have ever met anyone so believing!" Larry remarked, adding: "Vaya con Dios." (Go with God). I wished I felt like I had enormous faith, but at that moment, as he drove away, I felt quite forlorn and anything but a brave adventurer. I valued all his help getting me started and I was going to miss laughing about our language differences. But as one friend left, new friends arrived in the form of Toni and Kerry Hellum, who I met through a chain of contacts originating in New Zealand.

Later that evening I wrestled with assembling the cot, sitting on the ground, struggling to bend the legs and pop them in the bed frame. I had been advised to sleep in one to raise me above the creepy crawlies. It was very comfortable but the temperature plummeted and I woke up feeling cold. I didn't want to get up and lose the heat I had, and maybe step on a snake or a scorpion in my quest to find extra clothing in my unorganised pile of pack bags. Instead, I lay looking up into the clear sky, sprinkled with glistening stars.

When I consider your heavens,
the work of your fingers,
the moon and the stars,
which you have set in place.
What is man that you are mindful of him,
the son of man that you care for him.
Psalm 8v3-4 NIV

# A GARAGE SALE!

Everything bites and stings in Texas – it's armed to the teeth!
- Bill Rinehart

In the cool morning I heard beautiful piano music coming from the house nearby, and was invited in for breakfast by Irene Rinehart. I discovered that the piano was being played by John, a 6ft 8in giant. Bill and his three sons were all well over 6ft tall and I felt very small beside them.

"35 to 40mph winds…" said David, the youngest six-footer, reading from the weather forecast on the internet, adding: "…with gusts up to 50mph, and it will be freezing again tonight. We're a mile high here. As high as Denver."

"No wonder I was so cold outside last night," I thought. He explained that the temperature varied so much between the day and night because the atmosphere was so dry. When the sun drops, there were no clouds and vegetation to hold any heat.

"It rains July to September, if it rains at all. It's called the monsoons, but it's not really. Three years ago they came out of a ten year drought," Bill informed me, as I laboriously saddled up my horses and tried to fit everything in the pack. Although Toni and Kerry had already taken a load to Alpine the previous night, I still couldn't fit everything on the horses. To protect Smoky's back from the sores I had four saddle blanket covers – a soft wool blanket that I had bought at the Big Bend Saddlery the previous day, the half inch black foam, the air blanket and another one. Now I couldn't do the girth up! Riding over three layers, I could hardly feel Smoky underneath me and he didn't seem to feel me urging him on with my heels. It was exhausting. Then I realised that he was used to being ridden with spurs, so no wonder he didn't feel my feeble tapping, over several layers of saddle blankets, which made the saddle slip one way and then the other!

Maddie, Garry's daughter, showed me how to get off the property, avoiding the cattle grid (guard). Then on the first rise Smoky brushed up against a road marker and Pistol jerked the lead rein out of my grasp. I thought he wouldn't leave Smoky, as horses stick together, but he picked up speed, cantering down the main road, spreading the pack contents along the highway.

"Is a horse without a rider meant to be heading down the road?" one driver inquired, and drove on. Other cars and trucks whizzed by and I winced, for it looked as if they were driving over the contents of the pack. "Please don't run over my tripod," I pleaded.

I concluded that people wouldn't stop and help because they were afraid I could be a drug smuggler. At last a truck did stop and two dark men, one thin and one fat, caught Pistol and held him while I gathered my pack. Thankfully, I discovered that my tripod hadn't been crushed. I reloaded Pistol, tying his lead rope to the attachment on the back of Smoky's saddle so that if he decided to take off again, he wouldn't yank my arm out, and would have to take the Aussie saddle, Smoky and me with him. As I continued, I passed lots of padlocked gates marked "No Trespassing - Warning K-9's", which sounded like machine guns. However, Irene and Robert, who I had breakfasted with that morning, drew up alonside us and informed me they were guard dogs!

"This is loco weed and is poisonous to your horses." Robert picked a pretty looking purple flower before they continued on their way.

"I just wanted to check you were okay!" said Toni, my next visitor, jumping out of her car and patting both Smoky and Pistol.

"That's what we call a garage sale over here!" she laughed, after I recounted my first incident of Pistol strewing his load along the road. She took my heavy shoeing gear, useful tripod and tent, so I could trot on and cover some distance. She then escorted me with her car and flashing lights down the main road hill, for it had no verge (bar ditch), and we headed towards Alpine, a town set amid the desert. I'd almost completed 10 miles on my first day, with my runaway horse, Pistol, tied to the back of my saddle. This slipped from side to side on the many blankets, and I kept having to jerk it back into the central position on Smoky's back, while continuously tapping his sides with my heels to make him walk out. I could hardly believe what I had got myself into. Riding thousands of miles to Canada!

With God all things are possible. Matthew 19v26 NKJ

# HANDBAG HORSE

Larry Joiner sorting Smoky's bridle
Below: Trying out the Bronco Poley saddle, and accessories.

The wither bags that Colin Dangaard had included were inspired by the Australian Light Horse, a legendary cavalry, which made the most successful charge in recorded military history when, in 1917, 600 mounted men captured 75,000 at Beersheba, in the Sinai Desert.

Instead of carrying a gun in mine, as the cavalry had in the past, and Texans had suggested I should do now, I used it as my very durable handbag for my sunscreen, penknives, wire cutters, notebooks, passport and so on. They were so deep that I sometimes found an out-of-date sandwich at the bottom!

"In Texas you can pretty much tell where a man is from by the style of hat he wears!" Bill remarked. "Ours are more typical of South Texas, while Robert's is typical of this area. These hats are turned up more on the sides and are bigger than those from the panhandle. Hats with smaller brims are probably from East Texas, where there are more trees and more cover. Out here you want something bigger with a wider brim, to cover your face and more of your body because of the intensity of the sun. There can be some funky looking hats. As you travel up just take a look," added Irene.

Bottom left: Rattle snake we met in the Big Bend.
Below: John, Bill, Irene, Robert, David Rinehart and Maddie Dunshee.

"Cowboys can be as vain as anyone else. The only difference is they don't smile when they do it!" said Bill, with a laugh.

Our first American drive / ride
through fast food!

Tom enjoys watering the horses with the collapsable bucket.

# THE ONE CENT PIECE

*It is impossible to rightly govern a nation without God and the Bible. - George Washington*

In Alpine, Toni picked up a cent off the street and pressed it into my hand. As I looked at it more closely those small few words engraved upon it impacted my heart: "In God we trust." I clenched the coin in my hand as that truth was the reason why I was attempting such a journey. Toni and Kerry offered me their back garden (yard), in the town, to keep the horses in overnight. She also gave me a collapsible bucket, which was great to pack, and meant that if I couldn't get the horses to water, I could get water to the horses. We got some hay and hoped the neighbour didn't object to the horses, while I camped in the empty house that Kerry and Toni were renovating. It was fun having the horses coming right up to the back door asking for their breakfast!

The Rinehart family and Hellums couldn't have been more helpful. Bill bought me a beautiful penknife and Kerry gave me a bunch of leather strings, which I could use to attach stuff to my saddle. I had lost my raincoat on the trek to Alpine so Bill, all six foot six of him, gave me his extra large yellow one which they called a duster or a slicker.

"Thanks so much – I love the colour!" I laughed when I put it on, for the bottom touched the ground and I had to roll the sleeves up to find my hands. "This will keep both me and my horse dry!"

"How big is a section?" I asked when they took me out to eat barbecued spare ribs.

"640 acres – approximately a square mile," Bill replied and continued: "In the Big Bend area, they could have eight inches of rain a year and there would be one cow to one hundred acres, whereas they have sixteen inches up here near Alpine and a cow to 30 or 40 acres. In East Texas, you could find one cow to two acres, and 45 inches of rain. There are a lot of springs in this country, although they are seasonal. The invasive juniper and salt cedars, which were brought in from Asia for erosion control, sap the water from the soil and are now all over the west."

The following day my friends took me to scout out for water along my route. We drove through the Davis Mountains, along the highest road in the area, stopping at the Texas McDonald Observatory where they gave me permission to water the horses. We couldn't drop grain anywhere we wanted, for the wild animals would eat it before I got there with my horses. Water and grass for the horses were a real issue in the desert-like West, although we were more likely to find water in the Davis Mountains. On the other hand, the whole area was notorious for drug smugglers. Only the previous week, a smuggler, with a train of donkeys, had been caught there.

The following morning Kerry and Toni picked me up and took me to Grace Christian Church in Alpine.

"I see there is lots of angelic activity in your life," the visiting minister said, pointing to me. "Angels to support your work and to protect you, for you have such an active life! The Lord says, when I made her I have to have an extra stretch of angels! He's going to call you to where there is some danger, and the angels are going to protect you."

Then I had another prophesy from a man called Jim: "You're going to be given another saddle when you get to Santa Fe, although you have one already." After such a haphazard start I was grateful for this encouragement and my friends' support, and the fact that they never voiced any doubts about whether it would be possible to get out of Texas, let alone to the border of Canada! I felt in a shambles as I had too much stuff to fit in my packs, so Toni offered to send some of it back to my base in Palo Pinto. I bought some spurs, but I got rid of a lot of things, like the foam, which caused the saddle to slip from side to side. Without it, the girth did up more easily, although Smoky always breathed out and within a few steps it would need tightening before the saddle slipped. This happened frequently when I was leading him. I'd only notice when he'd stop abruptly, as the saddle, along with the heap of attached bags and coats were hanging off one side, only the cropper and breastplate keeping it from slipping right under his stomach. It was a struggle to right the whole load and often I would have to start all over again.

You have to be bigger on the inside than the problem on the outside.
- David Fees,
at Grace Church, Alpine

## 06 RANCH

"Ma-am, I don't think I can understand you!" drawled Chris Lacy.
"I'm riding to Canada and wanted to know if I could ride through your ranch?" I repeated slowly,
and he passed me on to Missie Cantrell, who was taking some rides through the ranch.
"You can't bring East Texas horses to West Texas. You'll kill them," Missie said.
"You won't make it to Canada," was how Chris Lacy greeted me, when I arrived at the 06 Ranch.
"Oh yes, I will, by the grace of God." I retorted sharply.
"Well, darn it – maybe you will!" he replied with a smile.

Faith is a living, daring confidence in God's grace ...so sure and certain that a man could stake his life on it a thousand times. - Martin Luther King

Missie, who ran Texas Horseback Adventures, joined me and guided me through the 06 Ranch. "This business is about riding horses through pretty country – the simple way of life," Missie explained. "That's why I like to do these primitive camps." I wouldn't have described it as primitive, but rather luxurious, for after a delicious steak supper, cooked over a campfire, followed by a tasty 'cobbler' pudding, she showed me my accommodation, in a Tepee with a comfortable thick bedroll and blankets.

"You just shimmy in. I'm leaving that hammer here. You're gonna have to beat the hell out of those stakes again as there's not much holding them in."

In the morning Missie showed me how to secure my pack with a diamond knot, which she made me practise. This prevented the contents of the pack from riding loose, especially as we trotted.

"African killer bees, ssh!" she placed her finger to her lips as we passed by a clearing. "They come up from Mexico."

Missie spoke proudly of her State as we rode through the rugged pale brown landscape: "Texans are a different breed. I have never let go of my Texas number plate. They're hospitable, patriotic and deeply grafted in their roots. Probably goes back to the Alamo, and David Crockett where 200 men fought the whole Mexican army."

It was windy and my lips were beginning to crack, so I reapplied the lip block constantly and pulled my scarf up around my nose. I usually wore gloves to protect my hands from sunburn, but they were buried somewhere in my pack. In the wind and dust I rode Pistol on ahead and could feel his back come up and hear him swishing his tail – I was ready for him to buck. I needed to pay attention while riding him, for he was green, whereas Smoky was relaxing to ride, even if he did need a little urging on.

"Tighten that crupper. I don't want that sucker (packsaddle) going over his neck, 'wise we'll have a wreck!" Missie warned at the top of a steep gradient. She gave me some blue iodine for Smoky's back – the third different medication I had used on him, and after many applications it did dry out the sores.

Above: Camping out in luxury in a Tepee on the 06 Ranch. Below: Missie Cantrell and her pink cowboy boots.

43

# FORT DAVIS

The town of Fort Davis was founded in 1854 among the craggy lava rocks of the Davis Mountains, when the US military established a post nearby. The Fort was built to protect travellers heading west over the San Antonio and El Paso Road overland trail. Troops from the fort scouted and mapped the surrounding territory, escorted the mail, protected stagecoaches and wagon trains, and guarded railroad surveyors against raiding Indians.

The Apache (thought to be a word from the Zuni tribe, meaning 'enemy') occupied southern New Mexico, Arizona and south eastern Colorado and western Texas. The Comanches, who were fierce warriors and skilled traders (often trading things they had stolen, including horses, women and children) lived in the plains from Nebraska down to Texas.

Kelly Fenstermaker, an elegant artist and journalist who had previously contacted me about a radio interview, invited me to stay in her little apartment with a balcony overlooking Smoky and Pistol's yard. She came to take photographs of me at the fort, which had been carefully restored, with neat rows of cavalry quarters. We stayed with Kelly for several days, enjoying Fort Davis, allowing time for the iodine solution to dry out Smoky's sores.

At a supper party I met Joe and Melissa Williams, who were in the cattle auction business and wrote out a long list of ranch contacts heading north to Canada. I also visited Jessie at the local veterinary practice, who gave me good advice on the land and the dangers.

"Water and food are going to be the main problem. The area way up into New Mexico is desolate, and it's dry around here until July through September. It will be really tough until past Carlsbad and Roswell," warned Jessie, and continued: "Be careful of African rue which looks like green tumble weed. It's very poisonous, as is willie purple locoweed, a bluish grass."

"What about anti-venom for snake bites?" I asked with concern.

"Nothing you can do, but give them medicine for swelling – pretty common in the scheme of things," she replied in a matter-of-fact way. "Most times they are bit on the nose as they are curious. It's when the nose swells up that you have a problem, as horses can't breathe out of their mouths. If the nose swells up, they run out of a way to breathe," she warned before adding: "Don't hesitate to get in touch if you need help, and, by the way, my husband's a farrier."

"I bet this is the first time you had a cavalry sergeant fill one of these out for you!" joked John Heiner, Chief of Interpretation, as he completed a photo release form. Every time I took a picture of someone in the US, I had to ask them to sign one of these forms, and unlike the other countries I had ridden through, I was discovering that paperwork and legalities were an important requirement in the United States. I only had a few saddle bags in which to file these release forms but I often had to search through them all before finding one and by then, sometimes both the model and spontaneity of capturing the moment with my camera had left!

The flag was at half-mast due to a shooting of many people in a university in Virginia, the previous day.

Top: Mike Sloan. Middle: Gail Ott, John Heiner and Floy Healer. Below: John Heiner and Jan Sloan.

# STAR GAZING

Kelly Fenstermaker outside her home and below riding through Fort Davis.

Below: Kelly, Jenny and Fonda on the Davis Mountains Nature Conservatory.

At the Fort, Gary Dondle invited me to his astronomy lecture as this remote area was famous for the clarity of its night skies, which are some of the darkest in the United States. Astronomers consider the University of Texas McDonald Observatory one of the world's best places for deep-space observation. I went along with the Rinehart family and Gary instructed us how to identify the stars with the charts he supplied.

Fort Davis is a delightful little town, more than 5,000 feet above sea level, and consisting of many 'adobe' houses, named after a brick made with a mixture of soil and water, and often including grass, straw and even dried dung. The mixture is shaped and left to dry for days in the sun, or fired in a kiln to produce stronger and lighter bricks. By burning out the organic materials, it leaves pores which accept mortar more effectively.

I rode Pistol and led Smoky on a ride with Kelly, and her friends Fonda and Jenny, who took us around the town and then into the Davis Mountains Nature Conservatory – an area of rugged wild landscape and a habitat for rare plants and animals including wild pigs which had rooted up areas of ground. We stayed in a beautiful log cabin, and put the horses in corrals. However, they had nothing to eat, so I hobbled Pistol out on the grass. After his first experience in Larry's round pen, he didn't move an inch and stood like a statue for 20 minutes while Smoky grazed nonchalantly on his tethering rope. Eventually, I let Pistol loose, so he would eat some grass, but returned to find that he had eaten my quarter bale of alfalfa hay I had saved for their overnight stay in the corral!

Later that evening, after cooking spaghetti for all of us, I used my star chart to briefly check out the sky. It was 30 degrees Fahrenheit and cold.

"The sky will be especially wonderful on Sunday before 6.15 am," Gary had told us, so, early the following morning, I took my cup of tea and my chart outside, and used the Big Dipper to orientate myself, remembering that it always pointed to the North Star. I couldn't remember exactly what I was looking for, but I did notice that the Milky Way was beautiful.

That morning, the girls rode with me part of the way and then we hugged and said our goodbyes.

"It's been a real joy to have you. I hate to see you leave," Kelly said, kindly. I thanked her for her wonderful hospitality and feeling my emotions rising, quickly said goodbye and turned north.

I am part of all that I have met. - Lord Tennyson, English poet

Williams' place, spotting available water along the way. The area was classed as 'free range', which meant I could water my horses at troughs in the paddocks if the gates weren't locked.

As I rode down Mike's track, my horses snorted as a wild pig ran across our tracks. A herd of horses and a mule approached curiously and, nearer the homestead, a friendly Boer goat and a black bulldog, with wagging tail, greeted us.

"Oh, I had a great welcoming committee!" I said.

"Ma-am, I'm proud they didn't get in your way," said Mike, apologising for not being there for my arrival. Mike took me out to feed the cattle and horses, and it was clear that all his animals were friendly and loved. When the nuts rattled out of the truck, a herd of wild pigs, followed by a string of piglets of varying sizes, appeared from out of the cholla and yucca cacti and scrambled for the nuts amongst the horses and cattle.

A good man is concerned for the welfare of his animals.
Proverbs 12v10 LB

After my horses had finished the grain and hay that we had dropped on our reconnaissance trip, Mike gave them some more, so when I decided to leave, Pistol didn't want to be caught (fortunately he was in a small yard!). Mike gave me some green salve for Smoky's heels, which had been repeatedly trodden on by Pistol, and also for his back to encourage his coat to grow back over his bald, healed saddle sores. As I collected this assortment of medication, I lightened my load by leaving my heavy shoeing gear with Mike, as it had continually unbalanced the pack. However, I kept the rubber shoof in case one of the horses lost a shoe.

"My grandfather was a Campbell," Mike recounted, as he drove me on ahead to scout out the availability of water for the horses. "He was in line to be the chief of the Campbell clan when his cousin tried to kill him. He shot him, but was saved by a cigarette case in his shirt pocket. Then he stowed away on a ship to Canada and came down to Ohio. Survived several bullet wounds and gangrene in World War One. Then came to Texas, and worked on a citrus farm near St. Antonio. I came up here from Marja."

We dropped the pack off at the truck stop, so that I could go faster on Pistol and give Smoky's back more rest.

"Can I pray for anything for you?" I asked, as I swung up into Pistol's saddle.

"Rain," Mike replied. "This country has just come out of a real hard drought and the land isn't holding half the stock."

I did as he asked and added to the end of my prayer: "But can we just ride out of this area first!" I leant out from my saddle and shook Mike's hand, thanking him for his warm hospitality. It was always hard to leave new friends.

"Dios te bendiga,"(God bless you) he said as I turned back up his track, urging Pistol into a trot, concentrating as Pistol took more riding than Smoky. It was midday and I had 27 miles to cover if I was to reach my pack at the truck stop.

# WIRE CUTTERS!

"I'd give you a gun, if I had one," a lean man offered. He helped pour water for the horses from an underground tap (faucet) into my useful folding bucket, while his friend was fixing their car at Kent on their way from Oregon to Mississippi.

"Thanks, but God's looking after me." I replied.

"Be careful," warned Alice the storekeeper.

I followed a track, which was meant to avoid the dangerous highway, but it ran into a lake. There was a broken down fence between us and the I-10 highway, so I stood on it while Smoky stepped over it, but Pistol wouldn't walk by me. When I eventually coaxed him to move he got the wire caught between his hoof and shoe, pulled back in a panic, and the wire got wedged deeper.

"Jesus help!" I cried out, for Pistol was pulling so violently against the wire that I was afraid he would damage his leg and hoof badly. I soothed him until he stopped. My heart thumping, I continued talking gently to Pistol, while I dived into the wither bags that Smoky was wearing to find the wire cutters.

"Thank you God!" I sighed as my hand located them. I cut the wire fence from Pistol's hoof and pulled it out with the pliers. Relieved that one incident was behind me, I was now faced with another big obstacle: having to get the horses over a bridge across the I-10 highway. On the verge (bar-ditch) I waited and watched the horizon for oncoming semi-trucks. As soon as it was clear, I cantered across the bridge. Pistol shied at all the rubbish on the sides of the road, but at last we got over, onto the opposite verge and to safety.

The steps of a good man are directed and established by the Lord, when He delights in His way,
He busies Himself with his every step.  Psalm 37v23 Amp

Serg, manager of the Borracho Ranch ('borracho' means drunk), had heard from Mike and pulled up alongside us. Much to my relief, he said he would unlock the gates to the ranch (locked as protection from drug smugglers) so I could avoid the highway.

We'd travelled a long way so I was very relieved to see Neil Braid, that evening, when he arrived to trailer us back to the Vaquillas Trading Ranch. Neil and Beth were contacts I had made through Sherry Evans in Capitan – a friend of Karen's in Santa Fe. Although I hadn't met either of them, they had a lot of friends who were so willing to help. As I was passed along a hospitable chain of ranchers, I was repeatedly reminded that this area, so close to the Mexican border, was notorious for crime.

Neil, who had a Masters in Agriculture and Range Science, had managed ranches in Northern California, Montana, Wyoming and Arizona, before Texas. He told me: "When we came three years ago they'd had a ten year drought. There wasn't any grass anywhere and there weren't any cattle left. There were no fences and no corrals. The house was unbelievable, so we lived in Van Horn for five months. It's taken three years to get it back to half way decent.

"To a rancher in an arid environment, grass – residual grass – is like money in the bank. It will buy you time, in other words. You never use up all your grass in one year, as you never know what the next year will hold. One thing about this country, which is so deceiving, is that there's a lot of different plants for animals to graze on: deep-rooted, perennial, wooded species. So it's got a lot of drought insurance built into it."

# CATTLE BUSINESS

The morning was beautiful, the air was still and the irrigated green grass was so refreshing and calming to my eyes after travelling through the dry, windy and dusty land.

"They put on two and a half pounds every day on this grass in the spring," Neil told me, as he weighed the cattle and turned the herd out on Bermuda and wheat grass. "We try to put on at least an inch of water a week. If it's hot you put on two. That's a lot of water and electricity. A lot of evaporation too. It's hard to water with this system on a hot and windy day without losing a lot, so we try to water more at night. I'm not an irrigation expert - I'm on a learning curve."

"It takes a huge amount of rain for an extended period of time to wet this ground really good because it just seals over, as the ground gets so hard between rains. The most rain comes in July, August and September, with pretty violent thunderstorms and flash floods. A lot of wind, lightning and a lot of run off, because the ground is so hard and alkaline it doesn't hold the water." I realised just how different it was from farming in England.

"The calves come in from Mexico, Mississippi and Alabama and we usually put a hundred pounds on them here. We plan our cattle around our irrigation so if you get rain it can reduce your cost by quarter of a million in electricity. It got over a hundred degrees every day for two months last summer, but I would run a pivot (water sprinkler) in their pasture to help them cool off. When you see them that hot, and then see them under the water, I kinda hate not do it."

Head to head! A trusting friendship had developed.

Above: William Baize and below: Neil Braid

# THE SACK
# ON THE POLE

Neil asked William, who trained horses, to run Pistol over some wire and give him some lessons after hearing about my scary episode with the wire fence and him continually shying at plastic bags on the roadside. With a plastic bag on the end of a stick, William first rubbed it all over Pistol to get him used to it and then got him to move around the pen.

"He's pretty impressive with the long stride. Sure pretty to ride," observed William.

"Why do you use the bag on the end of the stick?" I asked.

"The sack on the end of the pole is to keep their attention and make them understand I'm the authority – not to be thinking about other things while in the pen, but to respect me and pay attention," William explained. "I really enjoy working with horses, to get them to trust you and do what you would like them to do. There are a lot of theories on training horses, but the most important thing is to get them to trust you. To be consistent and always do the same things, to reward them when they do it right and discourage them when they don't. Never ask him to do more than he can take at one time. Just enough to think about."

"He's a fast learner," he added, as he taught Pistol to lower his head. "I like a horse to put his head down and to trust you. You can get the bridle on so much easier. Horses which carry their heads so high mean they don't trust and are excited. Some horses have been desensitised, working hard on ranches. Horses which are alert and pay attention are so much easier to train."

Diary: 25th April – Neil and Beth offered to give me Anne, one of their collies, to keep me company. I am so excited to have a dog again as my Jack Russell died recently and I miss him enormously... but I phoned the National Park Authority and was told I was not allowed to take a dog into the National Parks and as I'm riding through five I'll have to leave Anne behind – so disappointed.

# NEW MEXICO

New Mexico is a state of variety – of both cultures and landscapes – from rose-coloured deserts, to broken mesas and snow-capped peaks. Despite its arid climate, there are also heavily forested areas of wilderness, especially in the north, inhabited by people of Hispanic origin, mostly descended from the original Spanish colonists. It also has a strong American Indian culture consisting of Navajo, Apache and the ancient agricultural Pueblo Indians, who live in pueblos (villages) throughout the State.

Guadalupe Peak

# GUADALUPE MOUNTAINS

Although I had thought of following Goodnight and Loving's cattle trail along the Pecos River, it was flat and desolate. So I was pleased to hear I could ride over the Guadalupe Mountains and north to Capitan, travelling at a higher altitude, where it was likely to be cooler, with more rainfall and therefore more grass.

Beth joined me for a few days as I crossed the Guadalupe Mountains into New Mexico. We watered the horses well before leaving on the south side, knowing that there would be no water available until Dog Canyon – a long climb over the mountains.

"90 mph winds go through here," remarked one of the rangers as we departed, and I was thankful that it wasn't one of those days as we climbed the steep switchback track.

"Smoky, do you think you could watch where you are putting your feet rather than looking at the scenery?" I reminded him, for he was looking around inquisitively and walking too close to the edge. Occasionally one hoof would slip over and he would be startled by the rockslide he caused. We were all puffing and sweating as we led the horses over the rough stony terrain.

Beth's horse, Leftie, seemed to be more adept than my two from East Texas. I had Pistol tied to the back of my saddle until he decided he wasn't going to follow Smoky around a sharp bend, and pulled Smoky backwards. Realising that the consequences could have been much more serious, I untied Pistol and led him on a long rope behind us.

"Wow! We've just climbed up there!" Smoky and Pistol remarked looking back into Texas.
Below: Beth riding Leftie leading Smoky and Pistol.

*Casting the whole of your care on Him, for He cares for you affectionately and cares about you watchfully.*

*1 Peter 5v7 Amp*

# DOG CANYON

It took us three hours to get to the top and several more to get down the other side to Dog Canyon. Here, we were grateful to find some high pressure taps for our very thirsty horses. We gave them some water and let them graze. Smoky knocked into a metal bin, frightened himself, plunged and broke his hobbles, so I put him on a tethering rope while Pistol grazed loose, and Leftie grazed with rope hobbles.

Probably alerted by the noise, a park warden appeared, with a Doberman dog and a pistol hitched on his belt. "North of here is bad – there's no water. It's desolate," he warned, introducing himself as Carver and continued to tell us a story of how he lent a horse to a ranger who let it die of thirst. His words worried me, that windy night, as Beth and I anchored down the tent.

As we were packing up in the morning mist and drizzle, Carver reappeared with his dog. "These may help," he said, handing us two five-gallon plastic water containers and two oranges. We filled these, and every other water container we had, but it was so hard to carry them. The whole pack shifted under the weight – even worse than grain.

I decided to put the pack on Pistol, and to ride Smoky. Although his sores were beginning to heal well, I set the Bronco Poley saddle further back and kept the girth loose so as not to irritate them. Packing Pistol took much more effort, for he was taller than Smoky and I had to stand on tiptoes. I could have done with a stepladder as I practised getting the diamond knot tight enough. However, whenever we trotted, the water containers caused the pack to shift, and after just a few miles, we decided to let the horses drink the water, because any time we gained by trotting was then lost by having to re-set the pack.

On our route were a series of unused drop gates beside the cattle grids. "I don't know how I'm going to do this when I'm on my own!" I gasped, as Beth and I struggled to uproot and open these drop gates, which were embedded in the ground.

Early in the day, we found a trough surrounded by cattle, and watered the horses here. As the day wore on, and the horses got thirsty, we made several detours to investigate water towers, all of which were empty. We asked God to send someone along, who knew where to find water.

"Tracey, there must be water there!" Beth pointed enthusiastically to some corrals and water tanks, so we rode over… but after searching every tank, and all around the corrals, we found none.

O Lord, I know the way of man is not in himself; It is not in man who walks to direct his own steps. Jeremiah 10v23

"It's hard to believe there'd be corrals, but no water," I sighed, and asked quietly "what next?" when a grey pick-up truck, followed by a plume of dust, appeared a quarter of a mile away. I waved frantically.

"He must be a local out here on the dirt road!" I enthused, forgetting all warnings about drug smugglers. As he passed by, I cried, "oh no, he hasn't seen us!" but kept waving until the pick-up stopped and started to back up. A tall man got out, wearing blue jeans and a cap.

"Are you a local?" I asked. "Do you know where there's water around here?"

"No, I don't. I've never been here before. I took a wrong turn," he replied pushing his white cap back over his forehead with a puzzled look, and added: "But I'm in no rush in getting where I'm going, so I can help you find some if you like."

"Great! Thanks!" I exclaimed. "We were given water containers this morning. I'll come with you. I'm Tracey and this is Beth."

"Greg." He introduced himself as we shook hands. "Very nice to meet you!"

"Beth, will you be okay with the horses?" I asked, as I grabbed the water containers, which were folded up and tucked into Pistol's pack.

"Sure!" she replied, as we put the water containers in the back of the pick-up. After reminding myself that the passenger door was on the opposite side from cars in England, I hopped in.

"I was down in Juarez, Mexico, building houses for families for Casa de Christo," Greg explained as we drove off to find water. "I decided to go the scenic way home to Lubbock, Texas. As I was going down the highway I missed the turning, but as I got to the salt flat, I just happened to see the second turning and ended up coming this way!" We stopped several times, first at an empty dam and then an empty water tank. Then Greg spotted a homestead in the distance.

"In case they meet us with a shot gun, can you talk to them?" Greg asked with a smile as we bumped along a rutted track. "In Spanish?"

"Sure I can talk to them… but I don't know if I can in Spanish!" I replied, delving into my memory, for I had done an intensive, six-week Spanish course. I loved the sound of it, but through a lack of use it had become muddled up with my school French. I'd never been good at languages – not even English, as a child I was dyslexic. I remember my Mother saying: "I can understand you but no one else can!"

"Olah… directo… adoite… ithquierda …" I began practising. "Was that Spanish or French?"

"I don't know about French!" said Greg, with a chuckle, and as we approached the ranch homestead I continued puzzling how to say, in Spanish: "Hello, I'm riding horses to Canada. Please could I have some water?"

# AN ANGEL IN A FORD PICK-UP!

A very thin old man came to the yard gate, and when I told him what I was doing (in English!) he said with an American accent: "Ya'll wait here while I go get my wife. She's in the shower, but she won't never believe this story!" He kindly let us fill up the water containers from his hose and left looking puzzled.

"Will Beth think I've kidnapped you?" Greg asked. "We've been gone over an hour!"

"Oh, I'm sure not – you seemed like a nice guy!" I chuckled.

Beth and the horses were glad to see us and to have a good drink. Greg had worked in Colorado, packing mules for hunters, so he helped unpack Pistol. Mind you, both Greg and Beth were a bit perplexed by the girth attachment on the Australian Bronco Poley saddle!

"I don't think I would camp too close to those pens or logs. There's lots of rattlers around and that would be a good place for them to hide," Greg warned. He finished checking the horses' hooves and gave us some neatly packed and labelled food supplies from his pick-up.

"Someone must be looking after you," he said, as we thanked him and shook his hand.

"Oh, yes!" I replied with a smile, "only God could have arranged a meeting like this!"

Beth and I pitched the tent in the middle of the corral, driving the tent pegs into the hard ground, and draped the tarpaulin over the pack bags.

"Italian cookies in the south west, delivered by an angel in a Ford pick-up, wearing blue jeans and cowboy boots," remarked Beth, as we crunched on the biscottis, sitting on some logs in the moonlight.

"We call these biscuits," I said while taking another bite.

"Oh, our biscuits are thick!" said Beth, showing what she meant with her thumb and forefinger.

"Those are scones in England… and this is a torch!" I pointed to the light on my forehead. "You'd call it a flashlight!"

"Oh, a torch over here is a flaming fire," explained Beth, and we continued to enjoy exchanging British and American expressions.

Above: "Is that it?" Smoky asked, peering over the corral fence as they had finished off the sweet feed.

Left: I was glad to find out that my small tent was waterproof as Beth and I were squashed in it when a storm exploded overhead, followed by a deluge!

# NO SHOOTING - PLEASE!

"Thunderstorms are a pretty big deal all over the south west," Beth remarked the following morning, as the sky exploded with loud claps of thunder. "When it rains it usually comes in fierce storms."

The dust in the corral quickly turned to liquid mud and we pulled the ground sheet up to prevent the water coming into the tent. There was another explosion of thunder overhead and the rain hammered on our tent. The temperature had plummeted, so we piled on extra layers of clothing and trudged through the mud to feed the remaining grain to the horses, before packing up and riding north. There was no shortage of water that day, and the horses were able to drink out of puddles on the hard ground.

We were expecting to meet up with Neil, and were just about to mark a large arrow in the dirt road to indicate that we had taken a short cut cross country, when his pick-up and trailer appeared.

"Nothing beats rain and a storm in the mountains. Everything gets so clear afterwards," he said, as he arrived with sweet feed, alfalfa hay, drinking water and a tasty sandwich. He added: "It's getting a bit darker again. You might see the second wave!"

Neil's pick-up slithered over the muddy ground and we looked out for signposts, which were non-existent. When they unloaded me, further along the road, Neil poured as much sweet feed into my pack panniers as I could carry, and Beth gave me her denim shirt. "It won't show the dirt!" she assured me as we hugged each other and said goodbye.

"Get in touch if you need anything," Neil called out, as I rode over the rise in the hill, and I felt a wave of sadness to be leaving good friends.

After several miles I could feel the drizzle increasing. Looking through my binoculars, I saw the roof of a barn up the valley, so I pushed the horses faster, hoping to find shelter, for I remembered that my laptop wasn't in a waterproof bag. Soon the barn had dissolved in the driving mist and rain, and not knowing how much further we had to go, I stopped among some willow trees alongside a dry wash (stream). Here, I hurriedly untacked and erected my tent, but by the time I'd got the waterproof covering on the tent, it was wet through. So was my sleeping bag, which was supposedly contained in a 'waterproof' bag.

I tied the horses to a tree, using doubled-up lead ropes, for I knew that Smoky was very adept at undoing knots with his lips, and I wanted to avoid losing them in this vast expanse of country. As an added precaution, I also used Smoky's tethering rope.

I put my damp sleeping bag on the damp horse blankets in the damp tent and got inside. I was cold and my feet were icy. I considered getting some more socks, but that would mean having to go outside in the pouring rain and searching through my bags, under the tarpaulin, and I would get even more wet and cold.

_Diary 29th April: Signs are posted up, with ' NO SHOOTING FROM THE ROAD'. Does that mean they do shoot from the road? Camped not far from the road - horses tied to the only trees around. Concerned that Pistol is deer-coloured, but Smoky shows up well, so I tied him close by. Near a dry wash but a short distance away, as remembered warnings of flash floods that sweep down the arroyos (dry riverbeds) when it's been raining. Even in another area. -I will not be afraid of evil tidings; my heart is firmly fixed, trusting, leaning on and being confident in the Lord. Psalm 112v7._

To keep a lamp burning
we have to keep putting oil in it.
- Mother Teresa

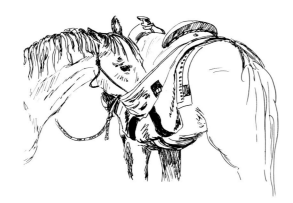

Smoky helping himself to the sweet feed from the pannier bag on Pistol!

*30th April: woke at 6 am cold and damp – everything's wet. Mud everywhere in boots, cooking pot, under fingernails and in hair. Exhausted after packing up – must eat more for energy – need to get more muscles in my arms!*

The morning sun was very welcome and, before packing up, I hung everything out to dry – including the sodden loo (toilet) paper! The panniers containing feed were so wet and heavy I could hardly lift them up over the saddle, so I moved Smoky into a dip to pack him up on one side, and then turned him around so I could pack the other side. Loading up the pack horse was the hardest chore of the day. I would do that first to get it out of the way and then finish up with loading the Bronco Poley on the horse I was riding as it was so much lighter. It took an hour to pack up every morning and I felt exhausted before I left our camp spot! It was a relief to then sit down in my saddle on the horse and ride away!

# PERSISTENCE !

No Trespassing. Private Property. No Shooting. No Hunting. There were signs all over the place. We hadn't got far when I came across another cattle guard, but seemingly no gate. I tied the horses to the fence and climbed over several more fences in order to knock on a homestead door, surrounded by junk. I could hear the TV, but no one answered. I looked around for a tap where I could fill up my water containers, but found none, so I filled up in a nearby river.

Time and again, we came across cattle guards, but no drop gates beside them to get my horses through. As I reached each one, I would scan the fence in each direction, looking for clues. "Why do they have to make it so difficult for horses?' I complained.

Sometimes, I would have to go through fences by uprooting them from the ground. At other times, I had to find the weakest place in the fence, use my pliers to let the horses through and then repair them afterwards. Wire was everywhere and suddenly we ran right into a mass of it. Fortunately, Pistol stopped still – he'd learnt after his last experience, and the training, not to panic.

These grids were a real test of persistence and I took all day to cover just 10 miles. Finally, I came to yet another cattle guard with a gate beside it, and at that point, an elderly man drove up in an old truck and invited me for a cup of tea. So I tied the horses at the bottom of the drive and rode up to the Flying H Ranch homestead.

"Wait in the truck while I warn my wife," said Rick, and I realised I did look quite filthy. Then he reappeared and beckoned me to follow him through a pack of large dogs.

"English Mastiff crosses," he replied, when I asked what breed they were. "The big one weighs 200 and a nickel (210lbs). That dog's vicious." He pointed to one barking fiercely in a cage. "It belonged to a police woman in Albuquerque who got shot."

"Would you like a shower?" asked Tip, Rick's wife. I gratefully accepted. "And you can stay the night."

"Would you have some hay, that I could buy for my horses?" I asked, and Rick took me to a hay shed and gave me a bale.

Once we had seen to the horses, he took me on a tour of some of his 12,000 acres – a ranch used for cattle and hunting. After I took a photo of him, I asked him to sign the obligatory release form. He refused. "Hell, people will think I've gone religious if you put a photo of me in your book!"

Terry, Rick's neighbour, arrived the following morning as I was saddling up. He'd found one of my saddle blankets which had slipped out from under the saddle the previous day, and had kindly tracked me down to return it.

"There have been several murders and killings around here," Rick told me as he gave me two pork chops, and added: "They will last you for a few days." (But I ate them both that day!).

"They say God looks after fools and drunkards!" Rick called out, as I rode off.

"Well, I thank God for that!" I replied with a laugh. "Thanks so much and have a good day yourself!"

"Oh hell, I don't want to!" he grumbled.

In the realm of ideas everything depends on enthusiasm...
in the real world all rests on perseverance.
- Johann Wolfgang von Goethe

# PARTY MICE!

The three great essentials to achieve anything
worthwhile are, first, hard work;
second, stick-to-itiveness;
third, common sense.
- Thomas Edison

"Don't ride on a full moon – a rustler's moon," a man warned me, introducing himself as Forest. He met me on the road and gave me the combination of the locked gate up ahead. "And keep an eye out for rattle snakes around the barns, they're on the move. I was struck at twice recently." Once I'd reached the gate, Forest returned to make sure I got through.

Soon I reached another cattle guard, with no gate, but fortunately a truck appeared. I explained my predicament. "No problem!" replied the driver cheerfully, introducing himself as Joe. He unloaded a huge four foot jack and heavy chain from the back of his truck, and used it to pull up a fence post, allowing us to walk through.

"Great timing. Thanks Joe!" I laughed. "Hey Smoky and Pistol, we're having a much better time getting around the cattle guards to-day!" Mind you, every time we approached one, my heart sank, and I wondered if there would be a gate, and whether I would be able to open it. Some drop fences had been unwired and rewired so many times that they looked like a maze of intricate knots to undo and do up again with my pliers.

The barns that Forest had told me about appeared on the top of the hill, surrounded by yards, and I was thankful to find one with grass for the horses. I put my pack inside and set up my cot before feeding the horses with a mixture of grain and molasses. They weren't the only ones to relish the sweet feed, for the resident mice had a party, nibbling any grain they could find. I turned on my torch and shooed them away, but they seemed to enjoy the limelight! So I wriggled out of my sleeping bag and hung the bags up, returned to my bed, and draped my shirt over my head to stop the mice running over my face.

The mice rushed for cover when thunder rocked the shed. It lit it up with lightning, and the wind howled and rain gushed through the open doorways. I dived deeper into my sleeping bag, but began to feel damp, and discovered a hole in the roof, right above me. So I got up to shift my cot, examining the roof for more holes by torchlight.

Once again, I had to dry out my sleeping bag in the sun the following morning. As I tacked up, putting the pack on Smoky's back (Pistol's withers were a little swollen with so much trotting the previous day), I saw a rabbit watching us. "Aren't you afraid of me?" I asked. "You're a friendly lot here!"

Usually I like to walk a lot, leading my horses – especially downhill – but Pistol wasn't good at being led on foot, so I rode him most of the way down to the Honda Bridge. As I was crossing the bridge to join the I-70 road, two semi-trucks loaded with half a house each passed by in front of me. The thought of riding along the dangerous two lane highway was out of the question, as there was no verge. If the horses shied, there was no escape, with the railings on either side.

"Are you OK?" asked a man, working on the bridge. "I was worried about you as it's going to rain."

"I'm fine," I replied. "I'm more worried about riding on the highway than getting wet. Thank you." And I whispered: "Now what do you think I should do, God?"

As I pondered my next move, a pick-up approached, over the bridge.

"You must be Tracey," stated a slim, dark-haired lady.

"And you must be Mary Jane Cooper," I replied, for Sherry Evans had called me and given me Mary's number that morning.

"Just wanted to find out where you were!" she added. I explained it was too dangerous to ride horses on the I-70.

"If you can wait an hour or so, I'll come back with the trailer and pick you up."

I was so relieved and let my horses graze in the rain until Mary Jane returned. On the way back to their attractive old sheep ranch in Black Water Canyon we dropped into school for her daughters' reading classes. Much to the horses' delight, Jim, Mary Jane's husband, gave them plenty of hay and grain.

I noticed the sheep in the yard next to the horses. "Are they Merinos!" I asked.

"They are, kind of. They're Ramboulet. The King of Spain gave some Merinos to the King of France in the 14th and 15th century and he developed his own breed."

Mary Cooper senior had prepared a delicious meal. As the whole family ate around the kitchen table, her husband John 'Coop' told of the time when the country was opening up, in 1900, and his 17-year-old grandfather and a friend herded a flock of sheep here, all the way from Oklahoma.

"That was after the land rush in Oklahoma, when a person could file for 80 acres. This increased to a section of 640 acres – a square mile," said Coop. "Wells and windmills were the greatest thing that ever happened for the West. In those days there was strong competition between the cattle and the sheep for water. The sheep had to water in the night and be gone by the morning, and the ranchers would stay with them constantly. Sheep numbers have probably fallen by 80 per cent in New Mexico over the last 15 years. Part of the decline was down to the market and government support, for it takes more labour to run sheep than cattle, and also the laws banning poisoning, trapping and shooting predators. You can't shoot a predator unless you have evidence: a dead sheep with bite marks."

Following a comfortable night in the guesthouse, Mary invited me in for another large meal of steak, eggs and potato. "I'm as well fed as my horses!" I said, gratefully. After breakfast Jim and Mary Jane took me along with Joyce Anne and Kate on horseback to photograph the ewes and lambs amongst the cholla cactus. But Smoky kept on doing enormous leaps over the spiky cactus as I held the camera in one hand and the reins in the other, while left in the yard at the homestead, Pistol's frantic neighs echoed across the canyon!

"Here are some things to take with you!" said Mary Jane, who was a vet, and handed me some bandages and bute paste for the horses.

Joyce Anne and Kate Cooper

Jim, Mary Jane and Joyce Anne unsaddling smoky.
Below: Jim with his Ramboulet sheep.

3rd May: Left the Cooper's ranch well fed and followed a track, through fresh smelling pine trees and over sparkling streams, which led us across the eastern side of the Capitan Mountains - a unique range, and one of the few to run from the east to the west, as most mountain ranges in North America run north-south. Loved the freshness and the sound of running water. The American south west is certainly dry compared to England, even though they say it's been the wettest spring in years! Met a main road and turned west, parallel to the Capitan Mountains. The evening sun was beautiful.

In Your presence is fullness of joy; at Your right hand are pleasures for evermore. Palm 16v11 NKJ

# CARRIZO RIVER RANCH

"We wanted to come and get you!" A girl in a cowboy hat, with a long plait hanging down her back, greeted me jumping out of a pick-up. She introduced herself as Cheyenne and her sister as Callie Sioux – Sherry Evans' daughters.

"That's Carrizo Mountain, and further to the west is the Continental Divide and the base of the Rockies." Cheyenne pointed to the mountains in the distance as we drove towards them through the beautiful evening light, which bathed the landscape in softness, and illuminated the shining coats of a group of wild antelope. As we approached the Carrizo Valley Ranch (meaning tall blue grass in Spanish) along a dirt rutted road, we were greeted by a Great Dane, and his Dachshund, Collie and Pyrenean companions.

"Roy, the Pyrenees, is an exceptional guard dog. Whatever you ask him to guard, especially sheep and goats, he will stick with it. He'll do a one mile perimeter patrol around the homestead, all through the night, fending off the coyotes, mountain lions and bobcats."

Callie had 21 Boer cross goats, while Cheyenne had a flock of 24 Hampshire cross Suffolk sheep. There were also six cats and several horses.

"Where were you a few nights ago when I needed you with all those mice?" I asked the black cat, who I discovered snoozing on my bed when I awoke in the morning.

"Howdy Tracey, at last we get to meet! " exclaimed Sherry, who had given me many helpful contacts. She hugged me, adding: "Sorry I wasn't here to greet you yesterday. I was at the National Day of Prayer meeting." Sherry, Walt and the girls made me feel like part of the family. Callie Sioux gave me a good-looking cowboy hat to replace my straw one, which had lost its shape in the rain. I had admired them in outlets while I had been gathering equipment for the expedition, but they cost several hundred dollars, and I didn't feel I could justify buying one when there were so many other more necessary expenses for the journey.

"Cowboys go as the country goes," commented Sherry, "depending on the terrain and vegetation. In south Texas, where there is a lot of mesquite (prickly scrub) they'll wear Levi jackets, thick leggings (chaps) and thick gloves, as the thorns will go right through you! On the open prairie they'll wear chinks to the knee and thin denim shirts. Up in the bush they'll wear wrist cuffs to protect their arms. The cowboys have different names, like the Buckaroos from Nevada, North California and Idaho, while in South California they have a real Mexican influence." Sherry added: "I was born to be a stock woman and privileged to work on ranches and see a lot of things you don't see anymore. I thought it would last forever, but I was on an end of an era!"

Walk in the ways of your heart.
Ecclesiastes 11v9

Above: Cheyenne, Shiney and Sherry overlooking the Carrizo Valley Ranch.
Opposite: Callie Sioux with her goats.

# BURNING ISSUE

Sid and Cheryl Goodloe control burning on Carrizo Valley Ranch.

Below & opposite: Sherry, Cheyenne and Callie Sioux fencing and on horseback.

I rode up to visit Sid, Sherry's father, and Cheryl Goodloe as they were burning on the ranch.

"This is a brittle enviroment. We have low humidity, high wind and low precipitation. When I came here, over 51 years ago, the creek was bone dry and there was no water on the ranch except three wells!" said Sid, continuing: "While working on ranches in the south west, in New Mexico and Arizona, I saw numerous petroglyphs (images engraved in the rock) from the 14th Century, suggesting that these dry streams originally held fish and beaver, so I knew there must be more water about. I figured out what the land had looked like: a savannah and open forest – the lower end was grassland and the upland open ponderosa forest. A ponderosa with a 12 inch diameter drinks about nine gallons of water in the winter, and 35 gallons in the summer. The reason the ponderosa is over populated is because we don't have fire anymore. Pre-Civil War there were nine to 15 trees to the acre, now there are 2,000. See, fire is as important in this ecosystem as sunlight, rainfall and soil. Here on Carrizo Valley Ranch we cleared the excessive trees and the underground aqua level rose, the springs came back and the creek ran again. If you don't 'control burn' an accidental fire can break out and rage uncontrollably. It can be a disastrous situation when you get a day with eight or 10 humidity, 40 mph wind and 80 degrees and you get an ignition and there is nothing you can do. These little trees are called latter fuels," Sid pointed to some trees, continuing: "A fire will go up through them to the tops of those bigger trees and then you have a crown fire and there's no stopping that. Flaming pieces of needle may go out half a mile ahead, you have spot fires, and then you have to evacuate people or they're gonna get killed."

After watching some burning, Sid and Cheryl invited me back to their their grand log home which they had built from ponderosa pine from the ranch, 7,200 feet up on a hill with extensive views to the Capitan Mountains. Here, Sid talked about his work in the Ministry of Agriculture and as an International Ranching Consultant for 16 years in many nations.

"I especially enjoyed Kenya, where I was the Provincial Range Advisor in the Rift Valley Province. Sid reminisced. "I went back seven times."

"My, you can almost hear it shivering!" he added, for it was cold as I left to ride back down the valley to the original homestead.

Cheyenne Evans going for a spin on Joe

We were up at 4.30am the next day and loaded up the horses, because we were expected at the Block Ranch at six, although we were a little delayed as the vivid sunrise impelled me to stop and capture its colourful display with my camera. Arriving at the ranch, we reloaded into another trailer to take the horses to the section where the cattle were grazing.

"The block ranch is 150 sections. It used to consist of hundreds of miles, but as time has gone, sections have been sold off. We used to have 12,000 mother cows, but at this point we're down to 500, or 10 to 12 to a section," said Dusty Wold, the foreman. "Yes ma-am, in time we'll see the end of ranching. Only rich corporations can make enough money. A lot of counties are buying ranches to maintain open space. And there are a lot of ranchettes appearing, like hobby ranches," he continued, springing up into his saddle.

He added: "With this water around, the herd are likely to be anywhere. These are pure bred, but we also have 'Brangus' cattle – a cross between a Brahman and Angus. The Angus has a better meat value while the Brahman travel better, cover more country and are also more parasite and heat resistant."

There are generally three stages in raising cattle, and usually three different owners. The first stage involves raising the calf, with the mother cow, up to 550lbs in weight. The second takes them to 800lbs (yearlings), and the third is the 'feedlots'. When they are finished they are 1,250 to 1,300lbs in weight.

"Most ranches sell them by video," Sherry informed me. "Different companies film them and the bids are done by watching TV."

# THE BLOCK RANCH

You make the outgoings of the morning and evening rejoice.
Psalm 65v8 NKJ

It was a fresh morning as we gathered the cows and calves and drove them back to the yards at the Block Ranch. Here, as the day progressed and the heat increased the calves were heeled, dragged to the fire, flanked, and then the team swarmed in to do their job of injecting, ear tagging, castrating and branding.

"There's a lot packed in those injections – a seven-way vaccine, including black leg, TB and tetanus. The white tag contains insecticide, to keep the flies away, and the ear notch makes it easier to identify a calf looking straight at you, especially in the winter time when they get so woolly you can't hardly tell the brand," explained Sherry. "Every ranch usually has its own earmarks. They'll be different shapes for heifers and steers.

"They have to be branded and peeled 30 days before they are sold, to prevent rustling," Dusty added.

At the end of the day Ruth, Dusty's wife, had prepared a spread of food for us all and as we sat around contentedly I talked to Sherry.

"I believe God must have created me to ride horses and work cattle because it gives me the most passion and the most joy, and also to be able to hand it down to my children!" Sherry enthused, adding, "there is such fun in having a branding day, working alongside your husband with your family and neighbours. There is something real special about it."

Above: Lee Starrit, Sherry Evans and Dusty Wold branding a calf.
Opposite: Bringing in the cattle and Walt Evans heeling a calf.

Above: Lesley Starrit spraying cattle against flies with Walt on horseback.
Below: Dusty Wold, Lesley Starrit, Sherry and Walt Evans.

# IT'S A WINDY WORLD!

Sherry with the horses while I climbed the windmill with Floyd!

"Get up here woman!" Floyd Goodloe shouted, as I suggested I could see well enough from where I was, to avoid having to climb out over the platform, which was 30 foot high up to the 50-foot tower.

"Don't look down Tracey!" I advised myself!" as Floyd grabbed my arm and gave me a heave up onto the platform.

"This is just a small one, I've worked on some more than double the size," he reassured me, nonchalantly balancing on loose boards while my legs trembled, standing on the only bit of wooden platform actually screwed to the tower! He continued: "One was over a 100 feet high! I've got 11 mills on this ranch. Most of them go down 32-150 feet deep to the water. Windmills have been designed to pump up to over 1,500 feet and have 24-foot diameter wheels. When you work on these mills, often you have to take the wheel off and then the tail and set the gearbox down, and all this gear weighs nearly two tons."

"It was wild and woolly back in the old days! Well, I guess I was young and it was a good way to make a living and there was the demand. Wind is the cheapest source of power out here and the most practical thing, as we've got all the wind in the world!"

"I have noticed!" I replied loudly, over the noise. My legs had stopped shaking, but I still had a firm grasp on the main pole.

"You have to be kinda crazy to climb up here and do what we have to do. Often we'd go out at 3am and work until 10 at night day after day. Sometimes you could only work on the mills at night as it was too windy in the daytime. I was out on one deal and a whirlwind came by and caught that wheel and spun me around four or five times. All I could do was to just hang on! That will certainly get your heart beating! That was early in my career. The other thing you don't do is work on these things in thunder storms as the lightning will get you seriously. Once the mill I was working on was buzzing and I got down off it as fast as I could when I saw fire flying from the static from the wheel. The air was charged and I thought wooo! It could have got us! It's not a job for everyone. We've had some close calls but nobody ever got killed."

"How many mills have you worked on?" I asked.

"Never counted!" he replied, "probably over 2,000, maybe 3,000. All over the South West I don't think there is a ranch I haven't worked on in Southern New Mexico!"

"Get up here woman!"

Floyd and friend!
"Are BIG tough cowboys supposed to have a lap dog!"

The wind blows where it wishes, and you hear the sound of it,
   but cannot tell where it comes from and where it goes.
      So is everyone who is born of the spirit.
         John 3v8 NKJ

"There are six, eight and ten foot mills in two foot increments up to 20 foot. The size of the wheel is determined by the depth of the well. The wind will tear it up if you don't have the right set-up. It's a lot of hard work when you have to replace the leathers, pipes and the rods, but then all you have to do is add oil, as it's the wind, which drives it. Many of them pump three to five gallons a minute." It was difficult to hear all his fascinating experiences in the high wind and I was glad we started our descent, although I held my breath getting back down over the platform again.

These multi-bladed wind turbines on top of a lattice tower made of wood or steel, enabled the South West to be settled and ranched, as vast areas of North America had little accessible water. The mills also contributed to the expansion of the railways by providing water for the steam engines.

"Now there are solar powered submersible pumps, run by solar panels. In New Mexico solar power is good because it's so sunny." Floyd remarked and added as I was soon riding north,

"Watch out for low water crossings (because of flash floods) and lightning on the mountains. Keep off the tops!"

# KEEP THE LOOP OPEN

Walt Evans teaching me to rope.

Below: Cheyenne demonstrating with an audience!

I had been impressed by the family's skill at heeling calves at the Block Ranch a few days previously, so I asked Sherry and Walt Evans to give me a roping lesson. They made it look simple, but I was about to learn it was a real skill and not just a matter of twirling the rope around your head, throwing it, and the loop just dropping over the target, as it tried to get away from you as fast as it could!

Sherry had professionally demonstrated roping in the past, but I couldn't keep up with her instructions, so Walt took over and patiently taught me, step by step, using a dummy calf.

"This is the hondo," he said, indicating the knot. "The loop and the second line here is the spoke – it's what you use to lock your rope – so you slide your fingers to make your loop longer or smaller. Your hand should be over the tip of your loop, and you can actually feel where it is when it comes around over your head. You aim that loop tip in the right direction and that's how you can cast your rope – like throwing a rock at something." He demonstrated: "Keep your hand and finger pointed out as you start swinging your loop and the back of your hand in the direction of the target. Keep your arm away from your body, remembering that your horse's head is going to be right in front of you."

Walt corrected my mistakes: "Your loop's not open because you didn't get it started in the right position and holding it too tight. As you spun it twisted, so let the rope move in your hand. Let's do it again. Your motion should be like this." He took the back of my hand and directed the wrist movement. "See how you can feel the tip. When you feel it going in the direction of the calf, let it go and the loop will come down over the horns. Then you take up the slack." As I continued to swing, the unused muscles in my hand, wrist and arm began to complain!

There was much more to roping than I had ever imagined and with a sinking feeling, I thought I may never get the knack. But thanks to Walt's patient persistence, the loop began to stay open as it swirled around my head. After having some success at casting the loop over the dummy calf. I advanced to one of Cheyenne's goats, who was tethered so couldn't escape! "Try to get the rope around my neck," she seemed to be saying, "not in my face." Finally, after all three of us getting dizzy as I ran in circles, the rope just happened to fall over her head!

Then the girls took me out to rope a real cow! Smoky remembered his past life as a roping horse, and enthusiastically raced after the one I had chosen because she was red and a distinct target from all the black ones. For a brief moment, I aspired to be a real cowboy, before losing control, as I tried to hold Smoky back with one hand and attempt to rope my dodging red target with the other. All at speed!

"Tracey, that's the fastest cow here!" Cheyenne shouted. "Why don't you try roping one of the quieter ones?" She was right. The black cows didn't seem to mind my rope hitting their backs, and as Smoky walked around them I practised swinging and aiming my loop. I made my first catch, although I was aiming at a cow nearby! My enthusiasm was rising, and I then had some success at heeling a few calves. I was completely ecstatic when I actually got the loop over the particular cow I was aiming at!

"No wonder you guys get hooked on roping!" I shouted, "It's so much fun!'

I thanked Sherry, Walt and the girls as I had so enjoyed their generous hospitality. I was sad to leave, but I reminded myself I was meant to be riding to Canada!

"I have to say one thing," added Sherry. "If there was ever an English girl who was truly a cowgirl at heart, it's you. You proved you don't have to be born in the western part of the United States, because here's a little English girl who came across the ocean, and who I watched rope, try anything and get so much joy. There's nothing like watching it on your face. You're just a cowboy at heart!"

Before I left Carrizo Valley Ranch, Cheyenne handed me some factor 30 sunblock saying: "You'll need this out in this sun at this altitude. You can burn in a moment." Sherry gave me some black boots and a scarf for my neck.

"Would you like a rattlesnake skin to take with you? I've had one in my freezer for seven years," joked Sherry. "You can eat snake too," she added seriously, and proceeded to instruct me how to catch and skin one – advice I wasn't at all sure I wanted to follow! "And quail are real easy to get if you have a pistol," she added.

Walt gave me his own advice about travelling in the mountains as he and Sherry took me to visit the Barraza's ranch.

"You can learn amazing things from your horse, like when you should be scared. Horses born and raised in this country learn a lot of things from their mamas."

"But Smoky and Pistol aren't mountain horses," I said, disappointed. "They came from East Texas!"

"Even if they're not mountain horses they can learn. They have natural instincts and can detect a bear long before you see signs of one. You'll see your horse flare its nostrils and turn its body, hunting for the direction of the bear. If you pay attention to your horse, a lot of times he will keep you out of a bind. It's a whole different ball game if you break your leg out in the middle of the mountains, and you don't want to get caught out on those real high ridges in electrical storms. Find a lower elevation camp, where you're not going to get hit by run-off water. Sometimes you need to camp earlier in the afternoon. Always go slow, take your time, watch your horse and if you sense something God puts in your heart, pay attention to it."

Arriving at the ranch, Sherry and Walt introduced me to the Barraza family.

"We had over 2,000 sheep seven years ago and now we've got ten. We lost 150 lambs to one mountain lion alone," remarked Joe Barraza as we stood in his large barn, with hundreds of dusty coyote traps hanging on the walls. "We just couldn't keep them alive. So we sold out on the sheep."

# THE HOMESTEAD ACT

Crossing the Double V Ranch and Dick Evans (below).

In 1862, the United States Congress passed a series of laws which totally transformed the American West. Land grants were given to the four transcontinental railroads extending from the Atlantic to the Pacific. Then came the Homestead Act, in 1863, affecting 29 states. It allowed anyone, who had never taken up arms against the United States Government, to file for a quarter section of free land (160 acres). This belonged to the applicant after five years if he had built a house on it, dug a well, ploughed ten acres, fenced a particular length and lived there. Additionally, they could gain another quarter section of land through a 'tree claim', which required the planting and successful cultivation of 10 acres of timber. These 'homesteading' families often came from Norway, Germany and Finland, although some were not farmers at all – more like land speculators – and along with the railroad companies got the best land. By 1900, about 600,000 farmers had received clear title, under the Homestead Act, to 80 million acres of farm and ranch land.

At the same time as the Homestead Act, the Native Americans were removed from their lands to reservations. Thirteen new territories, including New Mexico, were admitted to the Union, and land grants were given to each state and territory to establish agricultural colleges to encourage productive farming.

"The history of the West, the economics of the West, the culture of the West, is all water dependant," Dick Evans, proprietor of the Double V Ranch, told me. "One of the amazing things in the West is that you just add water and you get a miracle. Pecan nuts grow in Roswell and alfalfa hay is cut seven times."

Vicky, his wife warned me: "Take a flashlight and keep a lookout for snakes on the yard." As I left the homestead, I carefully picked my steps across the lawn and into the old saloon, where I was eyed by the head of a speckled longhorn cow with extensive horns, mounted on the wall!

The following morning, Dick drove me around a section of his ranch. "This used to be part of Mexico. We stole it fair and square!" he said light-heartedly, and continued:" New Mexico was separated from Old Mexico. It was a territory until 1914, became a state and then had the right to vote. John Chisholm claimed everything from Fort Sumner to Roswell.

"If you had cattle, you put a brand on them, for the 1870s and 80s was a very lawless time. It was open range with no fences until the 1940s. With the Homestead Act you could go and see the government land officer and file for half a square mile of free land. A husband and wife could each have half a section next door to each other. There were no fences and no water, except what came off the roof. If you had water you could graze seven cows, as 13 inches of rain wouldn't grow corn. But many of them would go broke all over again. Neighbours drew straws, gave their land to each other and moved to California. In the dust bowl every sixth person in Oklahoma went to California."

He added: "A mama cow, on a hot day, drinks twenty gallons. Seven sheep weigh and eat as much as one cow, but drink a whole lot less. One fifth as much. The Double V Ranch is 170 square miles with 2,800 mama cows. Five people take care of it and the 50 windmills have to be checked every other day otherwise you are killing cows. And then there are all the deadly plants: sorrel, milkweed, golden rod (kills them deader than a post) and loco weed."

As I left the homestead, I lost the veterinary bag that Sherry had repacked for me (as previously the syringes, for emergency injections, had become detached from the needles with travelling so she had put the liquids into bottles and wrapped them in cloth). I'd slung it over the horn of my pack saddle, but after travelling several miles on dirt tracks across the ranch, I noticed it was no longer there, so I headed back, looking for it, but without success. Fortunately, it was found by Dick, who caught up with me later!

# CORRIENTE & MESQUITE

The Corriente cattle originated from a breed brought over by the Spanish in the 15th century, chosen because they were hardy enough to withstand the ocean crossing and to adapt to the New World of Central and South America, the West Indies and south Florida. Over time, they have been bred for milk, meat and as draught animals. Although they have different names in different states, Corriente became the common term for these small cattle, now used by ropers in the North American rodeos.

The Corriente cows looked so alert amongst the fresh young leaves of the mesquite on the Double V Ranch. These amazingly hardy trees, armed with thorns and a deep root system, grow rampantly across the south west. There are three species, especially adapted to arid environments, which produce an abundance of large seedpods – a nutritious food source for wildlife.

The Indians ate crushed mesquite beans and, during the inevitable droughts of the desert frontier days, these beans became a primary food source for explorers and settlers, and were even used to replace coffee during the Civil War, when provisions ran out. They were fed to livestock when the pastures grass failed due to drought and overgrazing.

When the first Europeans arrived, their cattle not only ate and dispersed the pods, but they also stripped away the desert grasses, eliminating the competition and allowing the mesquite to spread. What's more, the pods become ready for germinating through being chewed, the seed parasites die when exposed to the animals' gut juices, and the moisture and nutrients in dung provide the perfect formula for growth. Even today, the historic cattle trails are defined by mesquite, which has gobbled up vast areas of ranchland, and is very hard to get rid of. Mesquite does, however, have its uses. It can be used for honey production, as a cure for arthritis and many other remedies, such as controlling blood sugar levels in people with diabetes.

# CUTTING HORSES

"Where are you heading?" a man in a black hat asked me as he climbed out of his pick-up. I was riding along the verge of the road north towards Fort Sumner.

"Canada" I replied.

"If you want to come back to my place here's my number. I train cuttin' horses." He wrote his name, Larry Reeder, on my pad. "Where are you heading tonight?"

"Jim and Carolyn Geiler's place," I replied.

"They'll know how to get to my place. It's the other side of Fort Sumner."

I followed the undulating, straight road north to the Geiler's grand entrance and long drive. As Carolyn gave me a lovely welcoming hug, I saw a big snake slither by Jim's feet. I shouted, causing him to jump, only to be told it was a bull snake, and harmless!

I enjoyed staying in the Geilers' beautiful home and, the following day, they took me to Larry Reeder's place, where we found a string of small horses tied along a mesquite fenceline.

"He was one of the best," commented Jim, as we approached Larry, astride a muscular 14 hand high bay called Wheresthecat. I asked him why they were small.

"Smaller ones seem to have an advantage," Larry remarked. "They can move well and turn fast."

"How can you tell a good cutting horse?" I asked.

"Short hock, short ground up to the hock, short cannons, good depth. I like to see a lot of heart depth in a horse."

"Why cutting horses?" I asked.

"When I started up I showed reining, halter, Western classes. I loved the cuttin' and the money was there. Horses was all I ever wanted to do!"

*Larry Reeder training a cutting horse while Smoky and Pistol take lessons!*

# HIGH DOLLAR DEAL

After sleeping in a bedroom decorated with horses – from the duvet cover, to the mat, to the light switch – I ate an American breakfast of cinnamon rolls, at 6am, with Larry and Pam Reeder, and then watched the cutting horse training. Derek, an Australian, and Fernando warmed the horses up for quite a while by trotting them around and around the corral, before they went into the arena, sitting back on their hindquarters and pouncing with their two front legs, eyeing the steers.

"He looks like he's primed with WD40. He's so fluid," observed Homer, Larry's friend as Larry sat astride a strawberry roan colt.

"That is something!" Larry replied as he walked him back to the gate. "He's got it all hasn't he."

"Are you drunk or sober, going to Canada?" enquired Carroll Brumley, one of Larry's neighbours, who had come to watch the training. "You are going to have quite a ride."

He went on to tell me about his sheep ranch near Marfa: "Back then everyone had sheep down there, but now all you can do is feed the damn coyotes, bob cats and, every now and then, a mountain lion that comes out of Mexico. The damn lions will kill everything."

I asked him to explain the cutting training as we watched. "The competitors can cut what they want out of the bunch of steers. They try to get one that will 'honor a horse' (one which looks at the horse) and they always try to cut a cow that hasn't been used."

"It takes a lot of cattle to make a cuttin' horse. What we work today, we won't work again," Larry added. "They get sorry and run over you, so we send them for fattening. I ride some horses for other people, I buy, train and sell. Just do it all ways, all different deals. My main business is to sell horses. It takes a good year and a half to train a horse."

"Do you do this training every morning?" I asked.

"Every morning." he drawled.

"When judging a cuttin' horse, it's style," explained Carroll. "How they do it, brightness on their face, and how they stop. They are given from 60 to 80 by five judges. They kick out the highest and the lowest. A real good score is 75. Larry's been at it all his life."

"Does everyone specialise?" I asked.

"Yeah, everyone's specialized. You've got reining cow horse people, you've got cutters and you've got reiners. Then you've got a bunch of team penners, team sorters, and barrel racers. All specialized. These are performance classes not rodeos. Cutting, reining, penning. Each group have their own associations and they will go on all summer and all winter. The cuttin' is a high dollar deal."

"Winning the Futurity is the greatest thing to happen to anybody in the cutting business," stated Larry in a newspaper article on the wall, referring to him winning the NCHA Futurity Championship at Fort Worth in 1978 on Lynx Melody. It continued: "Anyone can succeed at cutting if they are willing to pay the price, if they want it bad enough and will work at it."

The price of success is hard work, dedication to the job at hand, and the determination that whether we win or lose, we have applied the best of ourselves to the task at hand.
– Vince Lombardi

"OK, now you've seen what I was doing, it doesn't matter which one you take." Larry indicated the steers. "Just take one from the outside. Now go straight down towards that gate, and then straight back towards this gate, OK?" It was fun to have a try, and although Smoky had done some cutting in his past, he was out of practice (or maybe it was his English rider!).

"Now when you go, don't turn round this way. Never turn tail to a cow, that's a 'no-no.'"

After they had finished training, Larry pointed to his horse's hind quarters: "V slash lazy V. That's my aunt's brand – she gave it to me. In New Mexico there are real strict branding laws, you just have to have one no one else has got."

Larry invited me to stay on but I declined as I needed to keep going, so he dropped us off to avoid the busy roads and helped saddle up the horses. As I shook his hand and thanked him he said seriously in a deep drawl: "Now, if you need my help, you've got my number."

Left: Derek Detheredge, by the V slash lazy V brand on the barn door, said: "I was a city kid from Brisbane, Australia, an odd duck. I played in an orchestra and my teacher rode cutting horses. Now I'm here in America and learning from Larry."
Above : Trying out cutting on Smoky!

Las Madres Ranch

There is something about the outside of the horse that does good for the inside of a man.
- Sir Winston Churchill

# WATER HAPPY

I had been concerned about riding through New Mexico, as it was so dry and difficult to find grass for the horses. However, the hospitality and generosity of the ranchers was so consistent that I rode from ranch to ranch, and only slept out in half a dozen times.

As I approached Lake Sumner Ranch, Bill and Nancy Schade came to meet me and, once Bill had given the horses a generous amount of hay, they took me on a tour of their ranch, which bordered the Pecos River.

"The only thing we're famous for in this area is Billy the Kid!" said Bill Schade. He was a proficient killer whose violent life ended here in Fort Sumner." I asked about their ranch.

"We operate under the name Tres Angeles Land and Cattle Company, which is Spanish for three angels, named after our three girls, Lauren, Lainy and Katie," Bill told me.

"This pasture is just under four sections. There are 20,560 acres on the ranch. Just over 32 square miles," Bill informed me. "It's small."

"That's small, is it?" I exclaimed. "My family's farm in England is about 140 acres!"

"The problem is there are too many mountain lions, coyotes and bobcats. They kill the calves," Bill continued. "The mountain lions hang out in the salt cedars on the banks of the Pecos." He pointed to the river. "The salt cedars that you can see all along the banks were brought in for erosion, but now they're wrecking the West."

He added: "Out here, the number of cows that you can run is often determined more by how much water you have, than by how much land you have. When we ranched about 200 miles south west of here there was a ten year drought. The creek dried up, so we started running water through an old water tube, but it leaked and kept blowing apart. We only had two windmills, and there's only so much water they can produce, so we kept filling a 3,000 gallon fire tanker, and drove back and forth all night filling the trough. We'd get back to find the trough empty and the cows bellowing for more. When you live in the desert, any water makes you happy!"

"Certain grasses only grow when the soil temperature gets warm enough, like gramma grass. We depend on it growing all summer, to get us through winter. It's very palatable, nutritious and high in protein," Nancy told me. "Cool season grasses come up in the spring, if we have winter moisture, and this will get you by until summer. These grasses usually brown out during the summer, as they are not heat tolerant, but can return in the fall. They will green up after a freeze or after the soil temperature has dropped too low for the gramma grass."

After Lainy's graduation party, Bill and Laurie Riggins took me and my horses home with them to Las Madres ranch where we watched a video showing Laurie and her friends, Lora and Jessie competing in a roping class. Later they gave me more tips on my technique whilst we had fun roping a dummy until after dark.

"On this Las Madres Ranch (meaning 'the Mothers'), everything is based on babies, from Laurie giving birth to Taylor, to the cattle calving and even the goldfish who keep the water troughs clean by multiplying!" said Bill, who spoke about riding bucking horses out of school and now he loved to run horse clinics. "Everything pokes and bites you out here, but we just love this son of a gun," he indicated the ranch, "the land and the opportunity here."

Bill Schade

Bill Riggins giving one of his homemade halters to Smoky.

Greg Scott teaching me to pack up at Las Madres Ranch.

# LEARNING THE ROPES

"Pull harder," said Greg, demonstrating what he meant.

"More lead to your butt!" cheered Laurie and Lara, as they watched Greg teaching me to pack up. He had previously come to our rescue when we needed water in southern New Mexico. Now he had turned up again and brought his pack saddle from Lubbock, in Texas, to Santa Rosa to try out, as I'd previously been draping the panniers over the saddle and finding it difficult to get the weight even on each side.

"Try this saddle out, as it may be more stable where you're heading into the mountains." Suddenly, I remembered the prophesy I had been given in Alpine, Texas in April the previous month and before I had even met Greg: "you're going to be given a saddle, although you have one already."

"One pack has a buckle and the other a strap," Greg went on to explain. "It's usually best if you put the buckle on the driver's side. So if you end up in a wreck, or at night, you don't have to see it to find it."

"OK. American driver's side," I reminded myself (the opposite to English cars).

"Yes, the right side!" Greg joked. "You know what? It will be easier packing the panniers when they are already on the horse, rather than on the ground. You're not overloading the horse, but they are going to be pretty heavy to lift by yourself."

"Is this going to take much longer?" Smoky inquired with a yawn!

My next stop was with Ethan and Dianne Fuchs on the outskirts of Santa Rosa, where I appreciated Greg giving me another packing-up lesson.

"I have a friend who's an outfitter in Colorado. He's taught me a lot," Greg told me. "I have mules in Texas."

"There's a time and a place for mules," remarked Dianne.

"Yup, every time and every place!" Greg replied, as he lifted the bags in each hand, testing the weight. "A pound will make a difference. You have a dominant arm, so when the weight is almost right, swap them over and pick them up again." He demonstrated, and I was amazed at how I could feel the slight difference when I did as he instructed.

"If it goes lopsided, put a stone or two in the lighter one to even out the pack as you go along, and it should balance out perfectly."

I didn't think my packhorses would be too impressed! "Take that rock out right now," they'd say. "I'm not going any further carrying rocks!" I'd have to sneak them in without being seen!

My pack consisted of four separate bags. Two on each side, filled with clothes, a second camera, spare shoes, food and so on. My laptop occupied an entire bag on its own, which I had begun to resent, especially because it was struggling to cope with all my digital images, (the only reason I was taking it) and also it had lost its ability to connect to the internet.

"What are you doing?" Smoky looked enquiringly, "I don't want to carry the pack. Aren't I meant to be the riding horse?"

Hear counsel, receive instruction, and accept correction, that you may be wise in the time to come.
Proverbs 19v20 Amp

"Now hold that with your finger, and hold this with your fist, so you're not fighting it. You're doing alright – we'll have a pro here shortly!" said Greg, encouragingly, as he got me to practise the knots several times. Even when we put the pack on Smoky, who was shorter than Pistol, I had to stand on tiptoes to tie the knots at the top of the pack.

Greg offered me his bedroll. "Oh, I'd love to borrow it!" I enthused, for it consisted of a layer of two-inch foam with a warm sleeping bag, covered in canvas, which rolled up and sat on the top of the pack. My sleeping bag was meant to be suitable for minus ten, but I had been so cold and definitely needed something warmer for the ride into the Rocky Mountains.

"Wow, Greg, it's so comfortable I might not get out of bed in the mornings!" I said as I experimented lying on it.

"Oh no, she's taking my bed too!" wailed Greg, jokingly. "Be careful with it!"

He attached a string to the attachment on the back of my Aussie saddle. "This is a pigging string, and will save you having a wreck. Tuck in the rope under there so it doesn't look so pilgrimmie (amateurish)!" he instructed. "Now, that looks so nice!"

"I'm a bit nervous about damaging your sleeping roll."

"Good!" Greg laughed. "Very good!"

# SANTA ROSA

England and America are two countries
separated by a common language
- George Bernard Shaw

Tom and Sherry Green, Country and Western singers, who I had met in England with their daughter, Emiel Ross, had arranged for me to stay at several ranches and to give a photographic presentation at the Assemblies of God Church in Santa Rosa. Tom played the guitar, and along with an adept fiddler, created a great atmosphere for me to tell of my adventures in faith, crossing New Zealand, Britain and Ireland. As I talked I had to think fast, making sure I used words that Americans would understand, rather than New Zealand and English ones.

"Where does that lady come from? I can't understand a word she says!" a boy remarked to Greg afterwards!

"When you get excited, it is a bit difficult to catch all that you say!" Greg observed.

"But you guys have the accents!" I said with a laugh, "and especially Texans!"

Everybody had been so generous. Tom and Sherry gave me healthy herbal life protein drinks and energy bars, while Nancy brought a bag full of pasta and nut mixes, and fish food mix, having heard about my intention to try some fishing!

"She keeps on collecting things!" Greg remarked, knowing it was going to be almost impossible to cram anything more into my already bulging packs!

After eating at the Silver Moon with Keith, Emiel, Tom and Greg, I returned to the Fuchs' ranch, and met Ethan, who was just returning from giving my horses more grain.

"You think feeding horses takes a lot. You try feeding five boys!" commented Dianne who home schooled all of them.

"Our ranch is scenic. We don't have a lot of grass, but a lot of rocks. Mountain lions, coyotes and foxes all come down. The mountain lions eat deer and a calf occasionally, but they're not a problem to us, although sometimes we do find a skeleton up a tree."

Two of the boys, Joel and Seth, showed me their animals. They had quite a collection, including Spitfire the cow, two horses, a goose, salamander, gecko, tanks of fish, two live snakes, tarantulas (which they had caught themselves), a cat and 16 kittens. "One mother was got by a coyote so the other mother adopted the orphan kittens," said Joel.

I slept with the tarantulas in my room – fortunately, well secured in their glass tanks.

As Greg was teaching me to pack up we found a few rips in the packs. Then Smoky stepped on a strap and ripped it much more.

"You can hold your breath and fix that," Ethan told Dianne volunteering her expertise as a seamstress. "You're getting expedient service!"

Ethan suggested: "Plan to get going in the morning. In the mountains in the West it heats up and causes thunderstorms in the afternoon.

"It was so dry this time last year, you picked a good year to ride through!" added Dianne. "Everyone's in a good mood."

Tom Green, his daughter, Emiel, and grandchildren had come to see me off.

"Roy Rogers was the only guy who could run across the boulders with cowboy boots on!" joked Tom, studying my hiking boots, which had good tread on the underside and were sturdy for walking in. I wore leggings (half chaps) over the top for support and to stop being scratched by the vegetation.

To avoid a major highway, Ethan and Dianne took us to Jim and Tori Whiteker's place via a very old water tank. Here, Jim raised his own beef and marketed it in the farmers' market in Santa Fe, Los Alamos and El Dorado. He barbecued the most delicious steak.

I stayed a day and rode out over the ranch with Tori. Smoky and Pistol weren't used to avoiding the cactus as they were from East Texas and collected many spikes in their legs, which took some time to remove.

Jim gave me some sunglasses, and an extra flashlight (making four) while Tori had bought me some new denim jodhpurs, which fitted perfectly and gave me more protection from the mesquite and mosquitos.

Jim Whiteker.

# HEADING ON

*Creativity is the joy of not knowing it all.*
*– Ernie Zelinski*

As I rode towards Santa Fe the scenery changed, with layers of striped pink, orange and cream mesas, dotted with green juniper trees. Jim had some business to do in Santa Fe so had gone ahead with my pack, and I rode Pistol, so as to cover the distance faster. I followed the verge to Santa Fe, but whenever crossing the road bridges, I had to keep my eye out for traffic, especially trucks, as we hurried across between the railings. As we crossed one bridge, a car overtook a semi-truck, and at one point we were three abreast! I was relieved that I had traffic-proof horses. Travelling along the highways was stressful, for not only did I have the constant buzz of traffic, but I also had to keep a constant eye open for bottles, rubbish and gopher holes. I trotted the horses regularly, for at a walk we weren't going to cover the distance. No water was available on the roadside and I was annoyed with myself for leaving my useful collapsible bucket behind.

I needed extra concentration riding Pistol that day, as he shied regularly, but he did have a very comfortable canter. As I approached Santa Fe I was thrilled to see the Pecos Wilderness Mountain and the Rockies in the distance. I found it very exciting to be riding to places I had never been before!

Karen had arranged for me to ride to Chris and Kelly Sparks' place, where I was greeted by a beautiful man-made waterfall in the garden – so very refreshing in the dry climate. Their guesthouse was more like a museum, with a high ceiling above a wonderful room full of antiquities. Old bronze and copper pans, South American horse bits and 15th century stirrups adorned the walls. I sat in an old chair, decorated in stars and stripes, and enjoyed eating my way through a bowlful of dried and fresh fruit, carrot juice, milk, water and grapes, set out on an old table for me. I became absorbed by my interesting surroundings. A grand old Dutch dresser lined with jars, wooden chests against one wall, and a huge safe, emblazoned with the words 'The Hall's Safe and Co - Cincinnati', was set into a wall on the other end of the room (I imagined it would have had quite a story to tell!). Climbing up the winding wooden steps, I slept in a delightful little room, which looked out onto the big hall through an oval opening in the wall.

# WORLDWIDE NETWORK

Each new friend represents a world in us,
a world possibly not born until they arrive,
and it is only by this meeting that a new world is born.

– Anaïs Nin

I met Karen Lafferty and Jen Bullock, her assistant, at the Sparks' round pen, where Smoky and Pistol were eating the hay that Chris and Kelly had supplied.

"I have met so many of your friends around the world, and now at last I actually meet you, Karen!" I greeted her, and we exchanged hugs. They helped me brush Smoky and Pistol off, whilst they enjoyed the alfalfa and I thanked Karen for connecting me up with her friends who in turn connnected me up to their friends.

"What an amazing network of worldwide contacts God has taken to get me here!" I enthused, "I met your friend Christine Terreson from Sweden, while staying with Jan and Johannes Balzers in New Zealand. Initially I had met Johannes while doing a photographic job in Tibet for him and his Swiss partner, on the recommendation of another Swiss friend I'd met in Colorado five years earlier!

"Welcome to Santa Fe!" said Karen with a smile.

Karen was a composer, teacher, songwriter and musician. Although originally from New Mexico, she lived in Holland for several years, when she was with Youth with a Mission. She is also the founder of Musicians For Mission International and takes teams to many countries, holding numerous concerts and seminars for up-and-coming musicians around the world. She and Jen took me out to eat at Bobcat Bite, a small roadside cafe with character, where we sat at the bar and ate a tasty burger.

Karen Lafferty. Middle: Karen and Jen giving Pistol a brush down.

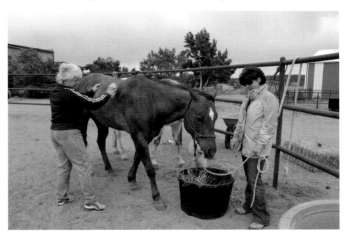

Below: Jen Bullock chosing a pair from the shoe tree on route 66!

# SANTA FE

Ropa Simms arrived with Karen Lafferty to escort me on her beautiful horse, Keller, into Santa Fe, alongside the Santa Fe railway. I appreciated the peaceful and scenic track, away from traffic. We were passed by just one slow tourist train, which I was pleased to see the horses ignored. We had a picnic, in style, for Ropa had brought cheese sticks and artichoke with a dip!

Santa Fe was founded in 1610 on the ruins of an abandoned Tanoan Indian village, and was the capital city for nearly 400 years – the oldest and highest capital in the United States. It once marked the end of the Santa Fe Trail, which was the earliest trade route linking the American frontier, back east, with the far west. It was also an international trade route between the United States and Mexico, and was followed by US troops in 1846 on their way to invade New Mexico, during the Mexican-America War. The trail helped open up the region to US economic development and settlement, and also served as part of the southern route to California during the gold rush of 1849. It was superseded by the railroads and later by a national highway, which later became Route 66.

In the early years the Trail was fraught with danger from Native Americans, lack of food and water, and lightning storms. There was no shelter and many died, because of lack of water and snakebites.

# BANDELIER

Karen and Jen took me to visit Bandelier National Monument, which was north west of Santa Fe. It was first visited by people hunting game animals. They did not build permanent structures, but used their spear heads to leave traces in the hard obsidian and basalt stone, which came from volcanic eruptions.

Later, the people became more sedentary, building homes of wood and mud. First, pit houses were built underground, followed by stone structures above ground. The people, who settled in the Frijoles Canyon are know as the Ancestral Pueblo people, and also as the Anastasia – a term of Navajo origin, roughly translated 'ancient enemies'. They were drawn here by the abundance of resources and the Frijoles creek ('the little river of beans'). These people made good use of the native plants. Ponderosa pines provided the ceiling beams for homes, while the yucca's broad, stiff leaves were used to create sandals, baskets and rope. They made soap out of the yucca roots and ate the plant's large white flowers.

The pink rock of the Frijoles Canyon wall is made of volcanic ash from the Jemez Volcano, 14 miles to the north west, which ejected a layer of ash up to 1,000 feet thick, over an area of 400 square miles. This compacted over time into a soft, crumbly rock called tuff, which is very easily eroded by wind and rain. Some components of the tuff erode quicker, and over time the exposed rock takes on a 'Swiss cheese' look. Ancestral Pueblo people used tools to enlarge some of the small natural openings in the cliff face, and the soft rock made excellent building materials for their homes in front of the canyon wall.

The heavens are telling the glory of God; they are a marvellous display of his craftsmanship.

Day and night they keep on telling about God without a sound or word,

silent in the skies, their message reaches out to the world.

Psalm 19v1 TLB

# TECHNOLOGICAL PROBLEMS

.... You can be sure that God will take care of everything you need.

Philippians 4 v 19 TM

I arrived at Hank and Judith Nowers' place on the outskirts of Santa Fe for a few days stopover. Hank took me into the local saddle shop to get some replacements for my ripped bags, then we went off to collect a bag of sweet feed and some bales of alfalfa hay, for which he generously insisted on paying the bill. The horses stayed at the Nowe's smallholding, while Karen took me back to her place. Jen had been preparing a delicious-smelling barbecue and a welcome card and a basket of goodies awaited me in my bedroom.

"It's been snowing up there in Colorado!" Jen remarked, and took me to buy gloves. Unsurprisingly, since this was the beginning of summer in the desert, they were hard to find! My time in Santa Fe was busy. Hank fed the horses every morning and sometimes I got to ride later in the day to keep them fit. Hank supplied me with necessities: a replacement pair of sunglasses, a stack of delicious protein bars, some lip salve, whilst Jim gave me some more substantial wire cutters.

Hank with Smoky and Shoe repairs by Joe Garcia.

"You can be hung for cutting fences!" Greg who was keeping in touch, joked over the phone.

"I only undo fences if there is no other way through, and then I do them up again," I assured him. Over 100 years ago, when the first barbed wire fences began springing up, and herds of cattle were still being driven to market, the trail cowboys would often cut fences to get through. In 1883, during a bad drought, fences were also cut to get livestock to water, but this led to fierce arguments and fighting, during which some men were injured and killed. So, in 1884, a law was passed, making fence cutting a crime, resulting in a one to five year prison sentence. Even carrying fence-cutting pliers on saddles became illegal.

Technology continued to be a challenge to me, and I suddenly found that 2,000 photos had disappeared from my laptop computer!

"Oh God, I can't believe this!" I groaned desperately, "please – there must be someone who is able to retrieve my photos,"

Jen, who was much more technology-minded than I, took me to the Albuqueque Apple store, but they couldn't retrieve the photographs.

"John from church has passed your computer on to someone, who might possibly help!" said Jen. "Let's just trust God he can!" Jen was leaving with Karen in the morning, to go on tour, so I copied all my most recent photos from my camera memory card onto her computer (which took me until 4am) and then copied them on to disks to safeguard them. After a few hours sleep I drove Karen's car to White Rock to visit John Tanski, who had already been working on my computer for several hours and was delighted to be met by:

"I have been able to retrieve your photos, but don't put so many on your computer as it doesn't have the capacity," he warned. He refused any payment, so I left him a few of my books, thanking him profusely.

"You're becoming too popular here in Santa Fe!" Judith remarked, adding:"You'd better get going!"

"Yes, it's a long way to Canada!" I agreed, "and I'm almost overwhelmed by peoples' hospitality here!"

Pistol and Smoky, well rested and cared for by Hank, were now restless, and had bitten each other, taking an area of skin off each ones' back. "I can't believe you boys!" I complained. "Here am I being so careful to protect your backs, and you go and take a chunk out of each other. You've definitely had too much rest!"

# A BATH AND BED!

I will instruct you and teach you in the way you should go;
I will counsel you with My eye upon you.

Psalm 32v8 Amp

Getting out of Santa Fe was a problem, as I was worried about riding along the busy and dangerous highways. I thought of going north and then west across the Jicarilla Apache Reservation, so I called the Reservation office, but no one phoned back. I then asked the State Highway authorities whether I would be on State land or Jicarilla Apache land if I stuck to the road through the reservation. They didn't know the answer.

"They have their own laws and could confiscate your horses," warned Richard at the BLM (Bureau of Land Management). Jim put me in touch with Donald Maestas, a livestock inspector, who bought a map and showed me a route going north and then west. Roper offered to take my horses out of Santa Fe and north, so we squashed Pistol and Smoky in with Keller, who was joining a party doing a ride to the north west. They dropped us off at Coyote.

I was very relaxed, trundling along with my horses in the beautiful evening light, with a lush green landscape contrasting with the pink and cream mesas. The wooden houses reminded me of Switzerland, and I hadn't seen such green grass since East Texas, two months ago. Then I suddenly realised I should stop dallying, and trot on to cover some distance. However, this caused the grain to shift the whole pack. Each time I attempted a trot, the pack dislodged and I had to retie it.

It was dusk when I approached some mobile homes, with bulldogs attached. It took everything I had to control the horses, and the pack shifted yet again. I shouted at the dogs and someone came out to call them off. "Where's Lala's place?" I asked, rather breathlessly, and he pointed up the hill.

It was dark by the time I tied Smoky to the white picket fence and knocked on the door.

"We had given up on you arriving tonight!" Lala greeted us and led us off to meet her neighbour, Orlando Madri. Here, the horses enjoyed the night in a field.

"I've got my bed roll to sleep in," I told Lala and her 94-year-old mother.

"No!" Lala said, handing me a clean T-shirt, " You need a bath and a bed!"

# A DROP OUT!

Matilda, Orlando's daughter, handed me some cookies as I left. I walked for the first five miles as I really didn't want the pack to tilt, but then I realised that if we travelled at the pace of Smoky's slow walk, we wouldn't make the 28 miles to Eunice Stevenson's ranch, so I began to trot along a smooth verge. Suddenly Pistol stopped in surprise as the bags dropped out of the bottom of the right panniers.

"Oh dear! Now what?" I asked, for there was no signal on my phone and I couldn't possibly carry the pack without the pannier to hold them. "Will someone come along and help us, or should I hide the pack over the fence on the far side of the road?" I asked, and waited for inspiration.

Within 10 minutes, Lala, Sam, Orna and Delores pulled up alongside me, on their way to do some grocery shopping.

"You are definitely God sent!" I laughed.

"Sure, we'll take the pack straight back home, because we won't have room for groceries now!"

I thanked them, and trotted on, as it was early afternoon and we still had many miles to cover. I had no idea how I would be able to continue without pack panniers.

A Scripture came to my mind: "So don't worry about tomorrow, for tomorrow will worry about its own things. Sufficient for the day is its own trouble." But Smoky, who was looking at the scenery, tripped and the sudden jolt knocked the wind out of me. "Smoky, please can you concentrate on where you're putting your feet, and stop admiring the view!" Then Pistol jerked, and snapped the pigging string tied onto the back of the saddle, but fortunately he continued trotting behind.

Later, an old truck, which looked like it was out of an old American film set, stopped and a cowboy ambled over and introduced himself as Poss.

"Have you read the art of classical horsemanship by Numo Oliveri?" he asked, as he rubbed Pistol's neck. "He said the only way I know how to express my love for God is through horses. God must love horses. To get to work with them is like standing in the river and letting the love come through." He also offered me a book by Helen Keller called 'Let us have faith'.

"Thank you, but I'm already overweight with too much stuff!" I replied. But as I dipped into the book, I liked what I read, so I rummaged through my saddlebags, found my pad and wrote down Poss's address so that I could return it. I tucked the book under Smoky's cropper. "Your portable office table!" Poss commented, with a grin.

Continuing on in the beautiful, but sinking sunlight, I was conscious that we weren't going to get to our destination before dark. Even though we were expected, I didn't like riding over strange territory in the dark, and I had no camping gear.

"I would love it, if someone could give us a lift!" I prayed.

But as for me, I trust in You, O Lord; I say,
"You are my God." My times are in Your hands.
Psalm 31v14 NKJ

# A LIFT

A few miles further along, a pick-up, coming in the opposite direction, swung onto my side of the road.

"Are you lost?" a young man asked.

"No, I'm following this road to the end. To Eunice Stevenson's place."

"Oh! She's my aunt. Would you like me to hitch up my trailer and take you up there?"

"That would be great! Yes, please!" I replied.

"I'll be back in ten minutes – you've only just passed my gateway." When he returned the horses were eager to hop into the trailer.

"What part of Australia are you from?" asked Matt Stevenson, my new found friend, noticing my Bronco Poley saddle.

"England actually!" I replied with a chuckle. He showed me his father's pee wee bit and gave me a pee wee T-shirt.

"Thanks, now I'll have something clean to wear tonight, as all my other stuff is back in Gallina!"

The state highway ended abruptly, and just beyond was the Jicarilla Apache Reservation. We unloaded the horses in the corrals, Courtney Stevenson brought them some food and Matt filled up a water trough. Her sister, Shelly, and her mother, Eunice, were at the house.

Life is either a daring adventure or nothing at all. The only thing worse than being blind is having sight but no vision.
- Helen Keller

Courtney Stevenson with Smoky showing Pistol's bite mark in his back. Below left: Matt Stevenson and (right) Poss giving Pistol a neck massage.

# HUBBA HUBBA WOMAN!

So I tell you, don't worry about everyday life,
whether you have enough food, drink and clothes.
Matt 6v 25 NLT

"What I expected was this hubba hubba woman!" Eunice humorously made a gesture with her arms to indicate someone quite solid when we met. "But this little girl appears!"

"You've come to the right house!" Shelly remarked, after I explained about my pack breaking. "A house full of girls!"

"Take what you like," said Courtney, showing me her clothes.

"Wow, what fun to wear some different and pretty clothes!" I exclaimed, as I tried them on. They were just my size! Eunice invited me to help myself to her make-up. "Suddenly I feel like a woman again!" I said with a chuckle.

In the morning, we all went to church back in Gallina. After I had talked about my adventure, they prayed for me, which moved me to tears. "Now, don't mess up my make-up!" Eunice joked as I wiped the tears away, smudging the mascara and started to laugh.

We collected the pack bags from Lala and, in the afternoon, Shelly climbed around the barn in search of her dad's old hunting pack panniers. "You want to see miracles. Well, you got one – we found them!" exclaimed Shelly. Then we scrubbed them down and Eunice sewed up a seam.

It was a fun few days. Eunice and the girls took me around the ranch, spotting elk in the evening, looking for old pottery, arrowheads and relics from the past, and floating on inner tubes in the water holes.

"This is the greenest it's been for 20 years. We came out of a 10-year drought at the end of last year." Eunice told me, and added: "Just be aware of leeches and rattlesnakes as you swim! Stay as long as you like!" she offered, generously.

"It will be better if I take you around the reservation and along the highway, as it would be too exposed to camp out there," advised Matt. He also suggested we postpone it for a few days, as the wind was reaching 70mph and the main road had been closed.

*Diary 6th June: Forecasted four to eight inches of snow in Wyoming tomorrow! Thank God I'm not in Wyoming yet! But dust is flying here! Eunice invited me to stay longer – I am tempted – But I really should get going when the wind dies down. I'm enjoying being here with the girls –*

*I have my own sleeping space in the hunter's accommodation in the barn and the horses are happy too – It's great they get on so well and stick together. Eunice saw Smoky jumping out over the cattle guard and then jumping back again as Pistol wouldn't follow him!*

# NAVAJO MISSION

"Yahee! How are you!" Leroy greeted us we arrived at the Mission, and Diane Bristow showed me where I could put Pistol and Smoky.

Leroy and his brother Howard were laughing as they had just unearthed a large bull snake while moving the water trough for my horses. Then Tyler Lopez, his sons, Howard and Leroy, and his daughter, Michelle, along with their charming sense of humour, took me on a tour of their Navajo reservation.

"This is what you call a low rider!" said Howard, as we scraped the bottom of the car down a grassy track.

"At the junction, watch out for the Rez Rocket. If you see dust coming, it will be an old reservation vehicle held together with duct tape and bailing wire," joked Leroy (a Navajo himself). He added: "Those crazy Indians!"

"We first came to help at the Mission for a few months and have stayed seven years!" remarked Duane Bristow, pastor of First Nations Gathering – a congregation mainly consisting of Navajos. Duane and Diane ran several classes, one of which was the Overcomers Program, helping Navajo men to overcome drug and alcohol addiction through a clinical and Scriptural combination. While I was there, Diane was simultaneously teaching Michelle to be a receptionist and helping another student with schoolwork. They held interesting seminars, and I was sorry that I had missed one focusing on horses and scripture.

"We love it out here and can't imagine being anywhere else," remarked Duane.

Monument Valley, Utah.

# UTAH
# MONUMENT VALLEY

The name Utah comes from the Ute Indian language, meaning 'people of the mountains'. This parched and barren expanse features many spectacular rock formations and dramatic landscapes, one of the most stunning being Monument Valley, home of the Navajo people. This is situated to the south, not far from the 'four corners', where the Utah, Arizona, New Mexico and Colorado borders meet at a single point.

# NAVAJO NATION

Monument Valley contains some of the most dramatic rock formations on the Colorado Plateau, with large blocks of compacted sandstone eroded by the weather. The reddish hues in the sand and rock are from the iron oxide, while manganese oxide causes the black streaks. This, with the remains of volcanic activity, adds up to a spectacular landscape.

The 25-mile valley is a Navajo Tribal Park, which was established in 1958, although the Navajo Nation's homeland is the largest in the United States and spreads far wider, covering approximately 26,000 square miles (17 million acres). It occupies north eastern Arizona, the south east of Utah and the north west of New Mexico. They traditionally call themselves Dine which means Navajo and as a nation independent from the US, as with other American Indians, they have the right to govern themselves.

Petroglyphs at the Sun's Eye.

12th June. What an amazing experience to ride through the red earth of Monument Valley – it was like being in a different world – a land of red desert... I sensed Smoky and Pistol asking, "Where are we? This is a long way from our home in East Texas." As I'm writing, Smoky is chewing a bit of bark... and now he has taken a page out of my diary just to let me know there isn't anything to eat around here! At the visitors centre I learnt John Wayne acted in a lot of Western films in Monument Valley. Greg's, come to help me move the horses around for the filming. I don't know how I could have managed without his great help. He's brought Pete his mule to show me some of the places he knows in Colorado.

The beautiful red coloured sand and rock gave us a stunning backdrop for photography and filming.

Ear of the Wind.

# THE HOGAN

The first known inhabitants of Monument Valley were the Anastasia Indians, who constructed the first cliff dwellings and then suddenly disappeared from the entire region around the 13th century. They attached religious significance to their homes, called Hogans – round dwellings constructed from natural materials and built by hand. The entrance always faced east towards the rising sun.

The history of the Navajos, like most of the other tribes, is a tragic one, for they were removed from their homeland and put in reservations across North America.

In the 1860s, as the white settlers established themselves in the west, the United States government marched more than 8,500 Navajo men, women and children hundreds of miles, to what is now Fort Sumner.

Many died on what is known as the 'Long Walk' and when they arrived at Fort Sumner plans for them to set up farms failed miserably. It was here that to stop the Navajos from starving the Army purchased the cattle Loving and Goodnight had brought from Texas.

Many Native American children were sent to boarding school in an effort to absorb them into the culture of the United States, but only a small percentage graduated, many ran away and the project was closed.

# THE CHURRO

Going for a slide down a very steep red sand dune!

*I could not, at any age, be content to take my place in a corner by the fireside and simply look on. Life was meant to be lived. Curiosity must be kept alive.*
*- Eleanor Roosevelt*

Navajo rugs are famous, and some Navajo people still prepare and spin wool the traditional way, using dyes made from native plants.

The Navajo-churro are descendants of the first sheep imported to North America in the 16th century and used to feed Spanish armies and settlers. Flocks of churros were acquired by Native Americans through raids and trading and became an important part of the Navajo's economy and culture. But these flocks were decimated by US government-sponsored flock reduction and crossbreeding initiatives, and the churro nearly became extinct. The turning point came in the 1970s when breeders began preserving the churro and reviving the Navajo and Hispanic flocks.

At Mexican Hat on the San Juan River, where we had penned the horses overnight we met some tourists, who had recently visited Bryce Canyon. They told me its colourful pinnacles were definitely worth seeing.

"Why don't we go and have a look?" I suggested to Greg. "It doesn't look very far away from here."

"Just a few hundred miles!" he said, estimating the distance on his map. "You'd better be careful when you say "let's just go" in this country, or we might end up in California! And anyway I thought you were meant to be heading north, not west! I've got to keep you on track heading north!"

"But I just love all these amazing landscapes and rock formations!" I enthused, "the wild west is certainly spectacular!"

# COLORADO

Colorado is the only state that lies above 13,123 ft (4,000 metres) in elevation. The eastern half is flat, contrasting with the magnificent Rocky Mountains to the west, where 53 peaks, known as 'fourteeners', rise to 14,000 ft and higher. The crown is Mount Elbert at 14,440 feet – the highest in the Rocky Mountains. An abundance of wildlife roam among uniform, upright conifers and whispering, shimmering aspen trees, which clothe the mountains at the lower elevation, while alpine vegetation bravely survives alone at the top.

# MESA VERDE

The scenery changed dramatically, from the red desert of Monument Valley, at 5,500 feet above sea level, to the green trees and snow-capped mountains of Colorado to the north soaring to and above 10,000 feet.

Before we journeyed into the mountains, we visited the ancient settlement of Mesa Verde in the south eastern corner of Colorado.

The first Puebloans (from pueblos, meaning 'village dwellers') were originally nomadic, but 1,400 years ago they began living in Mesa Verde (Spanish for 'green table'). Due to their skill they were also known as basket makers. The Puebloans settled, farmed and made pottery, dwelling in pit houses on the mesa tops or in the cliff recesses. Around 750 AD, they began to build houses above ground, with upright walls made of poles and mud, constructed one against another in long, curving rows, often with a pit house in front (Kivas). They later advanced to skilled stone masonry.

The population reached several thousand and, around 1200, they moved back to the cliff alcoves, perhaps for defence or shelter. Whatever the reason, it gave rise to the cliff dwellings at Mesa Verde, ranging in size from one-room homes to clusters of more than 150 rooms. In Cliff Palace the buildings were squeezed into the space available. The Puebloans lived here for less than 100 years, but then Mesa Verde was abandoned – no one knows exactly why. Perhaps because of drought or political problems.

"Strange is our situation here upon earth. Each of us comes for a short visit, not knowing why, yet sometimes seeming to divine a purpose. From the standpoint of daily life, however, there is one thing we do know: That man is here for the sake of other men." - Albert Einstein

Top: Cliff Palace at Mesa Verde.
Above: Greg and Pete travelling with us near McPhee Reservoir near Cortez.

# INTO THE MOUNTAINS

"Believe me it can be real steep in these mountains and I want to see you pack up properly before I dump you," said Greg, as we climbed up over 10,000 feet. It was much cooler up here, and I was grateful for a warm bedroll, with two inches of foam padding and a canvas covering.

"Gor, that's hard!" Greg remarked in the morning, after spending a night on my thermal mat.

"Didn't you blow it up?" I asked in surprise. "No wonder the ground was hard!"

"Now, if you were sending a parcel home, that would be the way to do it!" he told me, after watching me tying up the bedroll, and demonstrating a more efficient way. While I practise tying a bowline knot again and again I asked: "Why do you like mules so much?"

"Just 'cos they're more sure-footed in the mountains."

"Aren't they more temperamental?" I enquired.

"They have spirit and they have good endurance," he said, adding with a smile: "And they are prettier! There are mules just like horses. Good ones and bad ones. You just have to pick the right one. Mules are flat - burr-." He rolled his tongue and indicated smoothness of their motion with his hand. "They're generally smaller, but of course they make big mules too. I have a little red mule – the smallest, but the toughest on the mountain. He's saved my life. When we were both lost, he brought me out of the mountains. Mules have such great characters and it's good when they talk a bit so you can find them," he added, pointing to the tree cover. "I traded Pete for Edger, a horse that went right on the edge of the trail in the mountains. A scary little guy. Scared the devil out of me. I traded him and drew boot (cash)."

14th June: It's cold up here in the mountains! Glad of warm sleeping bag and more lessons on mountain survival and tying knots. My tent is meant to be a two-man tent but it only just fits me, my cameras, diary and front saddle bags/handbag (everything else has to stay outside!). Greg's tent is like a palace in comparison - He sure travels in style!

Pete

# WHEELER

"There's a place I know you'd like to photograph. Do you mind a short ride?" Greg asked, adding: "Silly question to ask a girl who's riding 3,000 miles!"

Greg had been travelling up from Texas to Colorado for the past 25 years, wrangling and guiding for an outfitter friend, who organised riding and hunting expeditions in the mountains.

"I'd get up early, catch the stock, pack up and hustle up the guests. Believe me you have to be a good judge of people, because you have to get them to some tricky places in the mountains. It's so steep, sometimes you can't get them out again!"

"I'm so glad you took me on this detour!" I enthused as we reached the Wheeler Geological Area. It was amazing. The area was named after George Wheeler, who surveyed much of Colorado in 1874, and is famous for its geology. Years ago, eruptions from massive calderas were followed by huge flows of ash and mud. As the layers of volcanic debris cooled down, crystals and mineral ores collected into veins and pockets to create large mineral fields. It also created the volcanic 'tuff', with its fragile capstones, needles and spires.

# JELLY LEGS!

The air was so much thinner, my legs felt like jelly and my heart beat overtime as I walked, trying to get myself adjusted to the altitude. I mentioned this to Greg, who wasn't surprised, although he had acclimatised over the years.

"Creede has an extra long runway for the airplanes to take off, because of the altitude," he added. Greg knew this territory, and continually scanned the horizon. Suddenly, he leapt off Pete, grabbed his binoculars and pointed into the distance, where I saw three elk.

"Elk move with the weather. Right now most of them are up higher, but this is their pathway to the valleys, their winter feeding grounds, down in Del Norte where they hang out in the alfalfa fields."

"What about the hunting seasons?" I asked.

"There are usually about four – there's black powder, archery and generally three rifle seasons. You can buy a tag (permit) for each," Greg informed me. "They issue a limited amount of tags for bear and moose. Of course, there are also deer."

Pistol was following behind Smoky, but didn't want to get his feet wet, so he pulled back as we crossed a stream and broke another pigging string. At the same time, he ripped off my second pair of saddlebags, which fell right into the water. I jumped off quickly to retrieve them, as they contained my video camera.

"If he breaks it too often, you can always double up the string. But promise me you won't tie the rope onto the saddle, otherwise you'll have a wreck," Greg warned.

Morning by morning he wakens me and opens my understanding to his will.
Isaiah 50v4b.TLB

"What are you reading?" Smoky asks as I read my Bible with my morning cup of tea above Creede.

# PEOPLE OF THE SHINING MOUNTAINS

Bighorn sheep

Hundreds of years before the Spanish explorers, trappers, hunters and miners came to the mountains of Colorado, the Ute people occupied and roamed over Colorado, and large areas of Utah, southern Wyoming and northern Mexico.

The nomadic Utes called themselves the "people of the shining mountains". They moved with the seasons, between the mountains and the valleys, hunting deer and elk, and gathering food. They harvested wild tobacco, gathered plants and nuts, and developed successful methods for catching fish.

When the Spanish brought horses to the Utes in the 16th century, it radically changed their lifestyle, as horses made it easier to hunt and to travel long distances. They gained a reputation for their horsemanship among the trappers and traders.

The discovery of gold in the San Juan Mountains was the beginning of the end, as Chief Ouray predicted. The Utes didn't suffer as much as the Indians of the plains, because Chief Ouray negotiated the Brunot Treaty with the United States in 1873, which allowed the miners and settlers to occupy Ute land in the San Juan Mountains. But, in 1879, despite his best efforts, there was a confrontation. An Indian agent was killed and hostages taken, and the Utes were forced to accept reservation land in Southern Colorado and Central Utah.

We shall fall as leaves from the trees when winter comes, and the lands we have roamed for countless generations will be given to the miner and the plowshare and we shall be buried out of sight. - Chief Ouray of the Utes Indians

137

Above and opposite page: Greg on Pete, with Pistol and Smoky, riding by the Commodore
– one of the greatest silver mines on earth.

Pistol just about to snap another pigging string as Greg waters the stock in Willow Creek,
which runs down past the mine and through Creede.

Creede

# THE SILVER DAYS

Nicholas Creede made the first silver strike on the Willow Creek in 1889. As word got out about his find, a town appeared along Willow Creek Canyon. Just one year later, its population had reached 10,000, with 24-hour restaurants, saloons and gambling halls. There was no law enforcement, apart from the self-appointed camp bosses, so shootings were part of everyday life.

In 1892, the town and the six bridges across Willow Creek were destroyed by fire. Almost as quickly as it had burnt down, the town sprang back up again, only to be swept by several other fires in succession.

Creede returned, after selling his first strike, and located the amethyst mine, from which $2 million worth of ore was extracted during the first year – some of it yielding $5,000 a ton. By 1892, $1 million worth was being transported out of Creede every month. Men made fortunes overnight, and it became world famous, known as 'Colorado's Silver Ribbed Treasure Trove'. But, in 1893, Congress passed the Silver Act which lowered the price of silver from $1.29 to 50 cents an ounce, bringing the heyday of Creede, one of the Old West's richest and wildest mining camps, to an end. By 1900, Creede's population had dropped to 900, although its mines still produced more than $1 million worth of gold, silver, lead and zinc every year. In all, the district has produced about 84 million ounces of silver from underground mining.

"There are plans to open up some of the old silver mines again, for the prospectors reckon there could be a whole lot more. They estimate there could still be at least 48 million ounces of silver in these rocks!" informed Greg, as we rode around the Bachelor's Loop and past the Commodore, one of the greatest silver mines on earth!

Ambition, fueled by compassion, wisdom and integrity, is a powerful force for good that will turn
the wheels of industry and open doors of opportunity for you and countless others.
- Zig Ziglar

# RULE NUMBER ONE!

I can't tell you how much I long for you to enter this wide-open, spacious life.
Open up your lives, live openly and expansively.
2 Corinthians 6v11,12 TM

After the dryness of Texas and New Mexico it was so refreshing to hear the gushing water in the creeks, as we followed the Rio Grande, the United States' third largest river, to its source in the San Juan Mountains. I had crossed this same river on the border of Mexico, far down its 1,800 mile journey towards the Gulf of Mexico. It's a river that has always been important for wildlife, travellers and settlers. Pueblo Indians based their agriculture on irrigation water from the Rio Grande, long before the Spanish colonists arrived in Colorado in the 16th century.

"It can snow any day of the year up here. Rule number one: stay dry," stated Greg. "It's pretty important, for even at this time of year you can get hypothermia when you get up high. Most hypothermia cases happen in summer when people aren't prepared."

"Thanks for the warning Greg!" I said, as I tried to get my digital camera to work. It kept flashing 'off'. "OK, why won't you work?" I asked it, feeling frustrated. I had only just bought a digital camera, wasn't carrying my instruction book, and didn't know what the problem was. For most of my life as a photographer, I had used two manual Olympus OM1 cameras, and then a Nikon F90X, mostly with transparency film. After deliberating for several years, I took the plunge and moved into the 21st century, although I still had my Nikon film camera in the pack as a back-up. Then I discovered that if I switched it off, gave it a rest, and then switched it back on again, it often worked fine. Technology!

"Wow, it's beautiful around here!" I exclaimed, taking photographs as we rode beside the Rio Grande.

# SUMMER GRAZING

Billy Joe Dilly, with whom Greg had worked for many hunting seasons, invited us to join him, along with some friends, as they moved cattle further up the mountain for summer grazing. He was the head cowboy on the Oliver's ranch and had been bringing cattle up to this allotment for over 35 years. It was leased from the National Forest Service, which set the dates when the cattle could graze on the mountain: namely, from mid-June to October 1st.

"How big is the allotment?" I asked Billy Joe.

"Twenty by twenty, 400 square miles. It's a lot of miles. It goes to Bear Crick," Billy Joe pointed, astride his roan mule. "Up that canyon, clear to Bear Town." Swivelling in his saddle he then pointed in several other directions, naming places. "It's about a 34 mile round trip from the ranch."

"How many cattle do you graze up here?" I asked.

"The permit calls for 179 large animals, so we bring 172 pair and seven bulls," he replied, adding: "We were later than ever this year because it was such a dry cold start and the grass didn't get started."

As the cowboys and girls pushed the cattle quietly along the flats they disappeared in and out of the dense willows along the river banks, flushing out cattle, and I hurried ahead on Smoky, leading Pistol. I wanted to strategically position myself out of the way of the mob of cattle, but somewhere I guessed they would be passing so that I could get some pictures and film footage. When the willow flats came to an end, the flow of cattle filtered onto a rough track,

which meandered upwards, constricted by dense trees on either side. However, the cows seemed insistent on taking detours through the trees and were flushed out, back onto the main track, which was once the main highway across Stony Pass. We passed a huge boulder called Bandit Rock, where outlaws used to hold up the stagecoaches as they passed by. The track once more opened up onto rolling high pastures. Here we stopped for lunch, while the horses and mules grazed contentedly around us. Then, leaving the cattle grazing, we rode into the next canyon to move another herd over the Rio Grande River to fresh grass.

"Do you get a lot of snow up here?" I asked Billy Joe, as we rode back down the mountain.

"We had a big snow last winter, but the biggest snow I ever remember was August 25th – we got 17 inches in camp. My daughter made a snowman and the grass and summer flowers were poking out of it! But it was short lived. In a few days you wouldn't know it had snowed other than it was real wet."

"What do the elk do in the winter?" I asked, adding: "Do you hunt then?"

"No, we only hunt in the fall. The elk migrate too. When the snow gets deeper and deeper, everything leaves, as it gets so deep they haven't got food," Billy Joe said. He continued: "We used to bring and guide hunters up here, with archery, rifle and muzzle loading. One year, the day before opening day, it began to snow and continued snowing. So we came out of our high camp – what we called Beaver Camp – and what usually took three and a half hours, took fifteen and a half as we busted through a lot of deep snow. It was tough," Billy Joe reminisced, adding: "But it's just a pretty good life! Never gonna get rich, but I wouldn't change it for anything. Don't want to go to work for Wal-Mart yet so we'll stick it out right here!"

We had begun early that morning, so we had finished moving cattle and were heading down the mountain by the time the clouds built up, preparing for a dangerous lightning storm. The following month I heard that three of these cows had been killed by lightning, along with a shepherd and his horse.

# INTO THE UNKNOWN!

We are all travellers in the wilderness of this world,
and the best we can find in our travels is an honest friend.
- Robert Louis Stevenson

It was time for Pistol, Smoky and I to contine on our journey.

"Everything you haven't touched needs to go away!" Greg told me, in a bid to lighten my load, which included surplus horse brushes, bandages, spare tack and paperwork, all accumulated along the way.

"Now, I reckon your pack weighs about 110lb in total," he said, picking it up. He swapped my head torch for a lighter one of his own, my battery-dependent water purifier with his hand pump, and then he checked my packing and knots once more.

"I've learnt so much from you, Greg. Thanks so much."

"Oh yeah, how to curse and how to spit!"

"You're not that bad you know!" I laughed, adding more seriously: "When God had you come along that dirt track in New Mexico he knew I needed to be taught how to survive in the mountains!"

"And, by the, way I need a pay rise!" Greg joked, lightening the moment as I stepped up on Smoky and he turned east and south with Pete. I laughed, and then swallowed, bracing myself for the separation of another good friend.

"Bye, Greg. Bye Pete!" I called, waved, and with resolve turned our faces west, into the unknown, along a dirt track lined with shimmering aspen trees. As I caught glimpses of the mountains ahead, through the notched, white, upright trunks, I wondered if our paths would ever cross again, for Texas was a long way away from where I was heading. As the horses' hooves thudded on the dirt track, and we gathered pace, I began to feel a surge of excited anticipation as to what lay ahead.

I rode over a tributary of the Rio Grande, with trout darting under my horses' hooves, and made camp beside the river, before we climbed higher to find grass and trees for shelter. I hobbled Pistol and tethered Smoky on a long rope, and was relaxing after pitching my tent, when I saw them both look up simultaneously and intently, their nostrils flaring. Within seconds they were off at a gallop.

# ESCAPE
# IN THE MOUNTAINS

I watched in astonishment as Pistol plunged past me, with both forelegs still hobbled, followed by Smoky, dragging his tethering rope. The last I saw of them was two silhouettes, bounding up the spur of the mountain and disappearing over the horizon.

I scanned the surroundings, but couldn't see what had spooked them. A mountain lion, or a possibly a bear? The light was fading, so I went after them. I scrambled up a scree slope, gasping for air in the high altitude, and flopped onto a dirt road. I followed it, upwards and westwards, spotting occasional hoof marks, until they were no longer visible on the hard surface. Here and there, I saw signs of deer, and at one point I saw large paw prints and I wondered if they were a lion's or a dog's. I hoped the latter. I prayed to find the horses, hoping they had stuck to the road, for the country was so vast that I could lose them for days.

There are thought to be 1,500 to 3,000 mountain lions (also known as cougar, panther or puma) in Colorado. They exist only in the Western Hemisphere, and their habitat ranges from desert badlands to sub-alpine mountains and tropical rain forests. In the wild their natural life span is about 12 years, and their favourite food is deer, although they also kill elk, porcupines, small mammals, livestock and domestic animals. Their most active hunting time is dawn and dusk… which I remembered as I followed the dirt track. Or maybe it was a bear that had spooked the horses?

Having left in such a rush, I had forgotten to bring either water or a torch. So as the dusk was fading into night, I was thinking that I might have to abandon the search until the morning. Then, suddenly, I saw the marks of a trailing rope in the dirt and there, around a bend, I found the tired horses with their heads hanging. Fortunately, the rope attached to the halter and tied around Pistol's neck had come loose, and he had continually stepped on it, jerking his halter and head which had slowed him down.

"Am I glad to see you guys!" I patted their necks in huge relief. "I gave you an easy day today, but you obviously needed a gallop! Now we have to go all the way back to camp." Pistol had lost his hobbles, and the only remains of Smoky's tethering rope was the sheepskin lined leather band around his coronet. We wearily retraced our steps, hoping to find the tethering rope and hobbles. In the twilight, I led them through a boggy patch, where they sank up to their stomachs and we were all splattered with mud. Then we slid and slipped down the same scree slope that they had bounded up and here, to my amazement, I found the rope and hobbles. Once I got back to camp, I tied them securely to trees for the night, praying and trusting they would be safe, for I wouldn't be able to hear them above the roaring of the Rio Grande. Gratefully, I collapsed into my tent.

Following the Rio Grande River to its source.

For God has not given us a spirit of fear and timidity,
but of power, love and self-discipline.
2 Timothy 1v7 NLT "

Below: Following the old route over the Continental Divide at Stony Pass.

147

# FISHING FRIENDS

I awoke at six, to find a frost (on June 19, almost midsummer!) covering the tent and pack. I was very relieved to see the horses still tied to the trees. Although my fingers were cold at first, after taking an hour to pack the horses, I had stripped off my layers and was sweating. I had a protein drink mix to boost my energy before setting off up the mountain.

Not far from camp, some fisherman stopped and the younger man asked. "How old are you?" Although this seemed a very common question to be asked in the United States it always took me aback – yet another cultural difference as I had been told it was rude to ask how big someone's ranch was in New Mexico. Apparently it was like asking how much money they had in the bank!

"It's rude to ask a woman's age where I come from!" I replied.

"Twenty!" Irvin, the older man suggested.

"That will do!" I replied with a giggle.

"I'm 84, and I was wondering if you would you like a cup of coffee?" he offered.

"Would you like some fishing gear?" Irvin asked, as I drank his coffee. "This is some of the best fishing up here." He handed me a reel and tub of worms. "Cast upstream. Let it drift out and down into a deep hole two to three times. Get a willow pole, six feet or so, cover the hook with the worm and let it loose and wriggle."

God alone is my refuge, my place of safety, and I am trusting him.

His faithful promises are my armor and protection. For he orders his angels to protect me wherever I go.

The Lord says, "I will rescue those who love me. I will protect those who trust in my name." Psalm 91 NLT

"How come you're doing this ride?" they asked.

"Because God put it in my heart. And by faith I believe and act on His word to me."

"The trouble is grizzlies don't read the Bible!"

"They might not!" I replied with a laugh, "It is written that God has given us authority over every wild animal and He has also given His angels to protect those, who believe and trust in Him."

After saying goodbye, we (Smoky, Pistol and my angels) climbed up to 12,650 feet at Stony Pass, where I had intended to follow the Continental Divide Trail northwards along the mountains. But I guessed it must have been buried in snow, as I couldn't find any sign of it, so I continued on the dirt road, heading west and plummeting thousands of feet.

# HIGH ALTITUDE

"It is called a wagon road, but the only means of using it was to 'take your wagon to pieces' and let it down several steep places by rope."
Ernest Ingersoll, Hayden Survey 1874

Stony Pass was the best route to Howardsville and Silverton between 1871 and 1882. Wagons, originating in Del Norte, hauled basic goods and mining supplies to San Juan City. From here, mule trains carried everything from food and clothing to machinery, pianos, livestock feed and fine china, over the Continental Divide and then descended 2,300 feet into the mining region of the Animas River. The Stony Pass freight route thrived until the Denver and the Rio Grande railway reached Silverton via Durango in 1882.

Smoky and Pistol were quite content to graze the verge, acting as my models while I fiddled with my camera, trying to get it to work. I appreciated the interesting information boards posted by the National Forest and Silver Thread, at the base of the Pass. One of them said: "The amount of wreckage strewed along the whole length of the wagon trail followed by us from this point, was sufficient evidence of the difficulties encountered by the pioneer teamsters of this region." Lieutenant E. Howard Ruffner, Army Corps of Engineers, 1873.

19th June: 2,300 feet was a long way down to get to Howardsville and I could certainly feel my leg muscles! All along the Animas River we passed old mining ghost towns. Riding along, I regretted not stopping to fish with Irwin. Then I met Chicago Jack, with his white ponytail. Apparently he came out every summer, as it was the best fishing and he gave me a Rocky Mountain cut throat trout for my supper!

Blessed be the Lord,
Who daily loads us with benefits!
Psalm 68v19 NKJ

Left: The Old Eureka mine and mining buildings at Howardsville.
Right: "People round here call me Chicago Jack! "A man with a white pony tail introduced himself giving me a trout. "What's that?" Smoky asked, "is it edible?"

# ROCKY MOUNTAIN CUT THROAT TROUT

By the evening, we were all exhausted after climbing up and down the steep mountain pass, so I started looking for a spot to camp. I chose my locations by the amount of grass for the horses, and nearby water, so that all of us could drink, and also for the view. I had found a spot that would almost fit our requirements, when a man asked what I was doing.

"Looking for a camp spot," I replied, but he informed me that this was private land. We both apologised. He for having to move me on, and I for not having seen the sign marked 'private'. So we continued on up the road to a spot opposite the old Eureka mine. Here I was happy to see that grass was more plentiful, but before I set up camp, I asked some nearby RV (recreational vehicle) campers if this was public land.

"We haven't been run off yet!" they replied, to my relief. Once I had the horses tethered out, I felt like just rolling out the bedroll and not bothering about putting up the tent. But then, I forced myself to do so, thinking of the midges, a possible thunderstorm or frost in the morning. Not wanting to overcook the trout, I fried it lightly. It was quite raw, for I hadn't realised that food takes longer to cook at high altitude, even though water boils quicker as the pressure decreases.

Then I pumped water from the Animas through Greg's purifier, which took some effort, because of all the minerals it contained. Once the horses had had a good graze and it was almost dark, I put them in some adjacent corrals and flopped into my bedroll.

# WELCOME TO THE UNITED STATES!

The value of life lies not in the length of days but in the use we make of them;
A man may live long yet live very little. - Michel Eyquemde Montaigne

*20th June: Woke up to frost again - oh, so good to have a warm sleeping bag! It's also good to know that the horses could move about overnight in a secure corral. These little things are luxuries - thanks God! Thinking of the miners in the past around here - of my own life - Father God, I want to accomplish all that You have predestined for me to do on this earth.*
*For we are His workmanship, created in Christ Jesus for good works, which God prepared beforehand that we should walk in them. – Ephesians 2:10 NKJ*

At first light, I tethered the horses in the longer grass and moved them around frequently so they ate as much as they could (as I never knew where the next grass would be). In between, I made a cup of tea, read my Bible and wrote my diary, as I had been too exhausted to do so the previous night. Sipping tea from my blue tin cup, I enjoyed watching the horses graze as the sunlight slipped down the mountainsides, like an incoming tide, which blanketed the deep canyon valley with warm sunshine. This was midsummer and cool, and I thought of the miners, who had worked in the Eureka mine opposite my camp spot over a hundred years ago, in deepest winter. It must have been a cold, hard life.

Once again, after spending an hour packing up the horses, I was hot. My RV neighbours kindly brought me a coffee, which I accepted gratefully… although I usually don't drink coffee, especially without milk! By 9am, I was travelling up the old dirt road, passing the remains of old mines, collapsed by snow and time. I couldn't help imagining what life must have been like back then, when everyone was desperate to strike it rich.

There were two passes to choose from, both of which would take us to Lake City: Engineers' Pass and Cinnamon Pass. I chose the latter. The climb was beautiful – it almost looked like Switzerland – but by midday there was a buzz in the air. Convoys of four wheelers and jeeps rumbled past, slowing down in consideration, but each covering us in layer upon layer of dust!

"Why aren't you riding?" one couple asked. I explained that I liked to walk and also give my horse a break.

"We're city folk. This is something else up here," exclaimed another couple in a jeep. "Where are you from?

"I've come from the Mexico Border three months ago."

"Oh, welcome to the United States!" they replied cheerily, waved and drove on up the mountain followed by their trail of dust.

# CINNAMON PASS

Then will you delight yourself in the Lord,
and I will make you ride on the high places
of the earth. Isaiah 58v14Amp

# DEEP SNOW!

*I will lie down in peace and sleep, for you alone, O Lord,*
*will keep me (and my horses) safe. Psalm 4v8 NLT*

Cinnamon Pass, 12,840 feet, Smoky reading the informative Alpine notice board
about the Alpine tundra, making us so much more appreciative of our surroundings.
Below: "This is a lot cooler than our old home in East Texas!" Pistol remarked. "Yep!
We sure didn't have snow lying around in mid-summer!" replied Smoky.

My leg muscles were stiff after the previous day, from walking up and most of the way down Stony Pass, as I alternated between leading and riding.

The water from melted snow was roaring and gushing so loudly that I couldn't hear if a vehicle was approaching around some of the deep snow-packed bends on the narrow track. One vehicle stopped and its occupants gave me a homemade muffin, a bottle of water and an energy bar, which gave me a boost as I descended into meadow lands, and then along a shelf road. I kept to the 'English side' of the road, for on the other side there was maybe a 600 foot drop, and I didn't want my horses getting spooked over the edge.

Once we reached the valley floor I regretted not stopping before, on public land in the National Forest, for down here there seemed to be 'private' and 'no trespassing' signs every ten feet. When we reached the river, we had to backtrack a mile up the canyon through territory marked 'keep to the road for the next 1.2 miles'. This made me feel intimidated and guilty, even though I wasn't doing anything wrong! So I rode up the middle of the road, taking care not to touch the verge on either side, in case someone appeared with a shotgun! After 1.2 miles we entered public land again, and I could breathe easy. The US Forest Service manages 193 million acres of public land which is usually not limited access. A wonderful gift to the people of America to enjoy the vast expanses. On my trek through the west I really appreciated the freedom offered by both the Forestry Service and the BLM (Bureau of Land Management).

On entering the Forestry, I noticed warning signs about bobcats and reintroduced lynx in the area. I was a little concerned for my horses so I decided to camp away from the roaring river so I could hear of any possible danger.

Pistol and Smoky woke me up at 5.30am, stamping their feet to tell me they were hungry. So I tethered them out to graze and kept a close eye on them, ready to grab them before they took off. Pistol still wouldn't hobble and so I was teaching him to be tethered on a rope. That morning, as I was eating porridge, he got his rope caught under his hind fetlocks and came crashing down. I flung my bowl down and rushed to untangle him. Some horses would have injured themselves, but Pistol was proving to be a tough horse, although his withers were a little tender from the pack pushing down on them as we descended steep mountains. That morning I packed Smoky instead, which was easier as he was smaller. I started out feeling cold, but I was sweating and exhausted by eight, so I sat on a log and had an energy drink before heading off towards Lake City.

# THE REALTY OFFICE

Lake San Cristobal

Arriving at Lake San Cristobal.

Cyndi Chadd, Dan, Michelle Murphy and John outside the Team Murphy Realty Office. (opposite top): David and Rosie Whitelock, Mike and Lynda Schell out side the Inn at the Lake. (below) Lake City.

Thanks to Delbert's good shoeing, and the boriem he had welded on Pistol's and Smoky's shoes back in Texas, they had lasted several months, but now I could hear them clanking loosely as we travelled along the road. I had a spare pair in my pack, so all I needed was a good farrier, who could put them on securely. We were all exhausted after our mountain climbing and were dragging our feet, when the horses pricked their ears, seeing two girls approaching, energetically pushing prams (strollers) as though they were marathon walkers. I took the slack out of Pistol's reins, expecting him to shy at the prams, but he didn't seem to mind them at all.

"Where are you going?" Jessica asked, introducing herself and Michelle, her companion. "Where do you keep your horses overnight?"

"Hopefully I'll find some public land," I replied. "We're heading through Lake City and then north."

"Go to the Team Murphy Realty Office. It's on the main street, just over the bridge and on the left," she instructed. "They will know somewhere to put your horses for the night."

Chatting to the girls was invigorating and shortly afterwards the trees opened to the beautiful Lake San Cristobal – formed about 850 years ago, during a particularly wet period, when a massive landslide, called the Slumgullion earth flow, blocked the Gunnison River. As I approached the far end, where there were some houses edging the water, a slim lady jumped out of her car.

"I heard you were travelling through!" she enthused. "I'm Kara Molinek, a reporter for the local Silver World Newspaper. Can I take some photos and interview you?" I liked Kara and her enthusiasm immediately. Simultaneously, as she was asking me questions, a local man gave me a big map book of Colorado, which later became very useful. I tore out some relevant pages, and these gave me an alternative scale to my maps of western USA, Colorado and other detailed versions.

I rode on through the pretty town of Lake City, following Jessica's directions, stopping at the traffic lights on the bridge and then turned into Team Murphy Realty.

"This is the first time I have been to a real estate office to find overnight grazing for my horses!" I chuckled to myself, as I stopped Pistol and Smoky in the parking area.

"I heard you were coming!" a red-headed woman appeared on the steps, introducing herself as Cyndi. "What can I help you with?"

"My horses need a field for the night and a good farrier," I replied, adding: "I have the shoes."

"I'll make some calls," she said, disappearing into an attractive wooden building. "Would you like a shower?" she asked, as she reappeared with some towels drapped over her arm. Just then, a patrol car pulled in.

"I can put on a shoe, but my back's not up to putting on a full set these days," said John, the local Deputy Sheriff, after I had explained my shoeing problem. I needed another solution. I had tacked on the odd shoe during my New Zealand expedition, but I much preferred having them shod professionally, so the shoes stayed on a long time. Also, after Pistol's first performance with being shod I was worried as to how he was going to react to having his second pair of new shoes.

Dan and Michelle Murphy arrived. "We've only been moved in here three days!" Michelle exclaimed, with a laugh. "We have a 100-day tourist season, so for eight months of the year, there's no income – we live here by faith!"

You chart the path ahead of me and tell me where to stop and rest.

Psalm 139v3 TLB

"We'll find a place for your horses," added Dan, showing me where I could leave my pack bags, in the back of the offices. It was the height of the season, and people were coming and going. I had a shower, while my horses rested outside the shop.

When Dan finished work, he gave me a lift. I sat on his vehicle tail gate, with the horses following on lead ropes, and we headed slowly through town to a large field, which backed onto the mountain. After filling up a large water trough, we went straight back to a barbecue that Cyndi and Jeff, her husband, had prepared at their log house, on the edge of beautiful Lake San Cristobal. I ate several huge elk burgers and met David, who knocked the breath out of me with his enormous bear-like hug. He offered me a room for the night at their lodge, called the Inn at the Lake.

"Thank you, but I'm fine at the estate agents'," I replied.

"Come and have a look anyway," he suggested, so I followed him over to a wooden building with balconies and overflowing, hanging flower baskets. 'Room 205', at the end of the second floor, overlooked the lake.

"Are you sure you wouldn't like room 205?"

"Wow, the view is wonderful! Can I change my mind?!"

# ROOM 205

Cyndi took me to fetch my pack bags from the Murphy Realty Office, and David helped me carry them up to room 205. He mentioned that he and his wife Rosie had lost their daughter in an accident, when she was 17 years old. "You remind me of her because she loved horses too," he said and my eyes filled with tears as I felt some of his pain.

My one night in room 205 stretched into a week, and we had many talks together, sitting out at the table in front of the inn. There seemed to be an empathy between us, for he had lost a daughter, and my father had left when I was 11 years old.

The next morning, Cyndi brought a delicious breakfast of sausages and eggs, in several large dishes, and I met more neighbours, including Mike and Lynda Schell, proprietors of Coal Creek Construction, who had built several of the homes and temporarily lived in a trailer just a short hop over the creek from the Inn at the Lake. Mike offered me his pick-up to take the horses to get shod.

"You're not lending her your pick-up are you?" a friend exclaimed. "You never let anyone near it!"

"This is a God thing!" Mike replied, and I swallowed, overwhelmed by everyone's generosity. He showed me his very smart, big, white, souped-up truck, made even longer with a borrowed trailer from Red Cloud.

"The right side!" I was reminded. I had just got back from eating in town with David and it was dark. Mike had parked it outside the Inn at the Lake, ready for a test drive.

"You hardly have to touch the brake. Just use this switch for the air brakes," Mike directed. "In this mountain country, you can burn your brakes out pretty quickly if you use them."

Early the following morning, I loaded up the horses and drove to Daryl Davis' place, near Gunnison, as Cyndi had arranged for him to shoe the horses. I was relieved to see how patient he was with Pistol, who didn't like the hammering – he never lost his temper when Pistol snatched his hoof out of his grasp. I kept soothing Pistol and massaging his neck so he relaxed.

"Of course, Smoky, you're perfect!" I patted him too, so he wouldn't feel left out.

Going for a swim in Lake San Cristobal!

The steps of a good man are directed and established
by the Lord when He delights in his way,
He busies Himself with his every step.
Psalm 37v23 Amp

Susie and Dan Rieple, friends from Colorado Springs, brought me several memory cards for my camera. I'd met Susie, who was also English (so we spoke the same language!) and a photographer, 10 years earlier at my Bible School rodeo in Colorado. She had worked for the BBC in England and come to America to join Focus on the Family.

"Susie why did you want to work for Focus?" I asked curiously, as most times I had been in touch with her over the years, she was either just going or returning from a far-flung overseas mission trip for Focus.

"The desire came through reading a book called Jerusalem to Irian Kiya – when I read the chapter on Christian Broadcasting, I thought this is what I want to do! I had always loved radio - because it's great for the imagination, and you introduce Christianity over the air waves in creative ways, and if the listener doesn't engage – they just switch you off!" she said with a laugh.

Her husband Dan was a custom furniture designer and maker, and they ran their business, Fine Ideas, just north of Colorado Springs. They were very supportive towards my ride and, at the beginning of my trip, Susie had helped me to gather equipment. During my journey, as I had no phone signal for long periods of time, I would pick up phone messages from her like: "I dreamt about you last night – how are you? Call me back when you can!"

Dan had given me a knife with a ten-inch blade. I kept this attached to my saddle for emergencies, in case my horses got caught up, but I mainly used it for replacing the many pig strings that Pistol broke… oh, and for cutting cheese when I had the luxury to eat it, as it wasn't a food that travelled easily!

# DEL CERRO

When we work from passion we are filling our niche in life
and work is no longer work - it is art.
Jim and Daniela Howell

Dan & Susie Rieple.

Dan and Susie escorted me to their friend's ranch near Cimarron, where Jim and Daniela Howell met us, with their daughters Savanna and baby Mia. Daniela, who was from Argentina, met Jim while studying in New Zealand and they had both worked on natural resource management projects around the world. Their business, called Del Cerro (meaning 'of the mountain'), blended the traditions of land stewardship, animal husbandry, herding, shearing, spinning, dyeing and weaving. They arranged for local weavers and textile designers to transform the organic fibres from the Howell's ranch into sophisticated interior designs.

"We are blessed to live, work and play in one of the world's most scenic and diverse landscapes, here on Colorado's western slopes," remarked Daniela.

"Why don't you just follow us up?" Jim suggested. Driving Mike's wide pick-up, pulling the trailer, I had to take a few deep breaths as I followed them up a dirt road, which was often very narrow and twisting, until we reached a cabin that Jim's dad had built.

"She's not a snuff-dipping, spitting girl," observed Jim Howell senior, on our arrival as his wife, Beverly handed around refreshing drinks. "Actually you are not what I imagined at all!"

"You look more like a California girl!" added Dan, as I was dressed in the denim shorts and T-shirt that Courtney had given me in New Mexico.

We left Pistol and Smoky in a grassy field by the cabin, and climbed further up the mountain to another, more rustic, camp spot, which Jim and Daniella had built. I felt as if I had walked into Africa, for this simple cabin had canvas windows, and nearby was an attractive lean-to, built from logs, containing a kitchen with a sink and shelves for cups and spices. Several hammocks were draped from the trees.

We had the most delicious dinner party, with several courses, including a juicy steak cooked over the open fire, and we sat at a long table top constructed of narrow logs, balancing our glasses on wooden coasters.

"A bear recently came through, trashed all the cups, got into the locker and drank the oil!" Daniela told us, "so we'll leave the dogs here tonight in case he returns." We didn't hear any bears as Susie, Dan and I camped in the spacious cabin, although the dogs did bark all night!

Dan, Jim and Daniela at camp.
Below: Daniela carrying Mia, with Marissa Isgreen, Savanna & Jim.

# BUMPER AND BB!

The following morning, I drove back to Lake City, and Mike swapped the pick-up for his jeep so I could do some more exploring around the area. He also set up a computer so that I could check my email and catch up on the office work. In the dusk, they took me out to look for elk, and showed me some great views.

I felt so welcome, and had made so many new friends, that it was hard to leave Lake San Cristobal and Lake City, but the pressure was on to get to the Estes Park Rodeo – the next location for the film. Before I left, I did a Riding by Faith presentation at the Inn on the Lake, and 40 people showed up.

"You look very different from when we first saw you arrive!" said Dan Murphy, for I was smartly dressed in Courtney's clothes, and just about to launch into my presentation.

"Amazing what a shower, clean clothes and bit of lipstick can do!" I laughed.

Afterwards, Kara brought her computer up to my room, for my technology skills were at full stretch, and I couldn't persuade the computer to copy my photos on to the external hard drive, to make space to load more photos from the camera to my computer. My Nikon digital still flashed 'off', unless it was having an 'on' day, and my other Nikon film camera wasn't behaving either. So I copied them onto Kara's computer, and then onto CDs, which took me until one o'clock in the morning, and then I was up at five to go up the mountain with Mike!

It was midsummer and I was shivering at 13,000 feet wearing four layers of clothes, gloves and a woolly hat!

"Six bucks with five pronged horns, which means they're four or five year olds." Mike informed me handing me his spotter (telescope) and I saw the sunlit elk, with their shadows mirrored on the snow. I couldn't get anywhere near them with my existing lens, and I realised that I would need a longer one to get shots of wild animals.

"OK boys, I want to show Bumper to Tracey," said Mike, who was dressed in camouflage gear, and looking through his camouflaged binoculars. "No, that's not him. He's got straight horns. Where are you this morning? You've got to be there – I want to show you off! Last year we had Droppie and Sweeper. This year we have Bumper and BB, or Big Boy."

He continued to talk as we bumped along in the jeep, and passed another elk. "She's older, I don't know her," Mike remarked and continued in his humorous way, "She's just wandered in off the street!"

Mike added: "I came from a hunting family. When I was hunting with my first BB gun, I could get up on the roof and hit people four houses away. Once I got the neighbour, and I didn't have a gun after that!"

Mike explained the hunting seasons, which start at the end of August and run through September. Sometimes they use dangerous, compound bows, with which he had killed bears and elk. Muzzleloaders had a 10-day season, while the rifle season, for deer and elk, continued into December.

"Archery is the hardest, so they use bows during the rut, because the bulls are pretty stupid then. The big elk don't get big by being stupid. Hunting elk is in the stalking," he said as we headed down the mountain.

At a lower elevation I had another close encounter with wildlife when I met Karen, who worked at the post office. She invited me home to see the marmots, which hung out in her back garden. They were also known as Whistle Pigs as when danger approaches they make a loud chirp or whistle, but even with this warning system they were still preyed upon by the eagles. These endearing, large, golden brown rodents, which live in burrows and amongst the rocks, eat grass and other plants throughout the summer, storing up fat reserves to hibernate all through the winter.

As I was leaving Lake City, and saying goodbye at the Murphy Realty Office, Kara rushed in clutching my sunglasses.

"I went to where you swam the horses yesterday. You remember the woman we met there? Well, she just handed me your sunglasses, and I wanted to catch you before you left town!" exclaimed Kara. "I'm seeing it for myself, what you were going on about – God's faithfulness!"

For your unfailing love is as high as the heavens. Your faithfulness reaches to the clouds.
Psalm 57v10 NLT

# THE GINGERBREAD HOUSE!

The horses were looking into the forest in the direction of an eerie crying sound. "It's only the crows, boys," I calmed them. That night the moon was so full and bright I didn't need a torch.

The horses stamped their feet to wake me early the following morning and I tied them out to graze while I drank tea and caught up with my diary until the insects found we were there. I hurriedly packed up, for the horses were swishing their tails and stamping, irritated by the biting. It was better to keep on the move, as the fly spray I carried didn't seem strong enough for the horses. The mosquitoes even bit through my jodhpurs.

As I followed the well-marked Colorado trail, through the pretty aspen trees, dappled with sunlight, a slim woman jogged past me and then ran back the other way.

"Do you need anything?" she asked, introducing herself as Cindy, and invited me to refill my water bottles back at her log cabin. It reminded me of the gingerbread house in the woods, from the fairy tale. Cindy offered me a shower and gave me tea and banana bread, yoghurt and apricots. She told me of the nearby 14,000ft peaks of Mt Shavano and Mt Tabeguache – both named after Native American Indian leaders. She said that her grandmother was part Ute Indian and her Swedish grandfather had opened the first bakery in Leadville.

"Grandfather and mother worked their claim in Leadville, 10,000 feet up – one of the highest mines in Colorado. It was back in the days when people took samples of gold and silver to make their claim for mining an area, but they had a Claim Jumper."(Someone else stole their claim).

I let the horses graze, until they got spooked and took off. I ran after them, retrieved them, and tied them up while Cindy poured me another cup of tea and continued telling me more.

"It was the real, rugged West. People were so harsh and evil. Two hundred people were staking claims at one time and there was a lot of bickering. This was the Wild West, you know, and people died – a lot of them in the mines. It was unusual to find a miner, who lived over 40 years. My grandmother died when my dad was 12. Leadville was a big mining community – an epic centre, bigger than Denver. People thought that if they went to Leadville, they would make their million, but few did."

# THE COLORADO TRAIL

We followed the Colorado Trail to the east of the Sawatch Mountain Range, through the San Isabel National Forest, which had several peaks over 14,000 feet. The trail was built by volunteers, and extends almost 500 miles from Durango, in the south west of Colorado, to Denver. It crosses seven National Forests, six wilderness areas, five river systems and eight mountain ranges. In the wilderness areas there was a group size maximum of 25 heartbeats, which included both humans and saddle/pack animals. So Pistol, Smoky and myself added up to three heartbeats! Mountain biking and motorised vehicles weren't allowed, neither could the trail crews use powered tools in these areas.

In some sections the Colorado Trail joined up with the Continental Divide Trail (CDT), which is at higher altitude, over rocky terrain and above tree level, therefore, more exposed to lightning strikes. The CDT was designated by Congress to run from Mexico to Canada, following the landmark divide through five states of Montana, Idaho, Wyoming, Colorado and New Mexico. Although we did follow the Continental Divide in sections and the views were spectacular, it was rough and hard going, especially for my horses, and definitely easier travelling at lower altitude where there was more shelter and grass.

Thanks to the snowmelt and regular summer thunderstorms, finding water in Colorado wasn't a problem, unlike Texas and New Mexico. The atmosphere in the West is so dry that Pistol and Smoky drank at most of the fresh creeks that we crossed. I had to resist the temptation to copy them, without first pumping it through the purifier – I couldn't risk getting sick. I was impressed by the signs at the trailheads, warning about the parasite guardia lamblia, which infests the digestive tract, and is spread through wildlife, livestock and human waste. There were also warnings of the dangers of extreme weather conditions, hypothermia and high altitude sickness, for low oxygen levels can cause headaches, nausea and dizziness. Thankfully, we were all well adapted to the altitude at this point.

1st July: Packing up the horses, reached for the saddle, and ran into a stub of a branch. Judging by the amount of blood pouring down my face into my eyes, I thought I had seriously scalped myself. Didn't have a mirror handy, so just mopped my face up, and then got a good early start. Stopped by a creek ('crick', they say) where there was plenty of grass. While the horses grazed contentedly I dipped into my book, 'Waking the Dead' by John Elredge, which I had acquired at the beginning of my journey in Texas. When entering a shop to buy tape, my eyes had locked onto this book and I had that knowing feeling that I was to take it on my ride. The author's writings were refreshing and encouraging. I liked his note on the scripture in John 10 verse 10 Jesus came to give us life and life to the fullest – " I don't think he meant fullest in having all the material possessions you could wish for – I believe he wants to set us free in ourselves to let the wild side in us out."

# REALLY LIVE!

*I came that they may have and enjoy life, and have it in abundance*
*(to the full, till it overflows). John10v10 Amp*

It was good to get going when the morning was still fresh and cool. On the outskirts of Buena Vista I asked some cyclists where the Colorado Trail continued.

"Did you have an accident?" asked one of them, in skin-tight clothing, and I remembered my forehead probably looked bloody.

"I walked into a tree!" I replied, feeling slightly embarrassed, for I was extra careful not to have accidents while travelling on my own with the horses.

It was a long, exhausting 12 hours to Silver Creek trailhead. The last seven miles over Cotton Creek pass were extremely steep, and we zig-zagged our way up about 1,000 feet to the snowline, and then down again the other side, over fallen tree trunks. I untied Pistol and manoeuvred him separately, since he didn't want to follow Smoky's route across the trunks, and snapped his pigging string on numerous occasions.

"Well, boys you are not acting like mountain horses, or even handy ponies yet!"

Smoky still had a habit of walking too close to the cliff edges and frightened himself when one foot slipped over the edge, causing a little rockslide! They forded bigger rivers, but panicked over little steams. Neither of them liked getting their hooves muddy! Smoky would jump six feet over two foot streams, which Pistol wasn't expecting so another pigging string would get snapped. To stop this from happening, I undid the lead rope and rode one horse across, and then returned to lead the packhorse across, positioning myself so they didn't leap on me or trample me.

Smoky had a more rounded back and, on him, the pack saddle tended to slip from side to side, especially when he scraped it against every tree he went past, to show his dislike at being the packhorse. I could tell, quite early on in the day, if one side was lighter than the other, and would sneak in a small stone or two to make it more even.

It was almost dark when we arrived at the Silver Creek trail head, and we camped back in the woods. I was so tired that I just got the bedroll out, but then thunder and lightning began, so I used the last dregs of energy to erect the tent. As I pulled off my boots, my socks stank, the soles of my feet tingled and my leg muscles ached from walking up and down steep inclines all day. My filthy shirt had a tidemark around the collar, and I seemed to have permanent dirt under my jagged nails, which I had given up trying to keep clean. As I lay back on the bedroll I thought of the immaculately dressed businesswoman, who I had sat next to on the flight to Dallas. She had handed me her card, with impressive titles, and asked in a concerned manner:

"What are you going to do about washing your clothes?"

At that time my head was full of so many thoughts and plans of horses, horse food, farriers, equipment, saddles, routes, pack saddle and survival. I replied: "To tell you the truth, how I'm going to wash my clothes hasn't even entered my head!" Lying there, I smiled and chuckled to my constant Companion, "What would she say if she could see me now? Exhausted, dirty, with a hole in my head!"

*We act as though comfort and luxury*
*were the chief requirements of life*
*when all we need to make us really happy*
*is something to be enthusiastic about.*
*- Charles Kingsley*

# FOOD FOR ALL!

"I guess I will be down the mountain in about 15 minutes," I told Chris Ott, a friend from Denver, over the phone as we arranged to meet at Clear Creek Reservoir. But then, examining the map further, I realised I was on a different mountain, and each of them was huge! Two hours later, in the moonlight, I approached the camp wearing a head torch, like a miner in the dark, and saw a light coming towards me.

"Sorry I'm a bit later than I thought!" I called to Chris, and I introduced Pistol and Smoky.

"It's so good to see you, and to meet you Smoky and Pistol," she replied, stroking their foreheads affectionately. "I have food ready for you all." She led us to her romantic camping spot, where a lantern hung from a tree, lighting up a couple of chairs at the edge of the river.

"Hey, Chris it's a treat to camp in style like this!" I exclaimed.

In the morning, she erected the shower tent and I had a delicious shower, washing away days of dust and sweat. Before we parted, she gave me her shower bag, which became one of my luxuries!

Pistol and Smoky always gave me my wake-up call by stomping their hooves, between 5am and 5.30am, before dawn. If it was earlier, I would tell them to be quiet and sleep some more. I'd then pile on the layers, and sometimes gloves, which I'd kept warm in my sleeping bag, crawl out of my tent, and tether them out to eat grass for a few hours in the fresh, cool mornings before saddling up. They would eat frantically at first, knowing we would soon be moving off, but as they filled up, they slowed down. In the middle of the day, I would stop wherever I could find good grass to graze, and then again in the early evening for two or three hours until dark. Getting enough food for my horses was one of my top priorities, and the availability of grass decided my route to a large extent.

Twin Lakes

I loved to watch my horses grazing contentedly, and although grain was difficult to carry and would only last a few days, I got hold of it whenever I could, because they needed it for such a tough and extensive expedition. By this stage of the journey both horses had lost weight. Smoky, being smaller and more laid back, looked great but Pistol concerned me more. He was that much taller, had lost more weight and it showed along his top line on his neck.

At night, I tied them to a picket rope between two trees to keep them secure, as I didn't trust them not to get tangled in their tethering ropes. Smoky was pretty relaxed and would move his legs to untangle himself, but Pistol panicked and sometimes ended up on the ground. Thankfully he survived unscathed, and gradually learnt to stay calm and wait, trusting me to sort him out. Often I would let him graze loose, so long as I had Smoky firmly tethered, and would keep a good eye on them. If he started to wander too far or they sensed any wild animals, I would immediately put him back on a rope.

The following day, Chris took the pack and grain on to the next camp spot. Not encumbered, we could go much faster. We trotted by Mt Elbert – at 14,433 feet, the highest mountain in Colorado – on our way to our next stop at the Mount Massive Trailhead. On our arrival, Chris greeted us:

"On the menu tonight is sweet feed for Pistol and Smoky, and spinach salad, sweet potato and rice noodles for us!" We set up beside the river with plenty of grass. She had already erected the shower and spread a checked red cloth over the picnic table for supper.

"Wow, what a treat!" I exclaimed. "This is fun having you meet me!"

# HALF MOON CREEK

## Mt Massive Wilderness

Chris slept in her car while I pitched my tent near the horses. I dreamt that a big bear was crossing the river in the night, splashing through the water so I deliberately turned over to switch dreams.

In the morning I heard a munching sound by my head. At first I thought of the bear, but then relaxed as I recognised the munching. Sure enough, when I unzipped the tent, there was Smoky's pink and grey nose.

"And what can I do for you this morning Smoky?" I enquired politely, knowing full well that he wanted to be first in line for the sweet feed breakfast! "I know you've got wiggly lips, Smoky, but that was really clever to untie your bowline knot!"

Nothing in this world can take the place of persistence. Persistence and determination alone are omnipotent.

- Calvin Coolidge

# GETTING PACKED

I was very surprised when an approaching walker called me by name.

"Tracey, your friend says to meet her at the Timberline Trail Head, as there is no grass anywhere else," he said, introducing himself as Mariano, and walked on his way. That day we seemed to be playing a game of overtake or relay, for I passed walkers, and then the same walkers passed me when I let my horses graze, and wrote in my diary. Then I passed them at a stream, and they had to move out of the way as Smoky and Pistol did their usual gigantic leaps over the creek. Once I was reunited with Chris, the same walkers passed us again.

Pete Turner and his wife Lisa, who operated the walking holidays, invited us for supper. They had a big marquee a few miles down the road.

"We're kind of ambassadors of the Colorado Trail," said Pete, as I tucked into a delicious chicken salad that Lisa had cooked. "When we see hikers doing the whole Colorado Trail or Continental Divide, we invite them in for dinner and give them water. We like to see their smiles! Some of them are burning more food than they can carry."

I thought to myself: "That's our problem!" Smoky, Pistol and I consistently needed more high energy food. We had all lost weight, because we were burning up more energy than we could carry to sustain us. It was great when Chris was with us, for she transported the grain, but when we were on our own, it was awkward to carry and only lasted several days.

"We've had a record hay season down in south west Colorado, with good early rains," said Pete, as we heard a rumble of thunder and a deluge began. It was Independence Day, when America celebrated independence from the British, in 1776. The first European immigrants had come to the New World in the 17th century, seeking freedom, but imperial Britain, with its constant desire to expand its territory, had tried to control them. Eventually, the American colonies won their independence.

I woke up suddenly, as something or someone fell into my tent.

"Have you seen a yellow tent?" a man's voice asked.

"Hang on, I don't know even where I am!" I replied, waking out of a deep sleep, trying to remember my whereabouts. "A yellow tent?" I repeated.

"Do you want to borrow a torch?" I asked, and then remembered that 'torch' had a different meaning in America.

"Have you got a flashlight?" he asked. Fumbling for one, I handed it out of the tent flap and saw a pair of very muddy legs and a dog.

"I am so sorry, I am so sorry," he kept on apologising. A few minutes later, he was back, and handed me my torch apologising once more. In the morning, I wondered if I had dreamt the midnight episode, until I noticed the yellow tent. I never saw him again.

At the trail head there was a group of boy scouts getting ready for a hike. I chatted for a while and then let Chris continue the conversation, because I needed to concentrate on getting the pack evenly balanced. Chris was driving back to Denver, so I gave her a bag of dirty clothes and a shopping list, including another bag of sweet feed for the horses. I could only pack enough for a few days, and as our mountainous route didn't take us near feed stores, whenever anyone was planning to meet us I asked them to bring a sack of grain.

With the new day comes new strength and new thoughts - Eleanor Roosevelt

4th July: Timberline Trail Head. Usually every evening I am exhausted, but by the morning I always feel revived and ready to go – that is after several cups of tea and several helpings of porridge! – I braced myself and tackled packing up the horses. The most energetic chore of the day. Earlier in the ride I wondered how I was going to keep on packing up each day all the way to Canada, but now I have developed more muscles and it is part of everyday life. Once I have the horses packed and ready I boost my energy by mixing a protein drink with water before setting off. I am becoming like my horses, eating and drinking at every opportunity!

# THE PLANK

By the time I left my camp spot, I was hot from packing up and from the sun, but within half an hour the temperature had plummeted and it had begun to rain. I rummaged through my saddlebags to find my waterproof trousers, gloves, sweater and long raincoat, and then rode through the drizzle, passing remnants of snowdrifts. I met several walkers hiking the Colorado Trail. Some were chatty, others very focused. I admired their stamina, as they were walking almost 500 miles, up and down steep mountains. Although we were travelling further, they were carrying heavy backpacks, and I was thankful for Smoky and Pistol, for not only did I enjoy their company, but they carried both me and my pack.

We crossed over Tennessee Pass, and continued until I found a grassy spot for the horses and a good view for me. I kept my gloves and hat on, because the mosquitoes were out in force. The following morning was cold and misty, so I hung the tent over some trees to allow it to dry out in the sunshine, before rolling it up and packing it. I hadn't gone far when I came to a narrow plank of wood, stretching ten feet over a deep black pool, and onto swampy ground. I was in a dilemma: should I take the horses along the plank (which was only about a foot wide), or wade through the water, which looked black and bottomless?

I unhooked my camera off Smoky's saddle, in case the horses fell off the bridge. Feeling uneasy, I stepped onto the plank leading Smoky, who took a few steps, crossing one hoof in front of the other, like someone on a tight rope.

"I will follow you," he seemed to say, "but are you sure it's safe?"

"No, I'm not sure," I replied, my heart thumping. Gently, I eased him back over the plank to the safety of firm ground, to everyone's relief. I didn't want to backtrack to Tennessee Pass, so now I asked for inspiration. How was I going to get across this area of swamp?

Let peace (soul harmony which comes)
from Christ rule (act as umpire continually)
in your hearts deciding and settling with finality all
questions that arise in your minds
and be thankful.
Colossians 3v15 Amp

# A ROLL IN THE SNOW!

May your trails be crooked, winding, lonesome, dangerous, leading to the most amazing view. May your mountains rise into and above the clouds.
- Edward Abbey

I searched for a way around the bog, and was extremely relieved to find a dry crossing on solid ground. I then rode and walked up the mountains, through some breath-taking Alpine meadows of wild flowers. One of my favourite flowers in the Rockies is the paint brush. At lower elevations, it displays its deep red colours in modified leaves, instead of flowers, known as bracts, which are pale yellow at higher altitude. It's a semi-parasitic plant, obtaining part of its nourishment by attaching itself to the roots of other plants.

I was going to take some self-timer photos from the tripod, but realised I had left the top of the tripod on the video camera, which was with Chris. So I had to find somewhere to prop my camera, and then run back and get into position before the shutter clicked!

I attempted this when crossing through some snow. I set the camera on a ledge on the far side of the snowdrift, ran back and jumped on Smoky. But the horses had never travelled through deep snow before, and when they felt themselves sinking, they panicked and plunged ever deeper, floundering around in snow up to their stomachs. I dived off quickly, rolling across the snow, avoiding Pistol's hooves, as he plunged after Smoky. After our rough and tumble we all arrived on the other side, breathing heavily, only to discover that the camera hadn't caught the action! I wasn't going to re-enact the crossing!

# 60 FOOT DASH!

Our way is not soft grass, it's a mountain path with lots of rocks.
But it goes upwards, forward, toward the sun.
- Ruth Westeimer

When we reached the Kokoma Pass, I could see no sign of walkers to ask to take a photo for me, so I draped my camera over the sign and tried to angle it so it took in both the mountains and me on the horses. I pressed the shutter, and had 40 seconds to get in position and ride across the camera's view. We repeated this several times, altering the camera angle each time, so it actually got us in the shot!

We climbed higher, and again I positioned the horses near a pile of stones and placed my camera on another pile 60 feet away. Then I pressed the shutter and ran over the stones and climbed on Smoky. The first photo showed me still climbing on, so I speeded up the next dash!

# ALPINE FLOWER GARDEN

For lo, the winter is past, The rain is over and gone.
The flowers appear on the earth; The time of singing has come.
Song of Solomon 2v11 NKJ

I felt honoured to have the opportunity to enjoy the magnificent display of wild flowers exploding into colour on the mountainsides. It was like going for a walk in a very big garden! Most of the plants are small so as to conserve their energy. Because of the thin soil, constant wind and long winters, they only have a few brief months to grow, flower and seed.

The columbine is Colorado's state flower and was almost loved out of existence at the turn of the nineteenth century, when trainloads of tourists came and dug them up for their homes and for commercial gardens. Then the Columbine Protection Act was passed, which made picking the flower punishable by fines and even jail sentences.

# BAIL OFF THE BALDIES

I was photographing and soaking up the beautiful scenery, carpeted in wild flowers, when I suddenly realised that thunder clouds were gathering, and we should get off the mountain before it brought lightning. After our last incident crossing snow, I tried to skirt over the rough rocks around the deepest patches, but Pistol fell into another snowdrift before scrambling back on his feet.

"Smoky, Pistol hurry up!" I tugged at Smoky's reins urgently, as I could see lightning in the distance, and remembered Greg's warning to "bail off the baldies". On average three people in Colorado are killed every year and 18 more are seriously injured by lightning.

"We've got to get off the mountain quick!" I urged them, for they were always slow downhill. I kept geeing them up, so that they gained a little speed over the rough ground. As we descended, we surprised a herd of elk, which took off at our appearance. It began to get darker, with forked lightning flashing over the surrounding mountains, accompanied by large rain drops.

I had planned to meet Chris again, who was bringing supplies to Copper Mountain town, but as we descended I was dismayed to hear the noise of heavy traffic and voiced my apprehension: "Boys, what are we getting into?"

When we arrived, amid bright, dazzling lights, we passed between the ski lifts and large hotels, where we waited on the pavement for Chris and our supplies before climbing back up the mountain to camp.

"I think I have a good place for your horses!" Chris exclaimed, when she found us. She hurriedly showed us up a cycle track and we tucked the horses behind some trees, before it was pitch dark. Pistol blended into the trees, but Smoky, being white, was more conspicuous. Chris showed me how to get out of town in the morning, and then gave me supplies: sweet feed for the horses, apples, new socks (my thermal ones had been cooking my feet!), protein and energy bars, dried fruit and six hard boiled eggs. I ate two eggs for supper, two for breakfast and two the following lunch. A pleasant respite from nut mixes!

"I can come early in the morning if you like?" Chris offered. "You're worth it, you know!"

"Thanks for the offer, but it's hours for you to drive up here and I'm planning to leave before the town wakes up!" Feeling exhausted, I could hardly believe I was camping near the loud interstate, making it the noisiest night I had ever experienced, even with earplugs firmly stuffed in my ears. At five in the morning, I packed up and I was riding down one of the main streets when some men in a maintenance vehicle pulled up alongside me.

"Are you planning to stay?" a man asked.

"No, just passing through, I'm leaving town right now," I replied.

"Well, are you going to clean up after your horses?" he asked sternly.

"In this dry climate it will dry out and blow away very quickly," I assured him.

"It has done five messes," he said angrily, adding in a threatening tone. "Do you want me to take you back and show you?"

I had heard of road rage, but was surprised that anyone could be so upset over horse manure, which was only digested grass! I backtracked and found one dropping, which had spread into five little bits, as Smoky had been walking at the time. Using my boot, I scraped it into the side of the road.

"Now, please Pistol, don't you do a poop, 'wise we'll be in more trouble!" I said, as we hurried through the resort town, passing its immaculate, mown lawns and golf courses. I thought of the first pioneers, followed by the lawless mining days, only a little over 100 years ago. What a lot had changed! I was sure they would have been more concerned about their own survival back then, not a bit of horse manure! This city resort, that I had mistakenly visited, somehow seemed so out of place in the rugged mountains of the Wild West. We were very relieved to reach the edge of town without another mishap!

Women are like teabags.
We don't know our true strength
until we are in hot water!
- Eleanor Roosevelt

# WHICH HIGHWAY?

Above: Our camp spot.
Opposite: Crossing over from Copper Mountain to Breckenridge.

*7th July.* On the way up the mountain, stopping to drink, Pistol got his foreleg over the lead rope, which brought him to his knees. I quickly backed Smoky up, a few steps, and untangled him. I was so thankful that he didn't panic this time - he's becoming calmer. So good to be back on the mountain with its spectacular views, but the horses find the steep climbing, over rocky terrain, so hard and the pack pushes down on Pistol's withers on the descents. He is very stiff and we're all exhausted. We've only got five days to get to Estes for the filming. The film dates are fixed and inflexible - if I don't show up I lose thousands of dollars and get no footage. Feeling uneasy about following the trail right across the mountain as it's so exposed to lightning and very strenuous for us all when we're all exhausted and we need a rest. There's no alternative, except the highway, which is too dangerous. Lead me in the right path, O Lord. Tell me clearly what to do, and show me which way to turn. - Psalm 5v8

The portion of the Colorado Trail we were following joined up with the Continental Divide Trail, across the tops of the mountains, with amazing views of the Rockies. I led the horses, and it was a tough climb up and down over rocks. This seemed a popular section for walkers, and energetic mountain bikers passed us on our ascent. I would wait at strategically good photo points, and ask the walkers or bikers to take a photo of us with my camera. We got to know each other better as the day progressed, for we'd overtake the walkers on the way up, and they would pass us while the horses were grazing.

Before we dropped down into another built-up area (Breckenridge) and got caught in suburbia again, I chose a camp spot in a grassy area beside a stream. It was only one o'clock in the afternoon, but we were all exhausted. Smoky lay down before I had even taken his saddle off, ate a bit more and then lay down again. It was a great location for us all to take the afternoon off after ten consecutive days climbing up and down mountains. It was so pleasant, in fact, that I put on my shorts, wrote my diary and studied the map, while the horses grazed, had a roll, a sleep and then grazed again. I saw that the Continental Trail didn't go directly north, but south-east, before wiggling its way north along the tops of the mountains. I was concerned about taking this route, since it was very exposed to lightning, with little cover to get down into for protection.

I usually put sunscreen on first thing in the morning and at midday, when I had sweated it off, but I was lax that afternoon, as the sun only felt pleasantly hot at that altitude. However, I soon got burnt. A few hours later I was pulling on the layers as it clouded, followed by thunder, lightning and hailstones, so I took cover in my little tent until it passed over. After the horses had grazed and rested for eight hours, I picketed them and crawled into my tent, listening to the coyotes yapping and howling and wondering which way I should go to get to Estes Park in time.

The Lord God is my Strength, my personal bravery, and my invincible army; He makes my feet like hind's feet.
He will make me as surefooted as a deer and bring me safely over the mountains.
Habakkuk 3v19 Amp & NLT

# WRONG TURN!

Do not, therefore, fling away your fearless confidence, for you have need of steadfast patience and endurance, so that you may perform and fully accomplish the will of God, and thus receive and carry away and enjoy to the full what is promised. Hebrew 10v35 Amp

As Pistol was still stiff and his withers tender, I put the pack on Smoky, who protested by scraping it against every tree he could as we descended through the forest, making it go squiffy. Pistol was the more obedient packhorse, and I could ride him out in front, but he didn't like to be led by the bridle while I was walking on foot to give his back a rest. Instead I used his halter and it almost felt like I was dragging him.

"Pistol, this is why you are the packhorse a lot of the time!" I said, feeling tired and irritable, "because you won't lead and because Smoky scrapes the pack on most of the trees he passes!"

I took a wrong turn, and ended up in a built-up area in Frisco. To get back on the right track, all I needed to do was follow the cycle road for a quarter of a mile, but there was a 'no entry' sign for horses. I remembered the unpleasantness on the public right of way in Copper Mountain, so I thought better of it! I should have retraced my steps, but instead I thought I would take a short cut up some very steep inclines, and ended up lost in a huge conifer forest (something that seems to happen to me all over the world!). I got my GPS out. People had tried to teach me to use it, but I hadn't got to grips with it yet, so I sat on a stone and decided this was the time to learn. I was pleasantly surprised that I could follow its directions to get me back on the right track!

Always bear in mind that your own resolution to succeed
is more important than any other one thing.
- Abraham Lincoln

"You're on it!" some walkers replied, when I asked where the Colorado Trail was, five hours after the initial mistake. As we passed a grand-looking house, the thought came to me that I should go and ask if I could fill up my water bottles, saving the effort of pumping it through the filter from the river. But I dismissed the idea, feeling too tired. I lay down in the grass, amongst some trees, to regain some energy, while the horses grazed around me, shaking their heads and swishing the mosquitoes away with their tails.

In a state of exhaustion I deliberated what I should do. Pistol was stiff in his hindquarters, and by now I had only four days in which to meet the film crew at Estes park and I couldn't afford not to be there. The actual cost of the ride was small in comparison to hiring a two-man film crew to meet me on five occasions. I felt like I had scraped the bottom of the barrel as far as my energy was concerned, and couldn't even think straight. I knew quitting wasn't an option, but I didn't want to even think about how I was ever going to get to Canada.

"Are you OK?" I heard a woman's voice, and a tall blonde lady appeared, leading Smoky. "I found your horse over by my fence, peeking through! He seemed to be saying, "this looks like a good place to stay the night!" Do you want to come back? I'm Mindy, Mindy Armstrong!"

"Thank you!" I replied weakly. "I'd love to!" She led Smoky, and I followed with Pistol, to the large house and barns, where I had previously thought to stop and ask for water. I smiled, for I hadn't followed the prompting in my heart so Smoky had taken the initiative and introduced himself!

Mindy led us into her large barn and, after washing the horses down, gave them alfalfa hay and a salt lick, which they relished. She refused any payment, and Zack, her son, appeared and handed me an energy drink. With the horses content, Mindy then made me a sandwich of ham, mustard and tomato, which was a refreshing treat to my taste buds!

I enjoyed my first shower for days, and other modern conveniences like a flushing toilet and a large mirror in which my reflection looked haggard! Mindy showed me to a bedroom on the third floor, adorned with her daughter's trophies and colourful rosettes, imprinted with titles such as 'World Wide Paint Horse Congress, Wichita, Kansas'.

"You were lucky I was home today, as I have a landscaping business and this is only my second day off in a month. I'm not usually here," she said, continuing: "The sun will come right in here in the morning." And she pulled the blinds down on the east-facing window.

"Make yourself at home," she added casually. "You all need a few days rest!"

Looks like a good place to spend the night! - Smoky

You chart the path ahead of me
and tell me where to stop and rest.
Every moment you know where I am.
You both precede and follow me.
You place your hand of blessing upon my head.
Psalm 139v3,5 NLT

# ESTES PARK

That the Lord your God may show us, the way in which we should walk
and the thing we should do. Jeremiah 42v3 NKJ

We stayed a couple of days. On the first day, I felt like a zombie in slow motion. Pistol was still stiff as I walked them out into the forest to graze and loosen up a bit. Early on the second morning, Chris came out from Denver and took me to breakfast in Breckenridge, where we shared a dessert. My stomach complained as it wasn't used to sugary foods after our very basic diet.

I realised I would have to get a lift to Estes Park to get there in time for the filming. Tanya Fallin, who was coming from Texas to be with me at this film location, put me in touch with Amy, who I hired to transport us up to Estes. I bought some hay and left the horses in her paddock, while she took me up along the highest major highway in North America – over 12,000 feet, at the top of the Rocky Mountain National Park. I looked for the best location for the filming, using the Rocky Mountains as the backdrop. This was essential for the documentary, since I was following the great Rocky Mountain chain – the world's longest mountain barrier, forming the backbone of North America, and running from Mexico to Alaska.

I marked promising locations on my map, and photographed some herds of elk, which were familiar with visitors. This was very useful, because I only had a 28-70mm lens, which would have been far too short for the really wild ones I had seen in the distance! By the turn of the 19th century the elk had been killed off, partly to supply miners with food. In 1913, however, 50 elk were re-introduced to the Estes Valley from Yellowstone, and now there are more than 3,000 in the Rocky Mountain National Park.

"No, I'm sorry, you can't take horses anywhere on the high ground in the park," the National Park officer informed me, when I went to arrange the filming permit. I was so disappointed, and thought of Isabella Bird, the Englishwoman who had freely ridden all over Estes Park 100 years ago. What a lot had changed! What was I going to do? The Rocky Mountains were the main geological feature for the film.

"Lord, please help. We need mountains for the filming. Where can I take the horses so that we can get a dramatic backdrop? The film people will be here within two days and I have to have it organised."

"You know the hunting season starts soon, and the hunters will shoot you and your horses – especially your horses," warned Amy, handing me a red neck cover for Pistol.

"Thank you so much," I said. "This will be very useful." As I knew the power of words, my habit was to negate words of death so I added: "We won't get shot. I'm relying on God's direction and his angels for protection."

"I tell you, you will get shot," she said insistently, apparently not hearing me. "People get killed."

"Well, we are not going to be shot or killed!" I confirmed.

It was good to see Tanya. We stayed with her aunt, uncle Billy and Joannna Harless, in whose garden several elk, made themselves at home browsing on the plants and flowers. I tried to back up my digital photographs, but my computer screen was blank. It had filled up one of four bags, and I had loaded it on and off my packhorses every day. Now, I seriously thought of leaving it behind as I continuously had problems with it, due to my technical inadequacies.

Death and life are in the
power of the tongue.
Proverbs 18v21 NKJ

Faith does not make things easy -
it makes them possible.
- unknown

The MacGregor Ranch is the last remaining working cattle ranch with horses in Estes Park and is also a youth education centre. Its original structures and museum collection offer a look back in time to the early homesteading days of Estes Park, in 1873, when homesteader Alexander MacGregor began his claims. He was followed by three generations of MacGregors.

# FRIENDS TO THE RESCUE!

*The moment I called out, you stepped in; you made my life large with strength.*
*Psalm 138v3 TM*

I called a friend, Peggy Colburn, in Fort Collins, who I had first met over 20 years ago while she was teaching jewellery at Dartington College of Art, near Totnes, in England. I hadn't seen her for 10 years, but I wanted to know if she and her husband, Jim, could suggest a good location.

"Tracey, we want to help you out," Peggy exclaimed. "We were just heading out the door to go camping, but we'd love to do anything for you!"

"Cameron Pass, just north of you, won't have snow at this time of year as it's lower," said Jim. "We'll pick you up and also check out Loveland Pass, back south, where you have just come from."

Tamara Thompson came to fetch me, and took me to Greeley, where her encouraging parents, Dave and Bonnie Duell, were preaching, which gave my faith a great boost. After a night with Brian and Tamara, Peggy and Jim drove me several hours south to Loveland Pass.

"Hey, Peggy and Jim, this is it!" I enthused on our arrival, as it was dramatic, with remnants of snow, and easily accessible to the film crew, who couldn't walk far from the road with the camera and tripod. Then we whizzed back to Estes Park. They took my computer to be checked out by Tamara's brother-in-law, in Fort Collins.

Tanya immediately whisked me off to the MacGregor Ranch, where we met Eric Adams to ask about filming here. The price he quoted made me gulp hard, but after a board meeting, he called me and offered the location for free! I was grateful for their generosity, for the ranch was beautiful, and I felt a little more relaxed as I had a location for the film crew, who were arriving the following day. Filming was by far the most expensive part of the journey and I needed to have everything set up to make the most of their time. Usually we ended up with one hour of raw film footage a day. Although I had completed several long-distance rides and published other photographic books, all of this seemed relatively easy, compared with the workings of the film industry which, I was discovering had different work ethics to those I was accustomed to. I was on a sharp learning curve, trusting a large portion of the proceeds of my business, which I had begun from nothing, 14 years earlier.

Tanya kindly helped me out by completing the permit application, but when we arrived on location, there always seemed to be hitches. I was still physically exhausted and worried about the filming, as I hadn't found any transport to get my horses back to Loveland Pass on the day after the shoot at MacGregor's ranch. I had called everyone I knew in Colorado with a horse trailer, put the word out in the rodeo, and contacted a recommended commercial transporter… but no one could do it.

"I need to talk to you about bears," said Bill. "They are the top of the food chain in North America and they eat everything."

"I've got to rush," I replied, excusing myself. Although I appreciated his concern my mind was too occupied by immediate problems. I added: "Can we talk about bears later!"

Peggy with Jim and Tanner Colburn on Loveland Pass.

Below Tanya Fallin with Tracey, Smoky and Pistol. Above: Creek crossing.

197

# ROOF TOP RODEO

"I'm riding to Canada," I answered a cowboy's question at the Roof Top Rodeo, at Estes Park.

"Are you kidding me?" he asked.

"I'm over half way," I assured him.

The glitz and glamour of the daring rodeo, now so thoroughly American, originated in the Mexican fiestas. The Roof Top Rodeo, looks like a stage set, surrounded by dramatic mountains, and full of glamorous people dressed in colourful attire, with shining belts and buckles. I felt rather underdressed for the occasion, in the comfortable, pale green shirt that I had worn from the Mexican/Texas border, as I cantered Smoky and Pistol around the arena for a moment of stardom. Smoky knew he was in the limelight, arched his neck and was unusually keen!

"I'm rockin' and rollin' tonight and letting her rip!" Chad announced, as music filled the air. "Friday night live!" There was saddle bronc riding, steer wrestling, tie down roping, bareback riding, barrel racing, bull riding and sheep riding

"We have kids starting to sign up for the Mutton Bustin in April," said Bo, one of the organisers. "There's a 55lb weight limit. We draw from a lottery and 14 mutton busters a night get to ride. They win a trophy that is as big as they are!"

This rodeo lasted for six nights, one of which was entitled "Tough Enough to Wear Pink", when all the cowboys and personnel wore pink and raised money for national cancer research.

"This is a unique rodeo," Bo shouted over the music, "because it's attended by tourists, who haven't been to a rodeo before."

"It won the cowboy's choice for Wyoming and Colorado Mountain States, four or five times," added Laurie, the livestock contractor. I could understand why, for there was a very hospitable and friendly atmosphere.

"We've been in the business right on 21 years," she told me. "Been here for 16 years. We put on almost 90 performances across the Country a year. We raise all our own stock, all the bucking bulls and horses."

I was interested to hear how the bulls and horses were bred and born to buck. "Some of these animals are $30,000 to $40,000, and bucking is natural," Bo informed me. "The strap they wear enhances their bucking, but doesn't harm them. The average workload of rodeo horses is two minutes a year. If they do ten, that's 80 seconds a year."

I was excited that I had an offer of a lift back to Loveland, but then discovered the offerer thought I meant Loveland the town, not the pass, which was in the opposite direction! So I continued to phone a commercial transporter, but there was no reply. It would take several days to ride back there – time that I just didn't have. Bob and Trip the film crew, who had been booked by me, would leave on Monday, and we had no film of the Rockies yet. This was the most important part of the journey, and I had to get some footage of it. This was one of those moments that I regretted having the idea of filming the ride, as it added so much pressure, and was certainly the most expensive and challenging aspect of the expedition. I whispered:

"God, I have no one to take me and my horses back to Loveland Pass. Have you any ideas of how we can get there?"

*Let him have all your worries and cares, for he is always thinking about you and watching everything that concerns you.*
*1 Peter 5v7 TLB*

*The credit belongs to the man who is actually in the arena, whose face is marred by dust and sweat and blood; who strives valiantly; who errs and comes short again and again; who knows great enthusiasms, the great devotions, and spends himself in a worthy cause, who at best knows in the end the truimph of high achievement, and who at worst, if he fails at least fails while daring greatly. - Theodore Roosevelt*

# THE TEXAS PICK-UP!

"What's too far?" Greg asked. "It's only a road trip! I'd like to come!"

I had almost cried with relief when Greg answered my call early the following morning.

"This could be a good opportunity to negotiate for a pay rise!" he added humorously, and I began to laugh, which helped to dispel the stress of the past few days.

"I'll leave Lubbock in about an hour, and be on my way," he confirmed.

While at MacGregor's ranch we filmed in the beautiful meadow settings for a few hours. Bob suggested lunch in the town. I was concerned they would be gone for hours and we would risk losing the afternoon filming opportunity, because of the very predictable storm patterns in the mountains at this time of year, so I asked Tanya to collect pizzas instead. After another two hour lunch break I trotted up and interrupted their picnic.

"Can we get a move on?" I asked in frustration, "there's a thunderstorm on its way."

Tanya had been kindly taking photos for me, but disappeared when the thunderclouds darkened the sky. "I don't do lightning!" she said quite sensibly, when I called her to find out where she was, since it was getting darker by the moment. Trip, the cameraman took over my camera and got wet by standing in the middle of the creek, getting splattered by mud and water as we crossed at speed. This was nothing new to him as from the very start of the journey he had been splashed while filming us, wading through the Rio Grande with the large camera. He took it in his stride in order to get the good shots, and would wipe the camera lens, only to get splashed yet again as we re-enacted trotting through the water!

After three hours of filming that day on MacGregor's ranch, Amy and Rob, her husband, took me down the road and dropped us outside the small settlement at Rollinsville. Passers by gave us some curious looks as Smoky and Pistol were tied to a lamppost and beside them lay a mountainous pile of pack bags and saddlery. I was quite amazed how all the pack could actually fit on the horses! As there was no phone signal I hoped Greg would spot us on the side of the road in the dusk.

It sure was good to see that grey, Texas numberplated pick-up, with the rusted cream trailer, come into sight again.

"600 miles in 11 hours! Not bad, hey?" Greg greeted me with a smile, and tipped his cowboy hat back off his head.

"Thanks for coming!" I enthused which was rather an understatement. Suddenly, I felt myself relaxing as I now had efficient and reliable help for the last day of filming.

"Well, You're showing me all these places I haven't seen before. Another country right on my back door," Greg said, lightly.

We drove south for several hours, and then turned off the interstate. As we drove through Empire, I noticed a nice-looking old building, up on the hill, slightly away from the road. It was almost 9pm when we arrived at this old guesthouse, and discovered they had rooms available.

Gary St Clair, the proprietor (and chef), kindly offered us his back pen behind the hotel for the horses, next door to where he kept his own mule, Angel, and two donkeys. He showed us where we could get water and we penned them in the smaller enclosure.

When they call on me, I will answer,...
Psalm 91v15 NLT

16th July. Loveland Pass, at 11,992 ft, near Breckenridge, where I had been the previous week, was ideal for the filming, with the dramatic Rocky Mountain backdrops. Left the Peck House at 6.30am and arrived at the pass at 7.30, awaiting the film crew. The blue sky was cloudless all morning. I had asked Bob to bring food to tide him over as we're in the middle of nowhere, and it made sense to get all the footage we could before the storm arrived. But we had to go down the mountain for a two-hour lunch break, while the clouds built up for a storm. When filming resumed we were dangerously exposed to lightning. Some warning signs are tingling skins, light metal objects vibrating or hair standing up on end – This was very obvious with the top hairs of Pistol's tail standing vertically (top right), during the last shot of the day, at about 4.30 pm.

# LIGHTNING STRIKES

*Living for a cause will prove as gallant as dying for a cause.*
*- Helen Keller*

While Trip filmed, under Bob's direction, Greg took the stills with my camera. He was a conscientious student and would hand me the camera for my opinion, to check the exposure and composition, before taking more until we got the shot we wanted. I had to re-enact crossing snow and although this wasn't deep, Pistol remembered falling over previously and didn't want to follow Smoky. He pulled back several times, snapping the pigging strings, so we had to do several retakes.

"It's a wrap!" said Bob, and we bailed off the high ground, as storm clouds gathered and the hairs on Pistol's tail stood vertical. Feeling concerned I asked Greg about lightning.

"I know it will kill ya!" he replied bluntly.

On average, lightning kills more people in the US than both hurricanes and tornadoes combined, with about 100 fatalities a year. 10 per cent of lightning strike victims actually die, and the survivors suffer life-long debilitation, mainly neurological. The states with the most casualties per capita are Wyoming, New Mexico, Florida, Arkansas and Colorado, where it is the most serious weather hazard. It can be deadly more than 120 feet away from the strike point, as high voltage currents flow across the surface, or within the soil, and there can be an upwards discharge from the ground for tens of feet, through people and trees. One year, lightning killed a herd of 56 elk.

The turbulent, swirling air inside the thundercloud creates a positive and negatively charged area, with the negative gathering at its base. As opposite charges attract each other, the positive charges form beneath the cloud and follow it. When the positive and negative charges finally meet, they complete an electrical circuit and lightning is produced.

It can strike many miles from the parent thunderstorm, outside the rain area and even beyond the thundercloud, or after the storm has passed. Lightning does not decide where it will strike until the 'stepped leader', descending from the cloud, is about 100 ft (30 m) from the ground or the object that is struck. That's why short objects can be struck by lightning, even if a tall object is nearby.

17th July: After filming, we came back to the Peck House, as it is close to the pass and a good, friendly place, where we can keep our horses and eat a good meal. We are staying a few more days catching up on notes and copying all my digital photos onto Greg's computer (mine is in Fort Collins being fixed) and then copying them onto back-up disks to send to England and Texas. Gary and Sally offered us a couple of rooms free of charge and Gary invited us up the mountain with his friend, Buff Rutherford. Horses and I still pretty tired.

No one can measure the depths of his understanding. He gives power to those who are tired and worn out; He offers strength to the weak. But those who wait on the Lord will find new strength they will fly high on wings like eagles. They will run and not grow weary. They will walk and not faint. Isaiah 40v31 NLT

Above, Gary, Buff, Greg and I at the Peck House. (below) Buff Rutherford on his horse Andy with Greg on Smoky, (middle) Gary St.Clair on his mule Angel, (right) riding up the mountain.

# PICNIC PARTY!

In 1980, Gary and Sally St. Clair had honeymooned at the Peck House, which looked out across Empire, returning every month until they bought it a year later. It was named after Peck, who originally came to Empire from New York in 1859, looking for silver. Instead he found gold, built a home and turned it into a refined hotel in 1862. In contrast to the primitive shanties, which miners hired for 50 cents, sleeping five to a bed, the Peck House had rooms with beds of maple, walnut and cherry.

Gary, along with his friend Buff, who needed an oxygen tank to breathe at this high altitude, took us up West Chicago Creek to the mountain. It was very pleasant to be meandering through the mountains with the three horses, Andy, Smoky and Pistol and Angel the mule. I'm sure 'my boys' apppreciated not having to carry packs on their backs.

"Just as well you penned the horses in one section, because a bear came through last night and ripped the fence off the next pen," remarked Gary

"Been hunting and camping in this mountain for 66 years, since I was 12," said Buff. "I killed an elk right here, and my wife got a five point (antlers on elk) here last year."

"There'll be raspberries, but they won't be ripe till mid-August," Buff remarked, clearly knowing every inch of the mountain. "But hey man, I can see some strawberries!" he added pointing down on the ground. He chattered on talking about grouse and wildlife, and then Greg pointed to a mottled brown ptarmigan: "Over there, gee!"

"I have already snuck into the cookies!" admitted Greg, with a chuckle, as we sat down for lunch in the drizzle.

"Life is uncertain, so it's best to eat your dessert first!" confirmed Buff with humour. As Gary handed us smoked trout, salmon and spicy cheese, he added: "Keep eating that fancy food, and the next thing you know, you'll be riding a mule!"

The men continued to banter back and forth to one another regarding mules and horses, as Greg and Gary both owned mules, but Buff preferred horses! "You ride what you can handle!" added Buff.

"Shall I take Andy for a drink?" asked Gary.

"Now, don't be trying to stretch those ears!" joked Buff.

In the light rain, there was a strong aroma of pines, vegetation and sweating horses. Greg helped to change Buff's oxygen tank, concerned that the it might not last the descent.

"Buff, short for buffalo – a nickname I got when I was playing Cowboys and Indians. I wouldn't play unless I was Buffalo Bill!" said Buff as we headed back to Empire. He pointed to the Stanley mine: "Strictly gold," he added. "There is a lot of iron, in the same vein as the gold. Mine tailings are usually orange in colour, because iron turns to rust. Silver tailings are usually grey, from the zinc and lead. I remember the mining – not the boom years though. The price of silver dropped by half overnight. The government bought the silver for coinage, but now they use gold to back up the paper currency. My dad and his partner didn't prospect for wages, but to pay the grocery bill! Then, in 1922, they found a silver vein and got $300 a day. They sold their shares to the company, knowing the vein could disappear as easily as it had appeared, and made enough to buy groceries for a year!"

After our ride, Greg copied the last of several thousand photos onto his computer, and then onto disks, saying: "Let's get this all sorted so I can boot you out! You need to get going north!"

"I want to catch the autumn colours," I added, visualising the amazing shades of the aspen trees, as they turned golden.

"The colour will be white, white when you get to Canada, if you don't hurry up!" Greg retorted, and transported me back north to Fort Collins, to the east of Estes Park.

Choose your passion, not your pension.
- Denis Waitley

# LUXURY FOR ALL

*I have learnt that a good friend is the purest of all God's gifts,*
*for it is a love that has no exchange or payment.*
*– Frances Farmer*

With Peggy Colburn and Tanner on her veranda in Fort Collins.

We sipped copious amounts of tea with real milk (no powdered milk lumps!), and caught up with the past ten years, in Peggy and Jim Colburn's back garden, in the fresh morning air – the only cool part of the day. Fort Collins, several thousand feet lower than the mountains, rose to the high 90s every day! Smoky and Pistol felt the heat too – having memories of their home in East Texas, when they sweated it out at Cindy Wright-Jones' place at Laporte.

"Is one of your horses an escape artist?" asked Cindy. "I came down one morning and Smoky's head popped up from the field next door. I asked him what he was doing there, and he replied: "What do you think I am doing – eating!" His expression was like a child being caught doing something he shouldn't. He had used his teeth to wiggle loose the railings, had taken off the two top rails and stepped over the lower one!"

At the same time as Smoky was taking the fence down, I walked right through a fly screen, splattering a jug of cream I was holding, like in a cartoon. It caused Peggy, Dianne, another friend and I to double up with laughter!

While Cindy fed the horses in the morning, I drove a car lent to me by Gerry Zell, a friend of Cindy's, and fed them in the evening as I was trying to get weight back on them. Pistol had lost so much from his back that the pack would come down onto his withers. Greg had given us another saddle blanket, with a section cut away to ease the pressure on the withers, and when he dropped us off, he said: "Get them and you beefed up!"

With Gerry's help, I learnt that I needed to arrange a veterinary inspection before entering Montana, and then again for Canada. She took up my cause, making enquiries in different directions on my behalf. She also gave me contacts for Yellowstone through a smoke jumper she was nursing, who had suffered many broken bones while parachuting in from a helicopter to fight a forest fire. She prayed over Smoky and Pistol and asked Kevin Spear, a farrier, to check out the horses' shoes.

"Be careful when you see moose for the first time," warned Kevin, as he tightened the clenches. "Something that is bigger and uglier – they can't figure it out."

While the horses and I ate and rested, I endeavoured to catch up on emails, using the Colburn's computer. Peggy lent me some of her clothes, making a refreshing change from my four shirts. I seemed to have mislaid two of them, until Jo Harless found them under the bed I had been sleeping in at Estes Park. She and Bill kindly brought them over to me, along with my book.

Peggy took me shopping, and we laughed and laughed as we tried on clothes, swapping them between each other at second hand stores (which are really good value in North America). I didn't have room in my pack for all the clothes and teabags that I collected while staying with Peggy!

Along my journey, I liked to dress up whenever I was invited to give presentations on my riding adventures. While I was at Cindy's place, I changed into Courtney's black trousers (pants), pink top and loopy earrings, along with Sherry's black shoes and Eunice's mascara. Once I had topped my outfit off with my red toe polish and lipstick, I immediately felt dressed up!

"I think you should stay for another week and let the snow fall on you!" Peggy remarked. "And you should have our phone number tattooed on you somewhere!"

"Oh, you mean if I get lost, rather like Paddington Bear: "If found please return to ... Peggy!", I chuckled.

"Yes! Happy trail to you, until we meet again! Roy Rogers said that!" Peggy laughed and waved as Gerry and Cindy took me and my horses back west to the mountains, just north of the Rocky Mountain National Park. As I rode north along the Laramie River Valley, it felt refreshing to be back at higher altitude in the cooler climate once again.

I woke up to a kestrel's cries and the calling of a fawn, as some deer leisurely passed by, grazing. I could tell by my horses' ears if there was wildlife about. Humming birds buzzed about my camp spot.

Later I passed the Forestry Information, where some volunteers from Florida kindly filled up my water bottles.

# WYOMING

Wyoming, the least populated State, containing dramatic, contrasting landscapes, is set on a plateau where the great plains are interrupted by striking mountain ranges. Several of these make up the Continental Divide, which stretches north-south across the central portion of the State, splitting in the south central part, called the Great Divide Basin. About half of Wyoming's vast stretches of forests and grasslands are owned by the United States Government and managed by the Bureau of Land Management which is responsible for 262 million acres of public land (one eighth of the US), and by the Forest and National Park Services.

Old miners' cabin.

Prairie dogs, small stout ground squirrels which dwell in burrows across 10 states in North America. Below: The Colorado Wyoming border

# THUNDER AND LIGHTNING

*When you get into a storm, use the panorama philosophy, the big view. Then you will know it will not last forever. With faith in your heart you can ride it out.*
*- Norman Vincent Peale*

Crossing through farming countryside in northern Colorado, after the high open trails in the mountains, I was again faced with cattle guards and drop gates. I had that same familiar sinking feeling as I did in New Mexico, each time I approached a cattle guard, wondering if I would be able to get through. On one occasion, there didn't seem to be a gate at all, but on closer investigation I discovered the log poles in the fence at one side of the cattle guard slid to one side. As I was doing this, Smoky got an electric shock from the nearby wire fence and took off back up the road with Pistol attached to him. I dropped the pole and ran to catch him. A little further on, deep clover covered the roadside verges. This nutrious feast was too good an opportunity for the horses to miss. I sat on the verge reading my book until they ate their fill and began to get restless and wander on along the road.

"You can water your horses at the Double Diamond Ranch if you'd like," said a young man on a four-wheeler bike, pointing to some large barns to the south. I thanked him, but said I was heading north. However, I was in two minds whether to turn back, because within half an hour it was as if a hot tap had been turned off, and a cold tap suddenly turned on. The warmth of the sun's rays were replaced with huge, cold raindrops hammering down on us. Thunder and lightning exploded about us, as I pushed the horses faster across the sage brush prairie. One clap of thunder exploded right over our heads, which caused us to dive off the exposed road down the bank. But we couldn't stay in the dip indefinitely, as there we were still dangerously exposed to lightning, so I rode the horses back up onto the road.

"Lightning, stay right away from us, in Jesus' name." I shouted as I pushed the horses faster and we trotted on across the high plains through the falling rain, under the heavy dark sky.

*"Have faith in God, for assuredly, I say to you, whoever says to this mountain, 'Be removed and be cast into the sea,' and does not doubt in his heart, but believes that those things he says will be done, he will have whatever he says. Mark 11v23,24*

# A LAND OF GIANTS!

After the first storm passed over, I could see another wave approaching from the south, so once again I pushed the horses on, heading northwards to find shelter as the storm chased us into Wyoming. The road rose before us, onto a higher sage brush plain, dangerously exposed to lightning, so we ducked down a track to some barns. We shared one open-ended shed with a couple of large tractors, as the rain hammered noisily on the roof and the lightning lit up the otherwise dark day. I really wanted to stay the night there, but there was no one at the nearby homestead to ask permission from, so I fed the horses the remaining sweet grain, and then repacked. After the storm had passed, we set off up through the prairie of sage bush, monster pylons and 20 foot snow fences.

Concerned that I needed to find shelter and grass for the horses before another storm and the night was upon us, we hurried across the wide expanse, under a dark sky. I was surprised to see so much sage bush. Having read the book 'Green Grass of Wyoming' as a child, I came to the assumption that the green grass must be in another part of the state!

Another conclusion I came to was there must be giants in the land of Wyoming judging by the monster pylons, snow fences and high drop gates, whose wire release was so high I had to climb up the fence just to try to unlatch it, looped tightly around the pole. Often, the only way I could do this was to use my pliers to loosen it first, before I could slip the wire over the pole and open the gate for my horses. Then it was almost harder to get it shut again.

It was 8pm when I spied an ideal spot, out of sight of the road, with a stream, trees, grass for the horses and enough room for my little tent.

The following morning, I walked into Woods Landing and called Neil Bailey, who I had contacted previously, as I was interested in his horse logging. He picked us up in his convertible trailer and took us on to another contact at the Johnson's 99 Ranch. On route I dropped my saddle into the Board Walk saddlery in Laramie, to have a few D rings repaired.

"My great grandfather arrived from Denmark when he was 16 years old. He came to lay the railroad tracks, from 1860 to 68, for the Union Pacific Railway. Indians often attacked, and after one skirmish he found that his brother was missing, so he stayed in the area," said Orville Johnson. "The Johnsons' 99 ranch has been in the family since the 1860s. It's 7,000 acres and we're working up to 500 cows. There's a lot more work in ranching than there is pay!"

"I don't want to tell you how many horses we have. Maybe 50, because we need to sell a few!" added Lindy, his wife. "We take on horses to break. That's why we don't get ours broke!"

I loved the 100-year-old barn and could feel that the interior was cool and well insulated, suiting both the hot summers and cold winters.

Above right: Snow fence to stop the snow blowing across the prairie.

Middle: On the way to Woods Landing. Bottom: Smoky and Pistol in a convertible!

The Johnson Family on the Johnson 99 Ranch

# RODEO QUEEN

While visiting the Johnsons' ranch, to the east of the mountains, I discovered the 'green grass of Wyoming' and a haze of mosquitoes at sundown! I also met Rodeo Queen Stacy Jo (Orville and Lindy's daughter), a former Miss Rodeo Wyoming who was crowned Miss Rodeo USA in 2006. I asked Stacy Jo about Rodeo Queens – another uniquely Western affair.

"A lot of girls, who want to be Rodeo Queens start when they are seven or eight years old. After becoming Princess and Junior Princess, they grow up through the ranks. If they practise their speaking skills and riding horses – which is the most important thing – they may become Lady in Waiting and then Miss Rodeo of Wyoming, or whatever their State may be," explained Stacy Jo. "I was riding before I learnt to walk, as a liddie biddie thing! But I didn't start to compete to be a Rodeo Queen until I was 16 years old, which was really late. You have to be 18 to run for a Queen, you can be one until you are 25 years old, and you hold the title for a year." As we chatted I learnt that there was a lot more to being a rodeo queen than just looking pretty on a horse!

"The 'looking pretty' part is probably the easiest!" added Stacy Jo. "We get judged on our appearance, hair, make-up and clothing. It's a really big deal in the Rodeo Queen world, because we are out in front of the public, and they want us to have the latest Western fashion attire that fits really nice."

"Western fashion?" I asked, surprised that there was such a thing, never having been a follower of fashion at all!

"Oh yes!" Stacy Jo replied. "They also look at how our cowboy hats are shaped and check that our boots are polished and our jeans are starched. We don't wear swimsuits, like the real pageant world, but we do wear leather dresses!"

"What else are you judged on?" I asked.

"Horsemanship is one of the main things. We get asked about training horses, and are judged on reining patterns (which is like dressage, but Western, with different manoeuvres) and we ride horses we have never ridden before. We're also questioned about our goals and lifestyles – everything and anything! We have to give speeches about our State and another subject of our choice – mine is nutrition and farming. So we're judged on a combination of appearance, reining, speaking, modelling, knowledge of rodeo, equine science and current events."

"What happened when you became Miss Rodeo USA?" I asked.

"I travelled all over and did some public speaking, mostly in the south and east of the United States, which was a lot of fun. Our job is to help people understand the sport and encourage them to come and see the rodeos. You don't have time to work while being Rodeo Queen, and all the travelling and clothing do cost a lot, so at my coronation party we had a silent auction. I raffled one of my horses off and we raised about $20,000 for the year. My committee helped me budget, to make sure it was used properly."

Stacy Jo continued: "Now I'm competing for Miss Rodeo America (there are two different rodeo associations), which is held in Las Vegas during the National Finals Rodeo in November.* No girls have held both titles so I might be the first. We'll see!" she added, with a big attractive smile. "When I'm not queening, I'm working on the ranch here, haying, calving, doctoring cattle."

Lindy gave me a lift to Laramie. Neil collected my saddle and took me back out to Fox Park, in Medicine Bow Forest, where I camped overnight. On the way there, he introduced me to some of his friends at the Buck Horn Bar, where I noticed a bullet hole in the mirror behind the bar.

"It's a dirty bitch to ride across that Great Divide Basin. Sage chicken, antelope and rattlesnakes. All up there is rattlesnake country," said Matt, Neil's friend, pointing to the middle section of Wyoming on my map. "Drop below 6,200ft and you're back in rattlesnake country."

* Stacy Jo was the first runner up competing against 27 girls in Miss Rodeo America, in Las Vegas. She won the personality, speech and miss congeniality awards.

Above: Stacy Jo Johnson, Rodeo Queen USA and below her niece Aurora Wand up and coming Rodeo Queen!

# LADY THE HORSE LOGGER

"I love logging. It's in my blood," Neil remarked. "I've been logging since I was a kid, and started logging horses in 1983. I've always liked wood, and I like to be in the mountains, so what could be better? A few years ago I just woke up, wondered what I was going to do, and decided "I'm going horse logging"."

Neil's Belgian horse was called Lady, and I was amazed at her strength and temperament, considering that this was only her second time out.

"When they're that big, you want them to be gentle, to obey your voice commands and pull. Lady's like a Cadillac. Loaded with a log, it's like she's got power steering and windows!"

"There used to be a sawmill, which owned the store and all the houses at Fox Park," said Mervin Brant, who stopped to chat while Neil and Lady were pulling out dead trees killed by a beetle epidemic. He continued: "At the turn of the last century lots of aliens worked in the forestry – Swedes and Greeks.

Back in the 1960s we had 12 to 15 horses and 20 men to log this sawmill, all year round. When my dad started, the horses would be hooked up, skid logs to the mill on their own, be unhooked at the mill, and return on their own to collect another. We didn't use mules, they're far too smart. The greatest thing about horses is they always want to go to work, even when it's 40 below and the tractor won't start. I had some machine equipment worth half a million, and it still couldn't do the work of the men and the horses."

'Why aren't you horse logging now?" asked Neil.

"Well, they still make the horses, but they don't make the men!"

Jim Nulle, on whose property Neil and Lady were working, invited me for breakfast and a shower. I asked him about the beetle epidemic, which was obviously affecting millions of acres in the mountains. The forest was peppered with dead, reddish brown and grey trees.

"It's a very serious problem, and it's only a matter of time before there's going to be a huge fire with all these dead trees," he said, clearly concerned, for his house was situated at Fox Park, in the middle of an enormous Medicine Bow forest.

A recent survey showed that 94,000 acres of the Medicine Bow forest alone were dying from the beetle epidemic, and increasing. There are two major contributing factors. One is the ageing forests, which are more susceptible to insects and disease, and the other is the extended drought, which makes trees dehydrated and weak, so that even young, healthy trees are unable to produce enough resin to combat the beetles. A tree will remain green for eight to 10 months after the beetles have killed it. Then its needles turn reddish brown, fall off and, eventually, the tree falls down.

The bark beetles, usually carrying a fungus, eat the inner bark, so not only do they spread the fungus, but also interrupt the transport of water and nutrients up the trunk, and this is what kills the tree. These beetles have always been present in the forests, in low numbers, but there hasn't been such a widespread infestation in recorded history.

The mountain pine beetles, each the size of a grain of rice, attack the tree en masse, tunnel under the bark, mate and lay about 75 eggs, which hatch and continue to eat the inner bark of the tree. These larvae spend the winter there, before emerging and attacking other green trees. As they multiply, so the trees die.

# QUAKIES

As I packed up the horses at Fox Park I was seen off by a group of people, who had gathered to watch the horses logging that morning.

"Grizzly bears get in a real bad mood if they are surprised, and want to biff you!" Neil warned me, adding, "You'll come across them in the mountains."

I waved goodbye and followed the long dirt road marked on the map, with had corresponding letters on the trees, indicating the different snow mobile routes. The continuous, dense conifer trees, edging each side of the road, made me feel a bit claustrophobic so I appreciated the open breathing spaces of sage bush and aspen trees.

A whole stand of aspen trees, also called 'quakies' because of their fluttering leaves, often grow from one root system. These roots can lie dormant in the ground over a long period, waiting for the right conditions of sun, space and moisture. Avalanches and fires create the perfect environment for growth.

Elk use the nitrogen-rich inner bark as late winter survival food, and the aspen is also the favourite food and building material for beavers, who can consume several pounds of bark a day and cut down hundreds of trees a year. But this stimulates saplings, and beaver ponds eventually dry up and become meadows, where new trees can grow. Aspen stands can shelter eight to ten times as many plant species and three times as many birds as the conifer forests. In the autumn their leaves paint the landscape in iridescent shimmering gold.

I see my path, but I don't know where it leads.
Not knowing where I'm going is what inspires me to travel it.
Rosalia de Castro

# MEDICINE BOW

*6th August, I think, as it's hard to keep track of the days!*
*Riding through the Medicine Bow forest last night, I met Duncan,*
*prospecting for gold with his two dogs. He explained that the*
*'GPAA' and 'private claim' signs on the trees meant that members*
*could prospect all over the country.*

*Camped in the damp forest. Don't know where I have left two*
*of my four torches, my GPS or the book I was reading. The torch*
*on my saddle had a flat battery so I searched for another, finding*
*it in my sleeping bag. Packed Smoky (always easier, as he is smaller)*
*because I'm trying to teach Pistol to lead on foot. Let them graze*
*in the middle of the day. The strap holding the pack on the bucksaw*
*snapped. Thank you God for bailing string!*

*Really could have done with my expensive GPS, as kept going*
*down dead end tracks – my sense of direction doesn't work well in*
*forests. Wasted hours of time and energy backtracking as my map*
*doesn't show all the trails.*

*At three, thunder and lightning began, – quickly put up my tent*
*by the little Laramie River, throwing the tarpaulin over the pack bags.*
*Then the sun came out, but decided to stay and get an early night*
*and early start as I didn't want to be on the exposed Bald Medicine*
*Bow heights in a lightning storm. The thunder was so loud and the*
*lightning lit up the night – rain pounded on the tent. Woke to my*
*alarm at 5 – still so dark. Tethered the horses out and after they*
*had eaten for an hour and a half, packed up and left. Following the*
*horses' intent gaze, saw deer as we followed rain-filled, slippery*
*four-wheeler ruts to Libby Flats. Felt claustrophobic, and having a*
*tendency to get lost in forests, it was refreshing to get out in some*
*space and see the Snowy Mountains, still wearing a little snow.*
*Though it was sunny, I was conscious of thunderstorms and*
*pressed on, frequently checking the sky to the west as clouds were*
*building up in the far distance and I didn't want to be caught in the*
*baldies in a lightning storm.*

The Snowy Range in the central south part of Wyoming is an extension of the Colorado Rockies and part of the Medicine Bow Mountains, which extend 90 miles from Elk Mountain Wyoming, and south to Cameron Pass, Colorado. The name is derived from the Native Americans, who first came to this area to cut mountain mahogany, water birch, and juniper for bow making, and to hunt and collect plants. Friendly tribes came to meet here for ceremonial pow-wows, to cure diseases, create medicines and make bows – hence the name Medicine Bow. They lived off the land in the Medicine Bow area until the mid 1870s, when the military forced them north.

French trappers arrived here in the early 1800s, including Jacque La Ramie, after whom the city of Laramie is named. He trapped along the Laramie River until he died in a skirmish with Indians. Other famous trappers, who passed through this area, were John Fremone, Kit Carson and Jim Bridger. In the 1860s, the Union Pacific Railroad reached the Laramie Plains, the city was established, and the ranching areas opened up to the eastern markets. The railway created the lumber industry in the Medicine Bow Forest, which became the major source of 'ties' (sleepers), used in railroad construction.

# THE SNOWY MOUNTAINS

I don't know what to do, but I'm looking to you.
2 Chronicles 20v12 TLB

The helpful people at Fox Park had given me a map, and directions on how to get over the top of the Snowy Mountain Range, through the Gap Lakes. However, I wasn't prepared for the boulder-strewn trail. Smoky, who still preferred looking at the scenery rather than where he put his feet, got caught between boulders, scraping one hind and one foreleg and nearly falling on top of me. Blood was pouring down his grey legs on to the pale stones, and I hoped the cuts weren't too deep. Pistol, seeing what happened to Smoky, refused to follow, snapping his pigging string. So I got Smoky across, and then returned to coax Pistol, who was more sure footed, over the boulders. When we arrived at the saddle of the mountain, I thought we would be over the rough going, but before us lay another glacial lake, edged with boulders and scree. My heart sank. We descended to the lake and saw walkers approaching from the opposite direction, scrambling over the huge boulders, having trouble even on two legs.

"Oh, you won't get horses across there!" one walker said, adamantly, as he passed me, confirming my fear that they could easily break a leg.

"God, now what can I do?" I asked desperately, as we became stuck in the middle of a boulder field. We couldn't go back, and there looked to be no way forwards.

The righteous face many troubles, but the Lord rescues them from each and every one. For the Lord protects them from harm - not one of their bones will be broken! Psalm 34v19-20 NLT
Are not the angels all ministering spirits, sent out in the service of God for the assistance of those who are to inherit salvation?
Hebrews 1v14 Amp

It was already midday, and the afternoon thunderclouds had begun to build. Here we were in Wyoming, the top state for lightning strikes, very exposed at over 10,000 feet, and in even more danger on the edge of water. I could feel my heart beating fast, knowing it was a race against time and the lightning. One thought was to swim the horses through the glacial lake, but it was a long way, the water was very cold and I wanted to avoid hypothermia at all costs. Also, I couldn't see into the black water. There were boulders to the edge, so there were bound to be more under the water, on which the horses could bash their legs or get caught.

I left the horses to graze and prayed as I scrambled over the boulders. I found a narrow ledge under the water, on the edge of the boulders and the deep, dark lake. The ledge still had gaping holes in it, but it was smoother, and the only possible way I could see to get horses across.

"Please God let the horses follow me through the water," I pleaded, my heart pounding.

There was no sense in procrastinating. I took my coat off Smoky, so that if we all fell into the lake, I would have something dry to put on. I also took my camera off his saddle and handed it to a man, fishing nearby. However nervous I felt, it was my job to get photographs, whatever the outcome.

"I believe we will get across, but can you take photos, whatever happens?" I asked him. I then laid my hands on Pistol and Smoky and prayed over them, asking the angels to keep the horses on the ledge, and declaring that none of our bones would be broken. Then, with a pounding heart, I led Smoky towards the ledge. Pistol pulled back, snapping another pigging string, I couldn't turn back so I left him and continued with Smoky.

"Now Smoky, please look where you are putting your feet. That's it boy! Don't panic, it's only a short way. Just keep on the ledge! Follow me, there you go, there you go!" I kept reassuring him, as he followed me into the water, onto the ledge. I had to be careful not to get in his way and get knocked over, but still be close enough to guide him and keep him on the narrow ledge, between the boulders on one side, and the deep lake on the other. Once committed, there was no space to turn back. I continued to soothe Smoky as we carefully picked our way over a 40 foot stretch of rocks.

As we reached the other side, Smoky realised that Pistol wasn't behind him, and started to panic, neighing frantically. So I wedged his lead rope between two boulders, trusting that the rope would hold and that Smoky wouldn't follow me back. Then I ran, scrambling over the rocks to get Pistol, who was afraid to move. With gentle persuasion, he hesitantly followed me, carefully stepping over the rocks, into the water and up over the boulders to join Smoky.

On the other side! Below: Our camp spot.

# ON THE OTHER SIDE!

"Oh, thank you God!" I sighed in relief. "Oh, you boys are so good!" I patted, stroked and congratulated them, and then took Smoky to a grassy spot beside the edge to wash the blood off his legs. One huge danger was behind us, but we had to hurry on to get to a lower and more sheltered elevation before the storm arrived and, with it, the lightning.

We continued past Cutthroat Lake (I wondered what happened there to give it such a name!). As I skirted Deep Lake, it began to thunder, so I quickly found a camping spot and put up the tent, which was still wet from the previous storm, and covered the pack with a tarpaulin. I hoped this storm wouldn't be too rough, as I was camped among some fallen trees, beside some others that didn't look very stable.

During the night, Smoky's frantic neighing woke me with a start, and I could hear him pawing the ground, as if something dreadful had happened. I quickly pulled my clothes and wet boots on, grabbed my torch, and leapt out of the tent into the cold night.

"Oh Smoky, you had me in a panic!" I said, realising it was only because Pistol had got loose and was grazing nearby. "Well, that's a surprise, it's usually you, Smoky, who unties himself!" I remarked, as I brought Pistol back to the picket line and retied him, patted them both and wriggled back into to my warm sleeping bag.

You chart the path ahead of me
and tell me where to stop and rest.
Every moment you know where I am.
You both precede and follow me.
Psalm 139v1-5 NLT

# GOING ROUND IN CIRCLES!

*Goals may give focus, but dreams give power. Dreamers expand the world. ~ John Maxwell*

In the morning, there was a crunchy frost underfoot. I walked round to a group of people across the lake, to ask if they knew about a path that was marked on the forestry map, but not on the OS version. They were having a family reunion, and I recognised Marti and Jeff as the couple, who had taken photos of me the previous day. They thought the route I was contemplating looked feasible, so we crossed over some very boggy ground, only to find that boulders blocked the way for horses. I left the horses to graze while I investigated every possible alternative way, but several hours later, we had to retrace our steps to take the long way around.

"Oh well, boys, it is beautiful!" I said, as we headed back through the marshland. On our way we met Jewell, a delightful woman, on holiday with her goats! After chatting, we continued on our seperate ways. Dreaming, soaking in the beauty, I found myself heading south instead of north and I came across the same family of walkers.

"We have now met you so many times that you feel part of our group, so please join us for a family photo!" they asked. I posed with them, said goodbye and backtracked yet again, determined to focus this time on where I was heading and not to continue going round in circles!

# SOLITARY BEAUTY SPOT

*There is an odd truth about our destination. It is this: The journey is actually our destiny.*
*We sometimes fall into the trap of waiting to arrive somewhere instead of living right where we are.*

*– Jill Austin*

I returned to Sheep's Lake and found no path to follow, so after examining the Forestry map, which wasn't very detailed, I headed north once again. I regretted leaving my GPS behind, for I couldn't tell exactly where we were, as we crossed boggy areas, fallen trees and manoeuvred around boulder fields. The trees were so dense that the easiest way was to skirt the bog at the edge of the tree line. Tiptoeing across the marshy areas, I had to be careful that my heels weren't todden on, as the horses would sense the softness and hurriedly follow closely behind me. Often all three of us sank up to our knees, splattering mud in all directions as we extract ourselves. With no sign of footprints or a path, I knew we were off course, so I kept heading north by my compass, negotiating bogs, fallen trees, and boulders. I saw deer and elk tracks, and although they tended to go west to east, instead of north, I often followed them while looking for one which turned north.

I followed a clear river, meandering through grassy marshlands, and spied a grassy bank, on a curve in the creek, which looked like an idyllic camp spot – one that was frequented by deer and elk, judging by their tracks. Although I didn't know where we were, I pegged Smoky out to graze and kept Pistol in view. It had been a long day, and it was satisfying to watch the horses graze and the trout jumping in the creek. I had a cup of tea, left my muddy boots out to dry (still wet from paddling through the glacier lake) and laid out my plastic shower bag, full of water from the creek, to warm in the sun. I was surprised there weren't clouds of mosquitoes in the swampy land, but realised we were probably too high. Using my tripod, I set up the self-timer on the camera to capture our beautiful camp spot and then, over my camp stove, I warmed up my portion of packaged tuna and ate it with couscous. After an hour or two in the sun, the water in the shower bag had warmed up enough to have a shower, which was a luxury, since the weather had been too wet and cold the previous evenings. But as soon as the sun dropped, so did the temperature. It became instantly cold and my feet felt like ice blocks by the time I crawled into my sleeping bag.

Smoky woke me about five in the morning, pawing the ground to tell me to get up, demanding his breakfast. To avoid my boots smelling out the tent, I usually kept them under the flysheet, along with my socks. I regretted it that morning, for I found that my boots were still damp and stiff and the tent white with frost. I tethered Smoky and let Pistol loose to graze, watching them closely, while I removed the frozen water from my metal cup and had tea and several helpings of porridge.

*9th August: The most beautiful solitary camp spot – with only the presence of animals. Smoky starts shaking when he sees anything. This morning got my gloves and woolly hat on in August! Water in the plastic shower bag, which I had thought I would use for washing this morning, is frozen solid! Waiting for the ice to melt so I can roll the bag up to pack it and also for the tent to dry out. Again, wishing I had the GPS – I can hardly believe that I only got to use it once! Well, the first pioneers wouldn't have had one! At least I've got a compass, but the forest from here on looks so dense – God, I need your direction how we're going to get through those tightly packed trees and fallen tree trunks piled on top of each other.*

You will strengthen me and harden
me to difficulties,
Yes, you will help, for the Lord My
God holds my right hand and says,
fear not I will help you.
Isaiah 41v10,13 Amp

When thou goest , thy way shall be opened up step by step.
Proverbs 4v12 FT

# LOST IN A FOREST - AGAIN!

*Yard by yard, life is hard but inch-by-inch, it's a cinch.*
*- Robert Schuller*

I decided to follow the creek north, assuming it would eventually flow into the large lake shown on the map, but the trees closed in on us, and it was often too dense for one horse to squeeze through, let alone a horse with a pack.

There were so many fallen trees, angled one on top of the other, that it was like a maze. I would leave the horses grazing and scout out ahead to find a way forward. Step by step, often having to go east and west, rather than north, I would cross and re-cross the creek, and slowly we made progress.

"Maybe we can walk in the creek?" I said, hoping for an easier way, but on investigation there were too many trees fallen across it.

"Even if we are lost for days in here, you boys have grass and we have the creek for water," I added, feeling very weary after climbing over fallen trees, scouting out the way ahead. I made myself sing.

Pistol would often get caught on the other side of a tree and snap another pigging string – he must have snapped 20 that morning by not following in Smoky's footsteps. I could imagine what it was like for those early pioneers – they must have been so tough and determined.

"If only you had your GPS," I told myself, "but you don't, so don't let it keep niggling at you."

"We need to get up higher and see where we are," I added, leading Smoky. We climbed up to a more open area, which had been burnt, scrambling over many fallen dead trees. In the bright sunlight, I reached for my sunglasses but realised they had been scraped off my head as we forged through the forest. Hoping to see the lake shown on my map, we kept pressing on and up, over the graveyard of trees. We reached the crest of the rise… and all I could see from here was mile after mile of conifer trees. My heart sank.

Suddenly I stopped the horses, as I thought I heard something. "Hey, boys do you hear what I hear?"

They pricked their ears and looked down the valley beneath us, where a small spiral of smoke was rising. Judging by the music and noise, there was a raucous party going on.

"I have never been so glad to hear a party!" I said, and we began to wind our way down to the source. Several dogs came out barking, followed by the partygoers holding beers. Thankfully they showed me where to go, along a gravel road. It was so bright that I missed my sunglasses. Usually I didn't like riding on roads, but after what we had just forced our way through, I said: "God, I will never complain about a road again! How did the early pioneers manage forging their way through this dense forest?"

I never did come across the big lake I was aiming for, which was marked on my map. On the edge of the Medicine Bow Forest I camped among the aspen trees at a much lower elevation. The following morning, finding I had a signal on my phone, I called Dale and Naomi Hitz, Dianne Fuchs' aunt.

"We'll be away, but make yourself at home," said Dale, and I scribbled his directions down and set off across the dry, stony rolling plains. I texted friends to let them know where I was, asking Greg to buy a longer lens for me, as I wanted to be able to photograph bears and other wild animals.

"God answers too many of your prayers 2 b asking for bears!" a text message came back from Greg, followed by another: "I'll take you 2 a zoo if you want to see bears!

16th August, I could hardly believe the contrast between the Medicine Bow Forest - from lush grass up over my knees in the boggy areas, to the dry and stony windswept plains just to the north. Pistol and Smoky are worried too with the lack of lush grass and stop to graze at every opportunity - which is often as I have to redo the pack. Got a long way to go today.

# HITCH HIKING

It is God who arms me with strength, and makes my way perfect.

Psalm 18v32 NKJ

I had 28 miles to cover to get to Hanna. But every time I trotted, the pack got dislodged, because of the extra roll on top, so the time I gained was lost by reloading the pack. I had four bags in the two pack panniers, plus the sleeping roll and tote bag on top. I was reloading again, when a young man pulled up alongside and asked me what I was doing. He introduced himself as Owen Williams, whose family owed the ranch.

"Retying the pack for the third time this morning," I sighed.

"Can I show you a double diamond knot?" Owen offered.

"Please do." I replied.

"I have used this knot to pack many goofy things and it seems to work," he said, as he wrapped the rope around the pack.

I was so grateful, for it really did work, and we trotted along and began to make up some time. A lady on a roan horse, with two dogs, gave me a friendly greeting, but I was so conscious of having to make over 20 miles before dark, so I waved back and kept trotting into the wind.

They were haymaking down in the valley as I made my way along the stony dirt road. Here we came across several cattle guards with drop gates that were so tight, it took all my strength to open and shut them. Then I found one that I just couldn't shut. I tried the pole on my shoulder, and then in the middle of my chest, but still couldn't get it closed. I was getting irritated when a pick-up, pulling a smart trailer, approached.

"Do you need help?" someone shouted in the wind. It was the lady I had passed earlier.

"Oh, yes, please," I shouted back. She introduced herself as Danette and with her extra shove, we got the loop over the post and the gate shut.

"Why are they so tight?" I sighed, thanking her.

"They have a sneaky tool! A ratchet to tighten the drop fences!" she replied.

"Does that hold three horses?" I asked, indicating her trailer.

"Do you want to load up?" Danette asked.

"You bet we do!" I replied.

"Where are you going?"

"Canada, but I'm trying to make Hanna tonight," I replied.

"Holy cow!" she exclaimed, as she opened up the back of her trailer and Pistol and Smoky eagerly stepped in, adding,

"You've got balls, I'd say!"

Danette took me back to Elk Mountain village in her comfortable, air-conditioned pick-up. There she gave me a large bottle of drink, which I downed in one. I had water with me, but I hadn't realised how dehydrated one could get in the constant wind. Danette reappeared with a bag full of trail mix bars.

"Is it always so windy?" I asked.

"Oh no, that's not wind. That's just a nice fresh Wyoming breeze!" she replied, adding: "When it's windy here you can't walk straight, but have to lean into it! In the winter the wind will blow you off your feet!" I learnt that Wyoming is often beneath the jet stream, or north of it, which accounts for its famous and frequent strong winds.

"This is the way to hitchhike, with your horses!" joked Tom, Danette's husband, who had just finished his train job for the day. As it was already mid-afternoon, he offered to take me on to Hanna, along with a bale of hay and some sweet feed.

"Right now, you'd be cooking across there!" Danette remarked, as they drove us across the prairie. "You're into snakeland now."

Once we arrived in Hanna, I checked the instructions I had scribbled on a piece of paper that morning, but couldn't relate them to our surroundings. As we stopped to ask at the general store, the passenger door flew open violently.

"There you are now, there's your wind!" exclaimed Danette. "Now, do you see the difference between the breeze and the wind?"

After driving along and investigating several dirt roads, we eventually found the Hitz's place, where Tom and Danette dropped us, with the horse food.

"Thanks so much!" I said. "I never would have found this place in the dark! And there was no grass or trees to secure the horses on the way. You guys are great to give us all a lift!"

The Hitz's door was open, and Naomi had left me a welcoming note explaining where to find food, and a map of how to get to the room where I was sleeping. The wind had unhinged the fly screen on the large window, so I wedged it back and then enjoyed the bliss of a real shower!

Danette and Tom Toth at Elk Mountain.

231

# LIFE IN HANNA

Rattlesnake in the sage brush.
Dale Hitz on Smoky.

The following morning, I met Lael and Axel, Dale and Naomi's sons, who had returned late in the night. They took me to lunch at Hanna's Wild Wonder Cafe.

"Pretty much the best sandwich place in the world," Axel told me, as I sunk my teeth into a tasty beef one and listened to the friendly proprietor, Kevin Asner, talking to Ken, a large elderly man in blue denim dungarees, about hunting snakes.

"A buck an inch for rattlesnake skins, used for belts and bags," he stated. "I don't take them under 30 inches. Last year I had me a 54 inch. The diamond back is much bigger – there was a 9 foot, 97 pound one last year. Prairie rattlers don't usually go a mile away from their dens, but one was tagged, and they found it went seven. And no, they don't taste like chicken, more like frog!" Kevin added: "I worked in government for 27 years. Then I walked away and started a business in Elk Mountain and said to myself: 'I'm going to run for governor in Wyoming. It only costs $200!' And I did!"

Kevin talked until we finished eating. "I love this business here, because you get to meet people. Think of all the great people, who have walked into this country with nothing. Wyoming could be an empire in the United States, because we have so much gas, coal, and natural resources. They say we have 200 years of coal."

Lael suggested we go to the museum, where we met a chatty lady, who knew the boys. She had lived all her life in Hanna and was proud to show us round. Hanna had been a major mining town, whose houses were all painted in 'the Rawlins Red'. The miners, who comprised many nationalities, rented these houses from the Union Pacific Rail and Coal Company. I read a moving extract written by a woman in her mid-80s, who told of her childhood in Hanna in 1908, which made my eyes fill with tears.

"I must tell you about the horses," she wrote. "They were kept down the mines all their lives, and people took hay down to feed them. Then they made a law that the horses should be taken to the surface every weekend, and they built a wire enclosure. Oh, what a sight to see! It's said their eyes shone like diamonds and their tails stood up in the air as they circled round the enclosure. When tired, they just stood like statues. I often wondered how they felt to go back down."

The next day, the Hitz family took me off in search of the Peruvian sheep herders, who get special three-year work permits. Their boss may have four or five different camps, with 1,000 to 1,500 sheep in each flock. We saw sheep, but no shepherds.

The Hitz family used to keep sheep themselves. "Once we went to church, and returned to find the sheep inside the house eating marshmallows!" said Naomi.

"That must have been so funny!" I chuckled.

"It wasn't funny," Naomi replied seriously, adding: "The sheep also liked to go to Hanna, because people watered their lawns."

"The Union Pacific train ran over 25 of the sheep on the tracks," stated Lael. "We would lose 50 per cent of our lambs to coyotes, bobcats and mountain lion. The mountain lions cut their heads off and the bobcats dragged the lambs away, even right behind the shed here." He pointed up the hill. "Even lambs weighing 100 pounds, ready for market. Then we got an Akbash dog, and then they only got a few."

"We would use black rams on white ewes because they grow faster and they have more meat," explained Naomi. "Black sheep always go through the fences, but white sheep don't. Once, we found our black ewe half submerged in ice, so we used an iron to warm her up. She was better behaved after that!"

# WILD HORSES IN THE GREAT DIVIDE BASIN

*To me, horses and freedom are synonymous. - Veryl Goodnight*

Greg appeared once more to help, with his truck and trailer, as he had agreed to accompany us cross the Great Divide Basin. This desolate expanse of 225 million acres, consisting of a desert of sage and alkali flats, has an average of six to eight inches of rain, which evaporates in the basin. This is BLM (Bureau of Land Management) land and home of pronghorn antelope, coyotes and wild horses.

Tom and Danette offered to help us find the wild horses. As I rode across the sagebrush desert, I was surprised to come across several small bands that were in such good condition, despite the dry environment. Transfixed, keeping at a safe distance, they watched us passing through their territory. Several times, they circled us with curiosity! Once, a few skipped across our path, kicking up dust, disappearing up over the steep-sided canyon. I thought they were gone for good, but they reappeared again, bringing a curious herd with them to see the foreign horses, carrying strange loads, passing through their territory. They looked magnificent in their freedom, strung out along the horizon. With their tails flowing in the wind, they stood alert, following us with their gaze down the canyon. Smoky and Pistol stared back at them, with their heads held high and ears pricked. I treasured these special encounters, although I did have to remind Smoky to look where he was going, as he was so intent on gazing at the wild horses in the opposite direction, he would trip up!

At night, when Greg brought food and water for my horses, in different locations across the basin, curious stallions would appear and linger, their heads held high and nostrils flaring, trying to decide who these domestic horses were. They sometimes exchanged neighs, and I wondered what they said to each other!

When the Spanish Conquistadors came to North America, they brought cattle and horses. Cortez, in his search for gold, brought cattle and 500 pack animals, along with 1,000 horses, which originated from the Spanish Barb, Arabian, Lipizzaner and other European breeds.

At the end of a 12-hour day, the evening light was so beautiful over the badlands that I set my camera on a tripod to take some self-timed photos. Soon afterwards, the sunlight disappeared and darkness blanketed the landscape. We headed for a distant location where I thought I had earlier seen the sun glinting off Greg's truck, but by the time we arrived, there was no one there. I was concerned that the horses had no water or food in the treeless desert, and was just beginning to look for a place to secure them overnight when, with relief, I saw a truck's headlights appear over the horizon!

Horses changed the culture of many Native American tribes, especially the Plains Indians, who became talented horsemen. They loved the freedom that horses gave them for hunting bison and fighting the white settlers. They were also a status symbol and chiefs took their favourite horses with them to the grave. They would capture the wild Mustangs, which mingled with the buffalo herds. Often, they chose the slower, in-foal mares to catch and break, but this was an energetic business, so they found it easier to steal already tamed horses from the Spanish haciendas on the frontier. Here, they faced little resistance and a continual supply, as the colonial government imported thousands from Spain owing to the constant demand from the settlers on the frontier.

The Nez Perce Indians in Idaho were the only tribe to breed horses successfully. Like most Indians, they preferred coloured horses, like the spotted patterns, which were commonly found in Spain. They also bred from those with the best confirmation, hardiness, speed and stamina. In the 1870s, the Nez Perce fled from the US Cavalry, with their horses and families, covering over 1,600 miles in 11 weeks. Eventually, the Cavalry caught up with them and took possession of 200 of their Appaloosa horses.

Wyoming is home to the nation's second-largest wild horse population, which is estimated at about 6,000. BLM, who manage the wild horse and burro herds in 10 western states, find this almost twice the appropriate management level. So every year they round up the horses and ship them to various places around the country on adoption programmes – the difficulty being that there are not enough homes for them all.

Sage bush stretched like a carpet, mile upon mile before us, as we crossed the Great Divide Basin, and I imagined what it could have been like to be a pioneer crossing the great expanse, for the main emigration route to Oregon and California passed just north of the basin. As we brushed through the aromatic sage bush, and I kept a careful eye out for rattlesnakes, an occasional jack rabbit would dart out and many pronghorn antelope seemed to materialise out of nowhere. At first, they were as surprised as we were and stood transfixed, before suddenly setting off in their jerky gallop, followed by a plume of dust. Amazingly, these antelope are among the world's fastest animals, with top speeds of up to 70mph! They are thought to be a true native of North America, as they are the only animal that cannot be traced back to Eurasia – all the others having crossed the land bridge that once joined Siberia and Alaska. At the beginning of the 19th century, they were almost hunted to extinction by the commercial hunter and settlers, until the hunting season was closed in Wyoming. Now, the State has approximately half a million pronghorns, more than any other State in North America, and these live off the abundant sage brush in the winter.

# SOUTH PASS

*There is no security in this world, only risk and opportunity...
take advantage of yours. - Douglas MacArthur*

The purchase of the massive Louisiana Territory by the United States, in 1803, opened up the Western Frontier to extensive exploration by the Euro-Americans. In 1804, Lewis and Clarke became the first white Americans to cross the western boundaries of the United States to reach the Pacific coast. They had followed the Missouri River, and crossed the Rockies in what is now Montana. However, this was a very difficult route, so others searched for alternative routes and discovered South Pass – which became known as the gateway through the Rocky Mountains.

For the next 20 years, trappers and traders trekked westwards from St Louis, followed by supply trains and expeditions travelling to the annual 'Rendezvous'. South Pass was the one place with water in the 2,000 miles of Rocky Mountains, where wagons could cross the Continental Divide without a difficult climb. Previous to the late 1830s, it was only used by Indians and fur trappers, when small groups crossed the frontier. They were called immigrants because the main trail began in Missouri, which was at that time the border of the United States.

By the 1840s, more immigrants were journeying west, heading for Oregon's fertile soil, fine timber and mild climate, to find gold in California, religious freedom and to escape the American Civil War. Even the the pony express used this route during its short life. Over several decades, 55,000 people migrated, traipsing thousands of miles over what became known as the Oregon and California Trail. They travelled in prairie schooners, stagecoaches, and even on foot, carrying their possessions in handcarts and wheelbarrows. It was a tough journey, which took five months, across semi-arid plains, deserts and mountains and by 1860, more than 20,000 people had died on the route.

# A YEAR LATER
## ... return to ride the High Line Trail

Many plans are in a man's mind
but it is the Lord's purpose for him that will stand.
Proverbs 19v21 Amp

Due to fixed, scheduled dates with the film crew in the Grand Teton and Yellowstone National Park, I'd had to miss out the Wind River Range in my ride from Mexico to Canada. As I had some unfinished business to attend to in the United States, I planned to return a year later to South Pass, to ride through these dramatic mountains with Smoky and Pistol.

Jen, who I had met the previous year in Santa Fe, dropped me and my horses off at South Pass for my five day trek. To get information on this route, I tried to find an elderly couple, who I met the previous year at the Atlantic City Mercantile – an amazing old pub, with huge stuffed animals gazing from the walls – but it was closed. In the bar next door a man suggested: "Go to see Steve Niles, he'll know, as he works for the Forestry Service. You'll find him last on the left, past the shop."

I found his house, and Steve helpfully pointed out the High Line Trail on the map.

"Take this," he said, giving me his map, which showed the whole range of mountains, and complemented my several detailed ones. "Take your lunch cos it's gonna take you a while!"

The following morning I set off across the plain, my hat anchored down around my chin as the wind battered us unceasingly, and eventually loosened the waterproof cover over the pack, which startled Pistol. Trying to find a way across a creek edged in deep willow, I spotted a moose. Fortunately the horses didn't even notice it, otherwise they would have been frightened and tried to take off! But within the few moments it took me to slip off Smoky and grab my camera, it disappeared into the willows.

It was so refreshing to be in the mountains with my horses once again and I was excited to be travelling the High Line. On the first night, I found a beautiful camp spot by a lake. The following morning, Smoky and Pistol gave me their usual wake-up call by stomping their hooves on the ground. I pulled on my gloves and woolly hat before leaving my tent.

"I don't want you guys spooking at any wild animals!" I told them as I tethered them out to graze. I then made a cup of tea, while keeping an eye on them. I was relaxed, savouring being back in the mountains, until Pistol got tangled in his rope. Last year he would have stood still, waiting for me to untangle him, but not this time. Suddenly he panicked, uprooted the tree he was tied to, and took off. He did a circuit of the open grassland, before disappearing, crashing off through the forest, dragging the tree on the end of the rope.

"Jesus, Jesus help!" I kept repeating, quickly grabbing Smoky, who was startled at Pistol's disappearance. I undid the tethering rope around his coronet and securely tied him to a tree. Then I rushed to my saddle and grabbed my 10-inch knife, quickly checking that Smoky was safely tied on a short lead, as he was screaming for Pistol.

I ran off in the direction that Pistol had disappeared, followed by Smoky's high-pitched neighing. I tracked his hoof marks in the dirt, over the rocks and rough terrain. Although I could still hear Smoky's frantic neighs, I was concerned that there was no sign or sound of Pistol. I was very anxious, praying and dismissing images of him lying somewhere with a broken leg, as I hurried through the trees scrambling over the boulders.

After what seemed like an age, I found him. He was frightened and shaking. The whites of his eyes were showing and blood was pouring from a deep wound in his near-hind fetlock. The tree that he was dragging on the end of the blood-stained tethering rope had stopped him, wedging between two other trees.

"God, don't let him have cut an artery!" I pleaded, as I stroked his neck, soothed him and then took a closer look. I winced, seeing that the cut was very deep and wide. As I untied his rope, I was aware, but puzzled that Smoky's frantic neighs had suddenly stopped.

Leading Pistol out of the trees, back to our camp spot, both Pistol and I were shocked to see Smoky on his back with his legs in the air, throttling himself with his halter, hanging from the tree. Pistol shied away and wouldn't go near him, so I quickly tied him to a nearby tree and ran to Smoky. I couldn't get to the lead rope so with the large knife, I cut his halter in several places, and he dropped to the ground, gasping for air. He then staggered to his feet. I was speechless and numb as I rubbed his head where the halter had cut into his face. One moment we had all been enjoying a tranquil morning and the next I had nearly lost both my horses.

Dexter Smith

I tied the horses side-by-side to give them some comfort, and gave Pistol some anti-inflammatory painkiller paste, and set about dressing his wound. I was grateful that both my horses were still alive, but very disappointed that with Pistol's deep wound, I wouldn't be able to continue my trek through the mountains. I packed up the tent and backtracked for several hours, down the dusty mountain trail, as it was urgent to get Pistol some antibiotics and his leg stitched.

At the trailhead, I met a couple, Dexter and Carole Smith, who were waiting for friends who were very late, to accompany into the mountains on horseback. There was no signal on our phones, so Dexter suggested he take me to a nearby lodge to phone a vet.

"That's why we like it up here because we have no communication!" muttered one of the four very laid-back men, who sauntered out of the lodge to see Pistol. The thinnest one, looking rather like a cartoon version of a cowboy, with bow legs, a cowboy hat, a red scarf wrapped round his neck and a cigarette hanging out from underneath his moustache, offered to look at Pistol's leg.

"That's bad! You won't be riding him again this season," he drawled, adding: "But it's a long way from his heart." I was concerned that he should have an antibiotic as soon as possible. The wrangler asked one of the others to get his veterinary kit. He said he was busy and another said he was cooking, but they both just hung around. The wrangler reappeared with a very extensive veterinary kit and Dexter knew what would be good to use on the wound. One of the men, whose eyes made me feel very uncomfortable, suggested that I stay there with my horses.

"That won't do much good. This horse needs a vet and stitches," Dexter replied. I felt relieved to be driving back down the drive when Dexter asked: "Did you ever see the movie Deliverance?"

"No!" I replied, shaking my head. After he told me a bit about it, and how the lodge reminded him of it, I added with a nervous laugh: "I never want to either! I thank God, He had you with me!"

On the way back to the trailhead, I asked Dexter to stop a car coming in the opposite direction.

"Are you going out?" I asked, jumping out of the pick-up and running over to his driver's window. "My horse has had an accident. Can you call a friend to ask her pick me up?"

"Sure!" he replied, "I'm Jim from North Carolina," and I scribbled Jen's number on a piece of paper. He confirmed: "I promise I will as soon as I get a signal."

Jen did pick us up. We got Pistol to a vet in Dubois. It was too late to stitch the wound, which was in an awkward place anyway. He did recover after several months. My charismatic Smoky was none the worse off, but I was very disappointed. I had made a big effort to return and had been much looking forward to riding the High Line Trail through the wind River Range as I had had to miss it out the previous year.

Later, on reflection, I realised I was clearly not meant to continue this section of the ride. The accidents to my horses were serious enough to stop even my own determination. I could only conclude that we could have been spared from something much more dangerous up ahead.

Green River Lakes

# THE RENDEZVOUS

Back in the early 16th century, it had become fashionable among the English upper class to wear beaver felt hats, for hatters discovered that beaver fur, with all its tiny barbs, created better felt than any other fur. European manufacturers could scarcely keep up with the demand and, by the late 1700s and early 1800s, the American fur trade began to grow in importance, led by the Hudson Bay Company, which had discovered the rich beaver resources of the Rocky Mountains and Upper Missouri River. In its heyday, 100,000 beaver skins were trapped each year for the production of hats, and increasing numbers of men headed west to profit from this booming industry.

The Rendezvous (French for 'meeting') began in 1825, when supplies were brought out from St. Louis to be exchanged with furs. The first gatherings lasted for a day, but as the trade grew, they stretched into weeks, attended by thousands of Indians and hundreds of trappers.

By the 1840s, the price of beaver fur had declined and the animal was becoming relatively rare. The South American nutria pelt replaced the beaver as a cheaper source of quality fur, the companies in the Rocky Mountains could not compete, and they abandoned the area.

Osprey

Hold fast to dreams, for if dreams die,
life is a broken winged bird that cannot fly.
- Langston Hughes

# A FISHY WELCOME

*17th August – hunting season is opening – there are a lot of hunters in the Wind River Range. Dropped down to Dubois to Mary Turney and Rick Liquice's place. Rick and Mary, great tour guides, are taking me and their relatives, Melissa and Eddie, around in their blue mini van, seeing Bighorn sheep, osprey, petroglyphs, a fish hatchery and their neighbour's beautifully restored shepherds caravans.*

"I have some friends in Wyoming, and they're the most hospitable people I have ever met!" Duncan, a connection in New Zealand told me.

"Make yourselves at home!" welcomed Rick, on the phone. "Use the washing machine – the door's open!"

There was a message on the door, and I opened it to be met by fishes galore! There were pictures of fish on light switches, toilet seats, lampshades, lights, glasses, cutlery … everywhere I looked there were beautiful fish, painted on the walls, floor and woven into mats. Anywhere it was possible to have an impression of a fish, there was one!

"That's why we came to live in Dubois and stayed for the past ten years – to go fishing!" Mary exclaimed. "But now we never keep them. We release them back into the river," she told me as we visited a fish hatchery, from which they release thousands of fish into the rivers each year.

Surrounded by badlands of beautiful variegated red, pink and pale rock, the Wind River runs through the attractive old town of Dubois, which was established over a century ago.

# WHISKEY MOUNTAIN

Ask in my name and you shall receive, that your joy may be full.  John 16v24 NKJ

We went in search of the Whiskey Mountain herd of Bighorn sheep, which we observed in three groups, coming down from the mountain through the sage, heading for the salt licks.

"We've never seen so many and we've been here so many times!" Mary exclaimed. "Tracey must have asked God!"

"I did ask!" I chuckled, delighted to be able to watch and photograph them, as they hung around for over an hour. Then we left to see several ornate petroglyphs of beetles and antelope, believed to have been engraved into the rocks by the Sheepeater Indians, who were part of the Shoshone tribe.

A storm was brewing, and on our way back to Dubois I had the opportunity to photograph osprey, although the wind was so strong that I had to brace myself, trying to hold my new long lens steady – which Greg had brought up from Texas for me.

The next stop was happy hour at the Rustic Pine Tavern. Entering the crowded room was like stepping back in time, with its long, old bar, lined with gnarled wood, and edged with cowboys and girls dressed in their boots and hats.

Animals which were once wild and now fixed on the walls, looked down upon us through their glass eyes, as Mary introduced me to several people: Jeff, a photographer, Lynn, a taxidermist, and Bill, one of Mary's former colleagues, who had worked in Denver for over several hundred thousand dollars a year.

"Now, I'm a cowboy on $10 an hour and much happier!" he remarked.

As usual, I was on a tight schedule, with the film crew arriving in the Grand Tetons in a few days, so Mary, having been to both the Teton and Yellowstone National Park many times, marked on a map where she thought the most scenic places were to be found. This would give us a head start, when it came to scouting out the filming locations.

# THE GRAND TETONS

The Tetons have loomed up grandly against the sky. From this point it is perhaps the
finest pictorial range in the United States or even North America –
Thomas Moran, while painting the Tetons in 1879

Great glaciers sculpted the Teton Range after the mountains rose and the valley dropped. Wind, rain, ice and glaciers then eroded and carved into the mountains, transforming them into the dramatic feature that they are today.

Glaciers are formed when more snow falls in winter than can melt in summer. The weight of the snow compacts into ice, and eventually begins to flow as a glacier. As it moves down, it collects debris from the mountains, and this gets deposited at the end where the glacier is melting. As the weather warms, the leading edge of the glacier recedes up the mountain, depositing material as it goes, which piles up and acts as a dam for the melting water. This can result in a chain of lakes, like those at the base of the Teton Range.

This is a small range, with seven mountains higher than 12,000 feet. The Shoshone Native Americans called it 'Teewinot', meaning pinnacles. In the 1800s explorers referred to the Teton as the 'Pilot Knobs', using them to guide their expeditions, since they are visible for 150 miles in every direction on a clear day. The French Canadian fur trappers, on the other hand, approaching from the west, named the tallest peaks 'Les Trois Tetons', or the three breasts.

# GREAT TIMING!

While Greg and I went to organise the film locations and permits, we left the horses with Larry and Sandra Rodeck on the outskirts of Jackson, who kindly fed them for several days, since horses weren't allowed in the Park overnight. I had been given the Rodeck's number through another chain of contacts: Diane Galbraith in Jackson, recommended by Diane, from the Navajo Mission in New Mexico. Larry also put us in touch with his vet Ernie Patterson, who gave me the necessary health papers for my horses to cross over into Montana and then into Canada.

"You can go most places," said Terry Roper, at the Grand Teton headquarters, much to my relief, "except on the road, as it is so busy." She marked places on my map that she thought were most suitable, most of which Mary had suggested earlier, so we went to scout them out. The Yellowstone National Park public affairs assistant and film monitor, Karen McEneaney, was equally helpful, and worked with us to plan a route for filming, for we only had one day to capture the essence of this huge national Park.

"I only received the film application on Friday. We usually require two weeks' notice, because you need a monitor and a guide, and I'm usually booked months in advance."

"How about this Friday?" I asked, almost holding my breath, knowing that the film crew couldn't change their dates, and Yellowstone was a very important part of the West, being the world's first national park.

"Well… it just happens I'm free this Friday!" she said with a smile.

But as for me, I trust in You, O Lord; I say, you are my God." My times are in your hand.
Psalm 31v14 NKJ

Moose have an intriguing make-up! The reclusive males have a huge rack of antlers weighing up to 80 pounds and, although they appear nonchalant, they can be dangerous. Their long legs are well suited for foraging in the willows beside the rivers and lakes, which are often deep in snow. They can hold their breath for a minute, so they dive deeply and scavenge underwater!

# THE SHOSHONE

The Shoshone Indians, were a peaceful tribe who lived in Yellowstone year round. There were several tribes: the Agaiduka (salmon eaters) and Kukunduka (buffalo eaters) and the Tukudauka (sheep eaters), who followed the Bighorn sheep migration. This sheep was a major part of the Tukudauka diet, and they made the carcasses into a wide array of tools and implements, including bows of sheep horn, made pliable from soaking in hot springs and boiling water. They traded these bows, plus clothing hides, to other tribes, who travelled through following the buffalo. Another prized material, which they used for trade and tools, was obsidian – a glassy, black mineral, deposited by volcanic activity, which they flaked into sharp arrow heads. Sheepeaters never acquired horses, unlike other tribes, as they used dogs to transport goods. Early explorers reported to have seen 30 dogs carrying skins, clothing and provisions for a dozen adults and children.

YELLOWSTONE NATIONAL PARK: Swimming the Yellowstone River!

# MAMMOTH HOT SPRINGS

By faith we understand that the universe was formed at God's command,
so that what is seen was not made out of what is visible.

Hebrews 11v3 NIV

For hundreds of years, Shoshone and Bannock people collected minerals from Mammoth Hot Springs to create white paint. These minerals, combined with heat, water and the limestone, have all contributed to the beautiful terrace structures,

Yellowstone National Park was once the site of an enormous volcanic eruption, which partially emptied a magma chamber and formed a giant caldera that covered an area of 30 by 40 miles. The molten rock in this chamber continues to provide heat for Yellowstone's hydrothermal features, including Mammoth – more than 20 miles north of the caldera. The water, which steams out of the ground, originates from rain and snow falling in the surrounding area, and seeping deep into the earth. Here, it is heated, and a network of fractures and fissures form a natural plumbing system that allows the hot, underground water to reach the surface.

Themophiles (heat-loving micro-organisms), algae, bacteria, and archaea create tapestries of colour where hot water flows among the Mammoth terraces. Billions of these micro-organisms live, die and are buried. Both colourless and yellow thermophiles grow in the hottest water and, elsewhere, orange, brown and green. The colours change with the seasons.

Heated deep underground, the water rises through the limestone and then deposits mineral calcite above ground. This calcite hardens, becoming travertine, and as the hot spring water continues to flow, vegetation, trees and thermophiles are engulfed. Rising waters at Terrace Mountain deposit over two tons of travertine here each day.

God made the wild animals according to their kind, the livestock according to their kind,
and all the creatures that move along the ground according to their kind. And God saw that it was good. Genesis 1v25 NIV

# A MULTITUDE OF ANIMALS

How many are your works, O Lord!
In wisdom you made them all; the earth is full of your creatures...
with creatures beyond number – living things both large and small.
Psalm 104v24-25 NIV

More wildlife is concentrated in Yellowstone National Park than anywhere else in the Lower 48 states (Alaska and Hawaii making up the 50 states of the USA). Most of these animals also inhabit the Grand Teton area and spill out from the safety of the National Park, into the surrounding states of Wyoming, Montana, Idaho.

The scientific name for the American buffalo is 'bison bison' – a mammal that resembles the Asian and African water buffalo. They once grazed the West in their millions, but were hunted almost to extinction by the turn of the 20th century. Today, they are again plentiful in Yellowstone.

"It's down to Tracey's faith that they are here!" said Karen, watching them carefully, along with Smoky and Pistol, as Trip filmed hundreds of them grazing in the valley. "They are still my favourite!" Karen remarked adding, "but you have to keep a careful eye on them as they look quiet, but can charge you. They gore people every year." Within a short time in the Park, we photographed many different animals.

"Now you can cross that off your list," Greg remarked, as I photographed a grizzly bear, recognisable by the hump on its shoulder, half a mile away on the hillside.

"It's too far away – the lens you brought up isn't that powerful!" I chuckled, squinting into my viewfinder to locate it, as it moved across the scree slope on the opposite side of the mountain.

The grizzly bear once roamed much of the North American continent, as far east as the Mississippi river, and south to Mexico, but was hunted out by the settlers. It was put on the Endangered Species List in 1973, but now that the numbers are well up, it has been removed from the list.

Unlike the deer, elk and moose, whose antlers are shed annually, Bighorn sheep have true horns, which continue to grow throughout their lives. Rams have thick horns that curl back and around, while ewes have thinner ones that curve slightly upwards.

Wolves were hunted to extinction under an old policy designed to remove all predators, so that the species they preyed upon, especially the deer and elk, would grow. Until the 1960s, an average of 1,000 elk were shot each year, resulting in a public outcry, so 14 wolves were brought in from Canada in 1995, and reintroduced to Yellowstone. Now it is estimated that 1,500 wolves inhabit Wyoming, Montana and Idaho, and the elk numbers have also dramatically decreased. Recently, the wolves have been removed from the endangered list and can be hunted outside Yellowstone National Park.

The red fox is the shyest of the canine family and most active at night. They have very large ears for their head size, which enables them to hear and catch mice under the snow. The reintroduction of wolves in Yellowstone caused a decrease in the number of coyotes, but an increase in the fox population, because they compete for the same food source.

Above and below: The Lower Geyser Basin. Opposite: Old Faithful.

# OLD FAITHFUL

*... a thousand Yellowstone wonders are calling.*
*Look up and down and round about you!*
*– John Muir*

A huge volcanic eruption, many years ago, spread debris for thousands of miles. The magmatic heat behind those eruptions still powers the Park's geysers, hot springs, fumaroles and mud pots.

Hydrothermal activity results when the surface water seeps down to meet the heat of the earth's molten rock, which can be three to eight miles below the surface in Yellowstone. It has the largest and most varied collection of hydrothermal features on Earth.

This hydrothermal efftect has altered and weakened the lava, making the rocks softer and leading to erosion. Cracks in the lava created the river channel and the 308 foot (93 metre) Lower Falls on the Yellowstone River. Later, glaciers contributed to the canyon's development, and melt waters from the end of the last glacial period carved the current V-shaped canyon.

Karen got us to Old Faithful just before its appointed time of eruption, for true to its name, it gives an amazing display, always on schedule. The first surveyors named it Old Faithful, for even then, as now, it erupts more frequently than any of the other big geysers. Its average interval between eruptions is about 92 minutes, and with each eruption it expels 3,700 to 8,400 gallons of boiling water, to a height of 106 to 184 ft (30 to 55 metres).

It was the first trappers' wild and wonderful tales of this area that sparked several major expeditions. One of these was the Hayden Survey, which included the photographer William Henry Jackson and artist Thomas Moran, whose photos and paintings documented the amazing features of this area. Seeing that it had no economic purpose, such as timber, agriculture or mining, Congress was persuaded to set aside 2.1 million acres and establish Yellowstone as the world's first National Park in 1872.

But although granted this special status, in the early years, wildlife was still poached, trees felled and thermal features vandalised. The Cavalry came to the rescue, and protected the park for 32 years, until the National Park Service was created.

Go confidently in the direction of your dreams!
Live the life you've imagined.
- Henry David Thoreau

# MI TSE A-DA-ZI - YELLOWSTONE

Yellowstone is at the core of what is known as the Greater Yellowstone Ecosystem, which covers 18 million acres, and is made up of Yellowstone, the Grand Teton National Parks, seven national forests, three national wildlife refuges and many private lands. It got its name when French Canadian fur traders asked the Indians in eastern Montana about the river which flows into the Missouri, whose source lies in the area of thermal activity. They called it Mi tse a-da-zi, which means 'yellow rock' or 'Yellowstone.'

When I visited, there was evidence of burning all over the Park, from the big fire of the summer of 1988 when 36 per cent of it was burnt. There had been a wet spring, but then virtually no rain fell through the summer. The Park's policy was to fight all human-caused fires, but to allow natural fires, usually started by lightning, recognising the important role they play in a healthy forest ecosystem. Fires sweep away the debris and open up the forest to the fresh growth of grasses, shrubs and wild flowers. The lodge pole pine, which can grow up to 75 feet (used by some Native Americans to make frames for their tepees or lodges) is the most common tree in the park, but needs the intense heat of fire to open its cones and release the seeds, and so sustain the dense green forests.

The fires, which broke out 20 years earlier, had started in June and were allowed to burn, as it was thought they would be put out by rain or would stop when they reached a river or lake. However, they raged out of control and 20,000 personnel (including the military) and convoys of fire engines, helicopters and planes, arrived from all over the country and became involved in the largest firefighting effort in the history of the nation. They succeeded only in protecting the buildings in the park, and the fires burnt until a quarter inch of snow fell in September.

On our travels through Yellowstone, we passed by the largest mountain lake in North America: Yellowstone Lake. It is inhabited by native trout and occupies the south eastern quarter of the large caldera. At several spots on its shore, steam rises from a fault line. All the signs indicate that the Yellowstone caldera is not dormant and could erupt once again.

Above: Bob Garner, Greg Scott and Trip Uhalt looking at footage beside Yellowstone Lake.
Opposite: The Yellowstone Lower Falls

24th August. Exhausted, I relaxed at this great camp spot which Karen had told us about, just outside Gardiner, with corrals for the horses! We've had a two-day film shoot, with 4am starts for Greg and I, since we had to keep the horses outside the parks and drive an hour to get to the locations. Also I wanted to make the most of the crews' time. We've accomplished more on this film shoot than any other, thanks to Karen and Greg who helped us cover many locations.

Bob gave me an estimate to edit the film of my journey which far exceeded what I had expected for a three minute film sampler! The film industry certainly is another world! Anyway, after paying for the film footage I don't have that money to spend on editing. Thank you God, You have 'a plan'!

Trust in the Lord with all your heart, do not depend on your own understanding,
Seek his will in all you do, and he will direct your paths. Proverbs 3v5&6

# MONTANA

Montana comes from Spanish and Latin, meaning 'mountain'. It is also known as 'Treasure State', 'Land of Shining Mountains' and 'Big Sky Country'. Although Montana is the fourth largest in the United States, it has the third lowest population density. To the west are the spectacular Northern Rocky Mountains – a great attraction to visitors, and also the home of the lumber industry. To the east, the Northern Great Plains stretch over half of the State, and provide ranching, wheat, oil and coal.

# ENGLISH BREAKFAST TEA ...

"There have been a lot of lightning strikes, and 13 fires in the area," the ranger informed me, explaining why the south of the Bob Marshall Wilderness was closed. He pointed to a map at the Lincoln station: "There were 47 fires burning in Montana at the end of July."

He gave me another phone number so that I could contact rangers, and find out which areas on my route had been closed by fires.

As I rode west, following a dirt road and skirting the danger areas, I found a camp spot, hidden from the road in the trees. I was startled by voices and saw three people appearing from out of the forest. They were just as surprised to find me and my horses, and introduced themselves as Bill and Shirley Morrison, and their grandson, John.

"We can tell you don't come from around here!" said Shirley.

"Be careful of the bears. They have been driven out by the fires," warned Bill. "We were very worried a few weeks ago, when this whole area was closed off due to fires – our cabin is just up the back here. We've had it for 40 years." He added: "Come up for a cup of tea in the morning!"

I would choose camp spots with available grass, hidden from roads, with trees to picket the horses and a stout branch where I could hoist my food bag, out of reach of the bears. They are opportunists with very sensitive noses, who can smell food, toiletry products, even when a woman is having her monthly period. Once they have found easy food, they lose their fear and people can be seriously injured or killed, so they have to be hunted and destroyed. I repeatedly saw signs saying 'a fed bear is a dead bear'.

The following morning was cool, with a light frost on my tent, so I moved it into the sunlight to dry it off, before I rolled it up and started packing.

Bill reappeared. "Are you coming for cup of tea?" he asked. "We just happen to have some English breakfast tea!"

"Thank you, I'll just finish packing and be right there," I replied, tying down the pack. I then led the horses along the track, over the wooden bridge and up a rise to a half-collapsed cabin, which was in the process of being restored. Inside, it was well established with a real stove, and I sat at the kitchen table while Shirley made a cup of tea. I had left the horses loose, to graze in the long grass. But suddenly their heads went up, and before I could get to them, they were charging off down the track. Pistol was still attached to Smoky and only snapped the pigging string when they reached the car, and he had to swerve to avoid it. I hadn't yet tightened all the straps and girths – I usually did that just before I mounted – and the bedroll was the first to fall off as they crossed the bridge. I was running after them, but by the time I reached the gravel road, a quarter of a mile down the hill, they were nowhere to be seen. I guessed they would go back the way I had come the previous day, and kept running until I reached a fork in the road, where some trucks with trailers had stopped.

"Seen some horses?" I gasped.

"It looks like you're OK!" said a cowboy outfitter. "When I saw your horses passing by, I said: "That ain't good. That's bad. I'm going to see who's balled up (in a heap) in the road"."

"I'm Greg Gilchrist , jump in, we'll catch 'em," he said as I climbed into the passenger seat. "Do you want to hear the good news or the bad news first?" he asked, as he drove along the gravel road.

Of all the liars in the world, sometimes
the worst are your own fears.
- Rudyard Kipling

# ...AND PORRIDGE!

"Just the good," I replied.

"The saddle was still on him!" said Greg, and I braced myself for the bad. "The bad news is it was underneath him!"

Immediately, I thought of my camera, which I carried looped under a stirrup leather and over the front of my saddle. My heart sank to think of it dragging along the gravel road.

"A tack yard sale – we're having a tack yard sale!" exclaimed Greg, as we collected my scattered belongings, spread at intervals along the road: a saddle blanket, then my water bottle, then more contents from my bags, then the saddle bags, then another blanket, my tent and tripod. I strained to see further up the road, dreading to see my shattered camera next.

"There's the lash rope," said Greg, "and the horses!" As we caught up with them, I jumped out and called for Smoky. Breathing hard and sweating, he stopped and turned around. Pistol kept going until he realised Smoky wasn't following him.

"What you need is a good mule pack!" commented a tall, blonde lady.

"How do you do such a trip on your own?" another asked, as I noticed with relief that the camera was still in one piece. The saddle had slipped, but miraculously the camera hadn't fallen underneath him.

"By faith with God!" I replied, feeling tremendously relieved that it was still intact.

"Oh you do have a good Aussie saddle!" said Greg, as he helped to reassemble both horses with all my gear, and showed me how to tie a quick release on the pigging string. "I see you don't need an outfitter!"

"You sure were a Godsend today, thanks so much!" I shook their hands, and they went one way, while I backtracked several miles to finish my cup of English breakfast tea with Bill, Shirley and John. I met them coming to look for me in their car, and John greeted me with a large tub of Quaker Porridge Oats: "We brought these to catch them. We know horses like oats!"

I smiled, for I'd never tried porridge oats with horses before, and thanked him. He walked back with me to the cabin, where I tied the horses securely to a tree. Shirley made me a fresh cup of tea and offered me a welcome chicken and ham sandwich and some cantaloupe melon.

"We'd like you to have this," said John, appearing with bear pepper spray, as I was making sure my girths were tight before leaving.

Bill showed me how it worked. "There's a lot of bears around because of the fires, and we are concerned for you," he told me. "Just make sure the wind is in the right direction before you use it."

It was hot and dry on the gravel road as we rode west. We were passed by several fire or forestry vehicles, who covered us in more layers of dust.

*29th August: What a start to the day! I was relaxing and drinking English breakfast tea, when the horses got spooked by something in the forest and took off again! After a long gallop, Smoky wondered why he was expending all that energy and stopped when I called him (dear Pistol was usually the leader, although they egged each other on). I had only seen one or two vehicles along this road yesterday, but when I needed help Greg and his outfit arrived – just on cue! Thanks God – your timing is perfect!*

You will keep in perfect peace all who trust in you,
whose thoughts are fixed on you!
Isaiah 26v3NLT

Fire fighters from New Mexico

Life shrinks or expands
in proportion to one's courage.
– Anaïs Nin

Kyndee on Smoky, Dee on Pistol and Ken and I on his Harley Davidson.

"We're from Silver City, New Mexico, and we're up here because of the fires," said some fire fighters. "The fire season down south ends once the monsoons start in July and August, so we're called up here to fight fires."

"There's a bear hanging around at Seeley. They like horse meat," one of them commented and once again I chose to overcome an opportunity to fear.

As I continued to Seeley Lake, the atmosphere became smoky and helicopters flew overhead, dangling large water buckets on long ropes. I rode into town, thinking I would get a phone signal, but there was none. A shop proprietor let me use her phone to call a local ranch contact, but there was no reply. I was just leaving town when a man offered me a drink, which I gratefully accepted.

"It's getting cold again in the mornings! You need to cuddle up to someone to keep warm here in Montana, unless you have a warm sleeping bag."

"Oh, I have a very warm sleeping bag!" I assured him.

As I headed out of town to find a place in the forest to camp, I passed a plumbing shop with a banner hanging outside saying: 'Thank You & God Bless'.

A lady with long dark hair greeted me: "It's a hoot, the tourists will think it's a real Western town with you and your horses!"

"What's the sign for?" I asked.

"For the fire fighters. A few weeks ago, Seeley Lake was the number one fire in the US!" she exclaimed, and I noticed the words 'Women of Faith' across her T-shirt as we chatted.

"You are welcome to stay the night here and put your horses in the back," said Dee, my new found friend. "We have an appointment now, but I can show you where you can sleep."

"Well, thanks very much!" I was touched at God's care once again, and followed her through a large, air-conditioned plumbing showroom, of pristine baths, sinks and taps, contrasting with attractive old bits of harness on the wall. At the end, there was a bathroom, a shower and a fold-away bed.

"Help yourself to whatever's in the fridge, and use the internet," she said, pointing to a computer. I found a message from Sandy, my business assistant in England, reminding me my flight from Denver to London was the following week! I had booked the flight the previous year and living another life altogether, I had forgotten the date. I was just in time to postpone it, thanks to Dee inviting me to stay!

The following morning, the horses had eaten every blade of grass, so I tethered them on the verge of the busy road, attaching them securely to a fence and moving them often so they could eat as much as possible.

"Would you like to put your horses in my paddock?" asked Dan, who ran the motel across the road.

"Overnight would be great!" I thanked him, and he told me about the recent fires.

"The motel was full of fire fighters for weeks. A couple of 'belly dumpers' came in from Canada – they flew into the lake to scoop up 1,500 gallons of water a minute. We're into the hundreds of millions of dollars for the cost of fighting fires in Montana," he said. "Most of Seeley was evacuated. The fire was coming in so fast and they said if the wind didn't change, it was going to burn Seeley down. It had national priority. We had an Alaskan hot shot team, a top-notch fire fighter team from Alaska, smoke jumpers, plus five helicopters, and the two belly dumpers. The fire was starting other fires by blowing embers over a mile ahead of itself."

"Well, I'm thankful I wasn't riding this way a few weeks ago!"

I led Kyndee (Dee and Ken's daughter), riding on Smoky, through the town to Dan's paddock.

"When these fires were going through, it was indescribable how thick the smoke became!" said Ken, as he picked me and Kyndee up and took us to a neighbour's to buy some hay.

"This is Montana and we don't sell bales of hay," said Laren Rose, refusing any payment. As we fed the horses Ken remarked: "It's been an unusual 105 degrees this summer. We have extremes here. Every few years it reaches 20 to 30 and sometimes 50 below. Most of the water lines are buried six foot deep and don't freeze up, but in the houses, it's a different story. So we have to get out and fix them and put more insulation in the walls and roofs."

The following morning, as I was leaving, Ken offered me a ride on his Harley Davidson motorbike and I jumped at the opportunity.

"Built for pulling stumps!" Ken remarked as we glided smoothly down the road on his 100 horsepower motorbike. Later, I rode out of town on my two horsepower and the speed was very different! Along the verge of Route 83, the horses shied at the carcasses of deer, knocked down by the traffic, and I had to be careful while trotting to avoid the horses stepping on the glass bottles, chucked out by passing vehicles and hidden in the grass. On my ride north, if I had an offer of a trailer ride along these fast roads I gratefully accepted.

That night, camping in the forest, I woke up in a panic, thinking the forest was on fire. I scrambled out, realising I had just reacted to a flash of lightning, which had lit up the trees around us. Smoky and Pistol were quietly resting. I'd heard so much about fires, that it was obviously on my mind! I calmed down and wriggled back into my sleeping bag, listening to the storm pass over.

# INTO THE WILDERNESS

"I thought you must be an Australian to do something crazy like this!" said a man, standing on the doorstep of the ranger station, after I told him where I was heading he showed me a route via Holland Lake into the Bob Marshall Wilderness. "Give me a call if you need my help. I have a trailer," he added, giving me his number.

I checked with the rangers that this route had not been closed by fires and was suitable for horses. I felt excited that I would be able to get off the road, after all, and ride through some of the wilderness. There was no phone signal, so I stopped at a lodge on the edge of the forest. A wedding was just about to begin, but I quickly used the phone at the bar to call Greg in Texas, to let him know of my altered route and to tell him I would contact him again in three or four days, when I expected to be out of the wilderness. I returned to my horses to find a man looking at them.

"You sure know how to pack!" he said and shook my hand. I felt very chuffed and told him a friend had taught me, remembering what a shambles my packing had been when I first started my journey, over five months ago in Texas.

The ride from the lodge, up the mountain, was very steep, with spectacular views over Lake Holland to the mountains in the west. But we didn't stop long – I was very apprehensive that if Smoky and Pistol got spooked by a wild animal, they could fall thousands of feet off the sheer edge.

The Bob Marshall, Scapegoat and Great Bear is the second largest wilderness in the lower 48 states, and borders Glacier National Park to the north. At the beginning of the 20th century, the elk herds had been decimated by hunters, supplying miners and settlers with meat. Then, in the 1930s, Bob Marshall, a pioneer forester and conservationist, helped the US Forest Service to realise the importance of conserving a 5.5 million acre portion of the vanishing wild lands. The Scapegoat and the Great Bear sections were added at a later date, and today it forms a continuous corridor of unspoiled mountainous forests – the home of grizzly bears, mountain lions and goats, wolverines, elk, moose deer and wolves.

I was leading the horses on foot when Pistol got spooked, snorted loudly and they both nearly ran me over. Then they stopped as suddenly as they had started.

"Thank you God for your angels!" I sighed, letting out a deep breath in relief, knowing that in this rocky terrain, they had probably picked up the scent of a bear or mountain lion. I liked to walk a lot during the day, especially on steep terrain, but I did think that maybe it was better to be on board Smoky, so that if the horses got spooked and bolted, and I stayed on, I would stand a better chance of not losing them.

For He will give His angels especial charge over you to accompany and defend
and preserve you in all your ways of obedience and service.
Psalm 91v11 Amp

Holland Lake.

266

Today is the 1st of September. I am noticing the reds and yellows in the scrub, and a few aspens with their branch tips tinged in gold. Smoky and Pistol were a bit surprised when we met an outfitter with a string of mules. I found this idyllic camp stop at dusk, on an isthmus surrounded on three sides by the lake. While unpacking, I found I had lost my tripod – must have slipped out while trotting on the road. Quickly put up the tent while the horses grazed. Thinking bears probably liked steak, I ate the last bit that Dee had packed for me and then hauled the provisions bag up a tree overhanging the water – hope it doesn't fall in the lake! Loved listening to the coyotes howling as I lay in my tent.

Pistol's loud snort made me instantly wide awake, every fibre on the alert ...he'd only snort if he had heard or caught the scent of a wild animal. I listened, ready to take action and protect the horses from any bears or mountain lions approaching the horses.

I will not be afraid, for you are close beside me, guarding and guiding me all the way.
Psalm 23v4 TLB

The following morning, I noticed that the sun was rising much later. I pegged the horses out to graze, and then sat on a stone with my cup of tea, watching the pink sunlight slip down the mountain, illuminate the trees and cross the water, where it warmed me and dried out the tent from the previous night's thunderstorm. Occasionally, the horses' heads would jerk up, eyes and ears alert, as we heard some rocks tumble underneath a wild animal's feet.

It was exhilarating being out in the unspoilt wilderness with my horses, and so relaxing. I took a big breath, and enjoyed the freedom from the usual constraints. I loved the solitude, peace, beauty and the thrill of being alone with my horses and God. Sitting on my stone, I saw a tiny plane flying far above us, leaving a white trail across the clear blue sky. It seemed so out of place.

Autumn had suddenly arrived, turning carpets of green into pretty yellows and reds. We didn't meet anyone that day, as we followed a twisting, well-maintained track, and then started to descend into denser trees past a rotund, almost tame ptarmigan, with bright red eyebrows, sitting on a branch, and a pine marten, a member of the weasel family, on another. I stopped Smoky and, eye-to-eye, we stared at each other for several minutes, before I reached quietly for my camera, and he was gone – obviously camera shy, I thought. I saw a lot of bear dung on the trail, and kept thinking black tree stumps might be bears! To avoid a confrontation, it's best to make a noise, but I could only sing or talk out loud to God and my horses for so long, so I eventually lapsed into silence, letting the horses' hooves act as a warning to bears – ringing loudly on the rocks, but quieter on the dirt. We reached Big Salmon Lake safely, to be greeted by a family of chatty coots, busily dipping and diving.

In solitude we give passionate attention to our lives, to our memories, to the details around us. - Virginia Woolf

Solitude is as needful to the imagination as society is wholesome for the character.
- James Russell Lowell

3rd Sept: Smoky and Pistol woke me up by pawing the pebbles. There's mist rising off the lake. The horses are frantically grazing the bright green grass between the pebbles, knowing they have to fill up in the few hours before we leave. Outfitters have been here all summer, with expeditions, leaving bare patches of earth. The horses only raise their heads when they hear the coyotes and wolves howl, or sense something nearby. I can see Smoky's nostrils dilate, as he smells the air intently.

I met Fred and Bob on their mules. They were working on the walkways with crossbuck saws, because no machinery is permitted in the wilderness. They recommended travelling on the eastern side. I nearly visited an outfitters camp until I heard a loud growl, which sounded as though a bear was there, so decided to avoid it and ended up facing the wrong way, after crossing several rivers. Suddenly the sun was in front of me, when it was meant to be behind me, and I realised that instead of being on the eastern side of the river going north, I was on the west going south! I apologised to Smoky and Pistol for taking them on a detour in the midday heat.

Big Salmon Lake

# SMOKEY HAZE

The atmosphere was thick with smoke haze from the many fires in the wilderness. We found some grazing at midday and then continued along the east bank of a river, through beautiful terrain, before heading back into dense forest, which made me feel almost claustrophobic. There was no grass, so I kept going through the dusk, desperate to find some for the horses. I kept them trotting until we arrived at the pack bridge.

The clearing on the wilderness side of the bridge looked barren, and appeared to be a regular camp spot for the outfitters, so I crossed over the deep ravine to investigate the other side, where at last I found some grass. There was one big drawback: it was near a cliff, beside a deep gorge. However, it was almost dark and we had to stop, so I pegged the tent out between the horses and the cliff. I moved Smoky on his tethering line several times so he could eat as much grass as possible.

In the dimness, something spooked them and Smoky broke his tethering rope. They both charged towards me, my tent, the cliff and the ravine.

"Steady boys, " I said calmly, and raised my arms, very conscious of the gorge behind me. My heart was pounding as they reached me, and came to a halt. I tied them side-by-side that night, but they were restless, and this made it impossible for me to relax, so I regularly checked them with my torch. A chipmunk insisted on rummaging through my saddlebags – I shooed him away, but he wasn't frightened, and made a meal out of the leather strap holding the water bottle.

5th September: Smokey atmosphere from fires. The horses are in 'go slow' mode. I'm not sure which is more energy sapping: riding Smoky and trying to get him to walk faster, or leading him, or rather dragging him, with his neck outstretched, looking at me in such a way as to say: "We haven't had enough food recently!"

"That's true and I'm sorry – I promise I will make it up to you! Can you just walk a bit faster so we can cover some distance today?"

The following morning the air was again acrid with smoke. I followed a narrow path, winding through dense forest, and hoped the fire wouldn't blow in our direction, for it was so thick that there wasn't a quick escape.

We came upon a clearing and a small creek, so I tied Smoky loosely to a branch and went to pump and purify some drinking water. As I was crouched down by the water, a black bear skipped nimbly over the creek, just upstream. I was excited to see a bear, but I knew that if Smoky and Pistol saw it, they would be off in a flash, taking the branch they were tied to with them. So I dropped the water purifier, sprinted back and grabbed the lead rope. Smoky looked at me in surprise, glanced upstream and then looked back at me.

"Did I miss something?" he asked. The bear's scent must have been blowing in the other direction, otherwise I would have been running after them yet again! Firmly grasping Smoky's reins, I led them back to collect the water purifier and we continued on our way across the creek.

Despite their names, black bears can be brown, blond, black or cinnamon, and can even have white markings on their neck. They have a straighter facial profile than the grizzly, with its more 'dished' face, and adults can weigh 100 to 300 pounds. Black bears usually have one to three cubs during the winter, in their dens, and these cubs stay with their mother for two summers. Grizzly bears vary from blond to black, with tipped (grizzled) fur on head and upper body, and can weigh from 500 to 900 pounds. They have a large hump of muscle above their shoulders, which are good for digging as are their two to four inch claws, which are usually visible in their tracks.

# HUNGRY HORSE(S)!

At the Spotted Bear ranger station I inquired if there was a way through the wilderness to Kalispell. They called another station to find out.

"The only route to Kalispell is a 55-mile road trip to Hungry Horse."

While at the ranger station, I noticed there was a swan-shooting season. They seemed to have seasons for shooting everything, so I put the red neck scarf on Pistol, whose colouring was too much like an elk or deer.

We set off on our 55-mile journey on hot and dusty gravel roads. That evening I found a grassy camp spot beside the river, hidden from the road, where it was warm enough to have my first shower for six days and wash some clothes. It was almost dark by the time I had finished the chores, hauled my bag up a tree, and secured the horses.

In the morning, I found that a squirrel had eaten a hole in my bag, which was up the tree! But I assured myself that a bear would have done far more damage.

We were all tired as we walked along the gravel road, passed by occasional vehicles, covering us in dust. The horses hadn't eaten hard grain for over a week and they were very lethargic. Smoky walked in slow motion, so I would remount and do some trotting just to cover some distance. We all needed a rest and good feed. I used to have an iPod to listen to music, to boost me at times such as this, but I had lost it along with my GPS and other things.

"God, we're so tired. I know you have done it before. Can you have someone give us a lift along this long dusty road?"

*If you abide in Me, and My words abide in you, you will ask what you desire, and it shall be done for you.*
*John 15v7 NKJ*

*Morning of 6th September: the trees are tinged with autumn. All tired, but have a great grassy spot beside the river. Thank God we've had so many lovely camp spots! Washed some underwear and changed a really dirty shirt to one not so dirty! It made me smile as I remember several people being so concerned how I was going to wash!*

"Where are you from?" asked a man in a cowboy hat, leaning out of a grey pick-up.

"Mexico!" I replied.

"You don't look like you're from Mexico to me!" he laughed deeply. "Do you want a cold beer?" He stopped his truck in the middle of the road, introducing himself as Ron and his attractive blonde companion as Kandy.

"I see you're packing metal?" he pointed to my saddle torch, clearly thinking it was a gun.

"Oh no, I'm riding by faith in God and his angels' protection."

"Hell, I don't even go to K-mart without packing a gun, and you've come from Mexico without one!" he roared with laugher again. "We were just talking about all the horse shit on the road, came round the corner, and I said, "here's our shitter"! It's great to see a rear end of a packhorse, although you know mules are better! By the shit on the road they have been eating enough!"

"Actually they are hungry horses!" I replied adding, "and I keep being told mules are better!" As we chatted and laughed I enjoyed their fun company.

"See here Kandy, they're legged up good," Ron indicated the muscles on Pistol's forelegs and thighs. "You know what you're doing girl!" he added, pointing to my pack.

"A friend taught me," I replied.

"Can we fetch you some real food?" asked Kandy and I offered to pay.

"We don't take money from strangers," said Ron. "You find a camp spot and we'll track you down!"

Feeling perkier, I carried on to find a camp spot beside the Hungry Horse Reservoir, where there was good grass. The horses tucked into it eagerly, as a hawk mewed, soaring over us. At dusk, Ron and Kandy found me and brought with them deep fried chicken, apples, chocolate bars and trail mix.

"Hush," Ron put his nose in the air. "I've just got a whiff of something." He flicked on his lighter to test which way the wind was blowing. "Grizzlies usually smell. They roll in what they have either found dead or killed, that's how you tell if there's a grizzly around."

As we chatted by the lake, Ron noticed the red necktie I had put on Pistol.

"In the hunting season, I put a red rug on my horse and the saddle on top. Otherwise they will shoot the horses from under you."

Just before they left, Ron said: "You've got balls. Big balls."

Kandy added: "I'd like you to come back and stay a few days. We could come and get you with the trailer in the morning?"

"Thank you, we'd like that very much!" I replied. Lying in my tent that night, trusting the grizzly wouldn't return, I was deeply moved as I thought about how God had answered my prayer for a lift and orchestrated my meeting Ron and Kandy.

Ron Smathers and Kandy Clarke with Smoky.

And in the sweetness of friendship let there be laughter, and sharing of pleasures. For in the dew of little things the heart finds its morning and is refreshed.
- Kahlil Gibran

Opposite and above: Our grassy camp spot on the edge of Hungry Horse Reservoir.

# A GOOD REST

His mercies are new every morning –Great is His faithfulness.
Lam 3v23 NKJ

"I've been a hunter all my life. Full time for three to four years, while I worked for an outfitter," said Ron, as he collected us the following morning. "I multi-tasked. Worked as a pack stringer. I did 682 miles, with nine mules – a full string. I'd pack the camp gear: supplies in, hay in, people's stuff in. Garbage out, meat out. Did twenty-two, 31-mile days in a row, without missing a day!"

"You won't believe it. Come and meet what we've found in the bush!" Ron called to the proprietor in the cafe at Hungry Horse.

We chatted to her later. "Holy cow, that's quite a trip," she said. "That's insane. What were you thinking?!"

I stayed with Kandy, while the horses had a good rest and feed a few hundred yards down the road, in Doyle and Eunice Catlette's paddock, right in front of their home. Kandy had worked hard on their peppermint farm most of her life, and the day Ron took her out for a drive, and she met us, was her first time down the South Fork Road!

After the filming in Yellowstone, Greg had dropped me in Montana, driven his trailer to Kalispell and left it there before flying home to Texas. So when I arrived here, I had the pleasure of having wheels! An English girl, driving a Texas-plated pick-up, on the other side of the road in Montana! I used it to drive the few miles to Jeny's to catch up on emails.

When I see the rainbow in the clouds,
I will remember the eternal covenant between God
and every living creature on earth. Genesis 9v16 NLT

278

# AND FEED FOR US ALL!

Jeny Running Brook Covill, is of Powhatan/Cherokee descent and a member of the Amonsoquath tribe of Cherokee. When my friends Johannes and Jan Balzar, in Auckland, New Zealand, had contacted some First Nation people in America, and sent them my route, Jeny had immediately responded, and was very welcoming. She was a dynamic woman pastor of All Nations Fellowship and founder of the First Nations Monday. She had arranged for me to speak at the Cowboy Church in Kalispell.

Kandy took me shopping. I bought black jeans, and she persuaded me to get a black belt, with silver hearts. She picked up a sparkly T-shirt.

"Isn't it all a bit flash?" I felt a little overwhelmed at wearing something glittering, after wearing the same clothes for almost six months.

"Trust me. You'll look great in this outfit!"

We left Smoky and Pistol making up for lost eating time. Jeny, who had initially made contact with Paul Arends, and also with Don and Toni Robinson, pastors at the Cowboy Church, all attended my photographic riding adventure presentation in Kalispell. I just told stories of God's goodness and faithfulness while riding through New Zealand, Britain, Ireland and the United States to a friendly congregation, many of them dressed in their cowboy hats and boots.

Jeny had contacted Robert Bremner of the Blackfeet tribe, and accompanied me over the Glacier National Park and the Continental Divide to meet him at Browning. We also met Robert's wife, Kati, and their friends Les and Stacy Costel, who invited us to stay on their Fox Creek Ranch on the Blackfeet Reservation. They kindly offered Jeny a horse to ride with us all to the border. Then Robert took us to the game and fishing department to get a permit for filming. Here, I noticed a sign, which showed $15,000 for a tag (hunting permit) for a bull elk (the Blackfeet speciality) and $6,000 for a Bighorn sheep. I braced myself to hear the cost of filming on the reservation.

"10 dollars please," said the official.

"10 dollars?" I repeated in surprise as it was so reasonable, when some of the other places we had filmed had required hundreds of dollars. It was clear that Robert was respected by the tribal Council leaders.

"Just as well you shoot with a camera instead of a gun!" Jeny remarked, with a chuckle.

The identical pick-ups with Montana and Texas number plates! Kandy took Ron's, while I took Greg's to get a round bale each, which were as tall as Smoky and Pistol, and provided the feast I had promised them!

279

# THE BLACKFEET TRIBE

"Remember when I was a cowboy," said Robert (Blackfeet Indian) to his wife Kati, as he explained that he had worked on two ranches for four years.

"No, I never did think of you as a cowboy!" she replied.

I enjoyed Robert's sense of humour, and he couldn't have been more helpful, taking the rest of the afternoon off to show us the Museum of the Plains Indian, which was very interesting.

"They seemed to use everything from the buffalo," Robert told me. "There are probably as many cattle now as there were buffalo in those days. When the Europeans settled in the West, we (the Blackfeet) were one of the few tribes that never moved out, even though we lost a lot of land." He explained many things as we toured the well-organised layout, displaying the intricate costumes, tools and way of life of the Blackfeet.

"There are four divisions of the Blackfeet: the Blood, the North Peigan, the South Peigan, and the Blackfeet," Robert informed us.

The Plains Indians had been in contact with the European explorers and traders since the 17th century. It was not until the United States purchased the vast Louisiana Territory in 1803, and after Lewis and Clark had made their historic western trip across the Great Plains to the Pacific Coast, that the Indians encountered the first thrust westward from the new nation in the east. Waves of prospectors swept over the Great Plains with the discovery of gold in California in 1840 and later in the Black Hills. US government troops inevitably ran into the Plains Indians, defending their homelands, and the fighting began in earnest. In 1876 the combined forces of the Sioux and Cheyenne made a bold and desperate effort to turn back the encroachment, at the Battle of Little Big Horn. Although they won, they ultimately lost out to the stampede of gold prospectors and settlers. During the latter half of the 19th century, the United States government placed the Indians in federal reservations, which their descendants still occupy today. After the freedom of their nomadic hunting existence on the Great Plains, they found the restrictive life in the reservation difficult. In 1890, the last bitter struggle took place between the US Government and the Sioux at Wounded Knee, in the Pine Ridge Reservation. The final years of the 19th century marked the end of the Plains Indians' traditional way of life.

Robert then took us to see his new place of worship, the Church on the Rock, just north of Browning. I asked if he was the pastor.

"I'm not the pastor, but an ordained minister – one of nine elders here – and have ministered on several of the reservations in Montana. Our pastor is Roy Wolf Tail, a wonderful person full of compassion and the fire of God!" he replied enthusiastically, adding: "Basically, six of us, with some other help here and there, spent many weekends and holidays building this church over a three year period. Money came in to buy the materials, independent of outside funding," explained Robert, showing Jeny and I its simple yet elegant interior, with international flags hanging from the walls.

"I'll send you a Union Jack flag!" I offered enthusiastically seeing it was missing.

# SNOW STORM

"You're so spoilt!" Greg remarked, when I recounted the story of meeting Ron and Kandy on the South Fork Road. He had flown back to take possession of his pick-up and trailer, and resume his position as wrangler, because Bob and Trip were flying in to film us riding to the border with some of the Blackfeet tribe. Meanwhile, Sandy, who had run my UK business in my absence, flew in from England.

Ron offered his horse, Buddy, for Sandy to ride with me for a few days, and Greg dropped us off at the southern part of Glacier National Park. This was north east from the Bob Marshall Wilderness, where I had been the previous week.

Drizzle was falling as we followed the Park Creek towards Two Medicine Pass. Buddy, ridden by Sandy, got upset about being tied to the trailer, pulled back, then jumped forwards several times and fell. Sandy somehow managed to roll clear, unable to understand what caused him to do this. As Sandy had only just arrived I wanted her to have a comfortable ride so we swapped horses and she rode Smoky. The pass to the north of us had been closed due to 'bear activity' (I wondered exactly what that meant!), so we chose the one to the south which took a little time to find. Then we climbed and climbed through the rain, which turned to snow. We saw mountain goats, sticking like flies to the scree face on the opposite side of the mountain valley, until our visibility was reduced to a short distance.

Above left: Sandy Marriott with Smoky and Buddy. Right: Packing up Pistol. Below: Climbing throught the blizzard. Opposite: Greg Scott.

"Nothing like breaking me in gently, Tracey!" remarked Sandy, bravely, as the wind was driving the increasingly heavy snow, and the path we were following disappeared. It was too dangerous to continue, in blizzard conditions with poor visibility and no track to follow over the mountain pass. Feeling defeated, we turned back down the steep mountainside, leading the horses over the slippery snow. When it did even out, I rode Buddy with my legs loose, as in the Western saddle it was too uncomfortable an angle to tuck my feet into the stirrups. I missed my Aussie one which was on Smoky!

I trotted on, with Buddy ahead. Sandy and I took turns singing loudly every tune we could remember to give the bears warning of our approach. Bears will automatically attack if they are taken by surprise and I certainly wanted to avoid running Buddy bang smack into one, at speed! When the light had completely faded, we found torches. Sandy used the small one that Jim had given me in New Mexico, and I forged on ahead, into the darkness, with Greg's wind-up flashlight. My feet were cold and wet, and I kept vigorously winding up the torch to generate both some light and in the process warmth, until the handle came off in my zeal! I knew I only had a short time before the wind-up light would fade, and we still had ten miles to go before we were out of the forest. We both needed torch lights as it was pitch black amongst the trees and we needed one to light the path and another to be able to see and follow the horse in front!

"Thank you God for Greg's organisation!" I said, as yet again, unknown to him, he came to my rescue. He'd left a spare flashlight and batteries in his saddlebag! Greg was expecting us on the eastern side of the Divide, and as we left he had said: "If you don't turn up before dark on the eastern side, I will meet you back here at the trail head."

"Sure!" I replied absent-mindedly, having no inkling we wouldn't make it across. Now, I had to get back to the agreed meeting point. We took seven hours to get to the river, and it was midnight as Buddy gallantly led the way across – it was much fuller than the river we had crossed earlier that day. Greg wasn't there, so we found a grassy spot to graze the horses and, in slow motion, I endeavoured to erect the tent. We had been riding for 14 hours and must have covered 34 miles in atrocious conditions. We were both utterly exhausted

"Hey, Tracey look!" exclaimed Sandy, as Greg's trailer appeared.

"I sure was worried about you gals – a snow storm has been blowing on the other side," said Greg.

"We sure are glad to see you!" said Sandy, laughing with relief. "I was so tired I was almost asleep on Smoky's back and couldn't even get off to walk. I feel as stiff as a board."

Greg had adapted the stock trailer so it could convert into living quarters. This involved scraping out the horse manure, throwing down a tarpaulin, hanging two boards on the sides to shelter from the wind and snow, and lighting a gas fire. We snuggled around it, drinking refreshing tea. It was a good feeling to lie in my warm sleeping bag on the trailer floor that night!

The human spirit,
once stretched
by an adventure of faith
will never return to its original size
- Unknown

_21st September:_ Woke up exhausted and
put on wet boots. Suddenly I realised
I was meant to meet the film crew
this evening to go over the last shoot
in Browning. Was grateful yet again for
Greg's assistance in getting us to the
film locations on time and bringing food
for the horses who I'm glad to see are
quickly growing their winter coats!

# THE CROWN OF THE CONTINENT

God has made everything beautiful in its time. Ecclesiastes 3v11 NIV

*22nd September.* Earlier on my journey I had asked for beautiful autumn colours and snow at the border, and I had been given both!

Les and Stacy Costel met us at their Fox Creek Ranch and invited us to use their trailer while they were in town. It was a lovely mobile home, with several little alcoves for bedrooms, and considering how cold it was outside, their offer was very much appreciated. It was luxury to be able to turn the heating on! They also thoughtfully lent us their phone, as ours didn't work in the area.

Greg had to put snow chains on the pick-up to get through the snow, but we made it to St Mary's Lake in Glacier National Park at dawn and watched as the sunlight turned the snowy mountains pink, before slipping down the mountainsides, illuminating the rich textures and colours of the autumn foliage. Glacier National Park, called Crown of the Continent and named after its 50 small alpine glaciers, has 200 lakes in its one million acres which straddle the Continental Divide. Robert informed us that the Blackfeet tribe had originally given the area to the US Government and in 1910, Congress established Glacier as a National Park. It has also been established as the world's first International Peace Park.

"You were reported for hunting elk," said a ranger, who approached us as we were filming, and asked to see our papers. "Interesting," I thought! Smoky and Pistol were probably more scared of the elk than the elk of them!

"You don't have a grazing permit, do you?" The ranger asked seriously, "so don't let your horses graze." Gulp! I pulled their heads up out of the grass and they tried to put them down again. They couldn't understand why they couldn't eat all the abundant grass at their feet for our usual policy on our journey from the border of Mexico was to eat as much as possible, wherever possible, because you never knew where the next meal would come from!

We had to go back and stand on the road and spent the next hour, while Bob and the ranger made a series of phone calls, trying to locate the necessary papers. The ranger was only doing his job, but I was frustrated that we were wasting valuable time, since every hour cost me hundreds of dollars, which turned into thousands a day when the film crew where on location. The ranger let us go on, but by early afternoon the permit problem was still unresolved and he asked us to leave the park, much to my disappointment, because I really wanted to capture more of the stunning scenery on film. Thankfully, however, we were welcomed to do more filming on the Blackfeet Reservation and later, I discovered I had a phone message from the park authorities, apologising that the permit papers had got stuck in Seattle!

"Eagle Ribs Mountain, Bearhead, Never Laughs Mountain, Dancing Lady Mountain, Rising Wolf Mountain!" Sandy read out some intriguing names from the map.

"One can only imagine the stories behind these names," I added, "like Bad Marriage Mountain, Skeleton Mountain, Brave Dog and Little Dog Mountain, and here's one called Almost a-Dog Mountain and Scalplock Mountain!"

# FOX CREEK RANCH

"We baby-sit about 260 cows here on summer pasture, from the first part of June to the first part of October. This is really good grass, with a lot more nutrients," said Stacy, whose family had been ranching for three generations. "They come from a ranch out east, which pays for the grass, and then they take their cattle back and graze them on the stubble and feed them hay for the winter."

"We rely on snow, rather than the rain, for moisture, to keep the creek full," added Les. 'It's amazing what a few feet of snow can do! And it can come really suddenly! We get plenty of snow in the winter. A lot of rivers originate up here – the further east you go, the less water and grass you'll find."

"At this time of year, we gather the cattle in and count to see how many more are still out there. We usually have to get them on horseback, as they run into the bush," said Stacy. "We all have full time jobs, so this is more of a hobby for us."

# LIVING THE DREAM!

Certainly Dreams come true!   - Norman Vincent Peale

I took my camera out on Smoky, and we both enjoyed moving faster than our usual steady pace, whilst enthusiastically rounding up the cattle coming in off summer pasture.

I must have been seven or eight when, riding my pony on Dartmoor, England, I played cowboys and Indians and dreamt of being in the 'Wild West'! Now, many years later, here I was in Montana being a cowboy (or rather, girl!), rounding up cattle with Indians, riding my enthusiastic Smoky in the most spectacular scenery. It was a taste of heaven on earth!

Delight yourself in the Lord and He will give you the desires of your heart.

Commit your way to the Lord, trust also in Him and He shall bring it to pass. Psalm 37v4-5 NKJ

Les and Stacy took us to check out the two border crossings into Canada, past an area of burnt trees.

"This was last year's fire, which spread from the park to the reservation. But all is not lost. If the wood is taken to the mill before it dries out, it can still be used," Stacy informed us. As we drove through Babb settlement, she added: "Don't blink – you'll miss it!". We reached the Piegan point of entry and met a stern official.

"You can come into this building, but if you don't have the right paperwork at the next building for your horses, you will be separated from them, and you will have to be escorted to Sweetgrass, in the east, for a veterinary inspection," he told us.

Instead, I decided that it would be more scenic at the Chief Mountain border crossing, in Glacier, just to the west, taking me into Alberta.

After rounding up the cattle at Fox Creek Ranch, we all sat outside around a large brightly burning log fire, and ate a warming chilli, along with fried beans.

"This is what we called S'mores," she told me, demonstrating the technique of a marshmallow on the end of a stick, melted over the fire, and eaten between two cookies.

"That's how we show our hospitality: by eating together. I do a lot of feeding, cooking and getting together – that's how we are!"

"The weather was nice today, but it can change fast here, from 56 above to 46 below in 24 hours! Supposed to be three feet of snow in the morning," Les said, adding, "in Alaska!" I wouldn't have believed it if I hadn't already experienced the sudden change of temperature, and snow a few days earlier.

Dreams only become reality
when we keep our commitments to them.
– Judy Wardell Halliday

Rounding up cattle on the Fox Creek Ranch, on the Blackfeet Reservation.

What is life? It is the flash of a firefly in the night. It is the breath of a buffalo in the winter time.
It is the little shadow which runs across the grass and loses itself in the sunset.
- Crowfoot, Blackfoot

# CHIEF MOUNTAIN

We set off early for the Canadian border, with the sunlight illuminating the tops of the mountains.
"That's Chief Mountain, sacred for the Blackfeet – a holy spot." Robert pointed to a spectacular flat-topped mountain. "They used to send young men, at 14 or 15 years old, up there for their Vision Quest. All Blackfeet had a protective spirit throughout their lifetime. They would go up there, and usually stay up there three or four days, to fast and pray, seeking their guiding spirit, their medicine, until they received their vision. For example, if you had a vision of a bull calf, that would become your name. Their main god was the one who created everything. They worshipped the earth, as they believed there was harmony in the earth, and we are all connected. A lot of Blackfoot names came from this vision – the eagle was pretty popular, as was the bear and the buffalo."

Chief Mountain

The Blackfeet were nomadic warriors, good horsemen and great hunters, hostile to surrounding tribes. They were highly skilled, making a variety of useful articles – especially clothes and buffalo robes, and exquisite quill decorations on tobacco bags and moccasins.

The Southern Peigan of the Blackfeet had a population of about 30,000 in the early 1800s, but the effect of the white man, disease, famine and especially the smallpox epidemic of 1876, reduced the population by about 70 per cent by the late 1800s. The Blackfeet territory had the richest source of beavers in the West, so encroachment of settlers was commonplace, and many people lost their lives.

The Blackfeet never had a written language, but passed it down orally. When the government put the Blackfeet into reservations, they took the young at five years old and sent them to boarding school. After about 40 or 50 years, there was no one left, who could speak their native language.

"When they took grandpa there, he couldn't speak English, so they gave him an English name," Robert recounted.

"America was ours before they came," added Stacy.

These striking statues at the entrance to the Blackfeet Reservation are made out of car parts!
Riding with the Blackfeet to the Canadian border.

Our land is more valuable than your money. It will last forever. It will not even perish by the flames of fire. As long as the sun shines and the waters flow, this land will be here to give life to men and animals. We cannot sell the lives of men and animals; therefore we cannot sell this land. The Great Spirit put it here for us and we cannot sell it because it does not belong to us. You can count your money and burn it within the nod of a buffalo's head, but only the Great Spirit can count the grains of sand and the blades of grass of these plains. As a present to you, we will give you anything we have that you can take with you; but the land, never.

- A chief of the Blackfeet Bands

Trust not in uncertain riches
but in the living God,
who gives us richly all things to enjoy.
1 Timothy 6v17 NKJ

Sandy, Brian, Jeny, Tracey, Robert and JR riding to the Canadian Border

Faith and works should travel side by side, step by step. First faith and then works, and then faith again and then works again until you can scarcely distinguish which is the one and which is the other - William Booth, James 2v12

Your unfailing love, O Lord, is as vast as the heavens;
your faithfuness reaches beyond the clouds.
Psalm 36V5 NLT

# THE BORDER

I left my escort party on the American side and together with my two horses, we approached the border of Canada. Emotions rose from deep within me, and tears filled my eyes and ran down my cheeks as I thought of God's great faithfulness in giving us this adventure, keeping me, Smoky and Pistol safe, and doing more than I could possibly imagine, in providing for us through many divine appointments all the way from Mexico to Canada. There, strung above us, like a banner in the sky, I clearly imagined seeing the letters: F A I T H F U L.

Then I realised the visionary banner in the sky was also for us – myself, Smoky and Pistol – as we had been given an assignment, and we had completed it. We had been travelling for six months, covered several thousand miles, met great people, including cowboys and Indians, fulfilling a childhood dream to ride horses across the Wild West of America.

This journey had consumed me. Riding with my two faithful companions, camping out in the open spaces, mountains and forests across America, had become a way of life. The journey hadn't been easy, but along the way it had changed me, creating within me stronger faith, commitment, courage and perseverance. Suddenly, I had reached my destination and crossed the border, which had seemed so far away, for so long, and I was shocked, almost numb – I felt rather apprehensive about returning to a normal kind of life, although simultaneously grateful and privileged to have been living my dream – it was indeed a multi-faceted gift!

O Lord, you have searched me and know me. You know everything I do; You understand all my thoughts.
You chart the path ahead of me ... Every moment you know where I am. You both precede and follow me...
Psalm 139v1-5

"I'm driving north to Alaska. Do you want to come along?" asked Greg. This invitation to visit Canada was God sent and helped me adjust from trekking on horseback for six months to my previous way of life!

Before I went north I gave Smoky and Pistol a big hug and left them with plenty of hay in Kandy's care.

"You are going the wrong way!" commented the Canadian customs official. "Don't you know it's cold up there – most people are coming out!"

He looked at me quizzically, handed me back my British passport, and said: "A Texas plated pick-up and trailer going to Alaska? There must be more to this story!"

Tracey and Smoky on Spring Valley Ranch

# EPILOGUE

Now to Him Who,...is able to do superabundantly far over and above all that we dare ask, or think,
infinitely beyond our highest prayers, desires, thoughts, hopes, or dreams.
Ephesians 3v20 Amp

On my ride in the west of America, I had been conscious of wild animals watching us travelling through their territory, but apart from the occasional glimpse they had avoided us, for which I was grateful as Smoky and Pistol got easily spooked (I'm sure they encouraged each other in this!) and high tailed it off at speed if they sensed wild animals. This meant an energetic and long walk on foot for me!

Although I appreciated the wild animals leaving us alone, I was disappointed I didn't have more opportunity to photograph them – that was until travelling through Canada when I saw far more than I could have even asked to see! They included; coyotes, caribou, mountain goats, stone sheep and both grizzly and black bears! One morning I had difficulty in focusing my camera as I was so excited to see five different bears!

After a photographic dash through Canada to cross the border into Alaska, we turned south again to collect Smoky and Pistol. Someone offered to buy them, but I couldn't 'just sell' them, not after we had shared so much together on this epic journey. Returning to the front range of the Rockies in Colorado, some friends offered to take care of Pistol and Smoky on their Spring Valley Ranch while I had to leave and return to England......

......You have done many things for us, O Lord our God; there is none like you!
You have made many wonderful plans for us. I could never speak of them all - their number is so great!
Psalm 40v4-5 G.N

... I would be coming back again!

What we do now on earth echos through eternity. - Maximus in the film Gadiator

I hope this account of my journey has stirred your dreams! Life is fleeting. Like the rodeo bulls and horses, born to buck, we are all born with special talents to do certain things. You can recognise them by your desires and passions – just as I did when I grew up playing cowboys and Indians! Several decades later, I followed my heart to cross North America on horseback, with my camera.

Jesus came to give us life, and to live life to the fullest – that's life everlasting in heaven, but also life to its fullest here on earth! Even before you were born, God had a good plan for your life.

You can say, "Yes! Lord Jesus, forgive me of my sins, come into my heart and be my Lord and Saviour and show me what I was born for!"

God wants to do more for you than you can ask, think, or imagine, and to take you on an adventure especially designed for you! "It's in Christ that we find out who we are and what we are living for." Ephesians 1v12TM

302

You are never too old to set another
goal or dream a new dream.
– C.S. Lewis

You can do what I cannot do, I can do what you cannot do, and together we can do great things. – Mother Teresa

My grateful thanks to the jigsaw of people around the world, who made this journey the adventure it became, through their prayers, support and hospitality.
And also to those, who helped and encouraged me while compiling this book.
God bless you all and God bless America.

Tracey Elliot-Reep

Grizzly bear cub

Coyote

# ACKNOWLEDGEMENTS

TEXAS
The Longhorns by J.Frank Dobie
Trail Drives of the Old West www.net.westhost.com
Big Bend, The Story Behind The Scenery by Carol E.Sperling
History of Texas http://en.wikipedia.org/wiki/Texas

NEW MEXICO
Bandelier National Monument Guide
Santa Fe Trail, www.en.wikipedia.org
Mesquite www.desertusa.com
Corriente www.corrientecattle.org/History.htm

UTAH
www.en.wikipedia.org/wiki/Churra
Monument Valley - www.en.wikipedia.org

COLORADO
Mesa Verde National Park Guide, U.S Department of the Interior.
www.coloradotrail.org/wilderness.html
Colorado Divison of Wildlife Information
Utes - Museum of the Mountain Man, Pinedale
Creede, Colorado Boom Town by Leland Feitz
Silver Thread, Colorado Scenic and Historic Byway Information -
BLM, US Department of the Interior, Colorado Division of Wildlife

Under the Sun at Lake City by Jack Nichols
Estes Park Information Centre and Guide
MacGregor Ranch - macgregorranch.org/
Lightning - www.lightningsafety.noaa.gov/ams

WYOMING
Beetle Epidemic -Trees and Shrubs, Forest Service, Dep of US Agriculture
Medicine Bow National Forest Map, US Department of Agriculture
Bureau of Land Management Wild Horse and Burro - www.blm.gov/adoptahorse/news.
The Noble Horse - Collins Publishers/David Bateman Ltd
Museum of the Mountain Man, Pinedale
Grand Teton National Park Guide and Moose Visitor Center
www.yellowstoneonline.com
Yellowstone: The complete guide in association with the National Park Service
Mammoth Hot Springs Trail Guide by the Yellowstone Association
Yellowstone Guide -National Park Service, US Department of the Interior
Yellowstone The Story Behind The Scenery by Roger Anderson & Carol Shively Anderson

MONTANA
Bob Marshall Wilderness Forestry Information Board
Museum of the Plains Indian, Browning

With many thanks, to those who took photos for me, helping to make this photographic travel book.

Front Page, Greg Scott
4, 5, Larry Joiner & Trip Uhalt
8, 9, Jen Bullock
31, 32, 33, Larry Joiner
34 - 37, Larry Joiner & Trip Uhalt
39 (middle), Larry Joiner
40 (left & right), Toni Hellums
44, 45, 46 (middle), Kelly Fenstermaker
55 (bottom right), 60, 61, 63, Beth Braid
67, Kelly Fenstermaker
80, 81(main), 84, Cheyenne Evans
91, Larry Reagan

94, 95, Laurie Riggins
96, 97, Emiel Ross
102, Roper Simms
113, 114, 116, 118, 120, Greg Scott
121,122, 124, 125, 127, Greg Scott
129 (bottom right), Trip Uhalt
130, 134, 146, Greg Scott
160, 161, 162, 163, Kara Molinek
178, 179, Chris Ott
196 (top), 199, Tanya Fallin
197, 199, Tanya Fallin
199 (middle), Trip Uhalt

199 (bottom), Jan Jones
200, 201, 203, 204, Greg Scott
202, Trip Uhalt
204 (bottom left), Sally St.Clair
204 (bottom right), Greg Scott
206 (top left), Leeann Zuelling
206 (bottom left), Gerry Zell
216, 218 (bottom), Greg Scott
220, 221 Michael R. Brown
222, Marti Freund & Jeff Borchert
224, Karen Borchert
232 (top) 233 (top), Greg Scott

236, 237, Greg Scott
238, 239, Jen Bullock
244, 245, 247, Greg Scott
254 (top), 256, 257, 260, Greg Scott
264, Caroline Jenkins
279, Josh Clarke
282, 284, 285, 287 Greg Scott
282 (top right), 286 Sandy Marriott
294, 295, 296, 298, 299, Greg Scott
301, Terry Theken
302, 304, 307, Greg Scott
Back Cover, Greg Scott

Thank you to Susie Rieple,Terry and Nancy Theken for looking after Smoky & Pistol

Other books and products by Tracey Elliot-Reep

Riding by Faith Through New Zealand
Riding by Faith Through Ireland
A Celebration of the Dartmoor Pony
Dartmoor Booklet
Dartmoor Calendar
Country Greeting Cards

**w w w . t r a c e y e l l i o t r e e p . c o m**

Tracey grew up on a farm on Dartmoor in South West England where she has her base, producing cards, calendars and books. Her faith, love of horses, adventure and photography has led her to many places including Africa, Tibet, Israel and Russia. She has ridden horses from the top of Scotland to Land's End in England and around Southern Ireland, and has published photographic books on her journey through Southern Ireland and her 2,000 mile expedition through the North and South Islands of New Zealand.